Adaptations of Mental and Cognitive Disability in Popular Media

Remakes, Reboots, and Adaptions

Series Editors: Carlen Lavigne, Red Deer College and Paul Booth, DePaul University

Broad-ranging and multidisciplinary, this series invites analysis of remakes, reboots, and adaptations in contemporary media from videogames to television to the internet. How are we re-using and remixing our stories? What does that tell us about ourselves, our cultures, and our times? Scholars use multidisciplinary approaches from areas such as gender studies, race, sexuality, disability, cultural studies, fan studies, sociology, or aesthetic and technical research. Titles in the series set out to say something about who we are, where we've come from, and where we're going, as read in our popular culture and the stories we tell ourselves over and over again.

Titles in the Series

Adaptations of Mental and Cognitive Disability in Popular Media edited by Whitney Hardin and Julia E. Kiernan
The Paths of Zatoichi: The Global Influence of the Blind Swordsman by Jonathan Wroot
The Superhero Multiverse: Readapting Comic Book Icons in Twenty-first Century Film and Popular Media edited by Lorna Piatti-Farnell
Woke Cinderella: Twenty-First-Century Adaptations edited by Suzy Woltmann
Gothic Afterlives: Reincarnations of Horror in Film and Popular Media edited by Lorna Piatti-Farnell
Screening Gender in Shakespeare's Comedies: Film and Television Adaptations in the Twenty-first Century by Magdalena Cieślak
Netflix Nostalgia: Streaming the Past on Demand edited by Kathryn Pallister

Adaptations of Mental and Cognitive Disability in Popular Media

Edited by
Whitney Hardin and Julia E. Kiernan

LEXINGTON BOOKS
Lanham • Boulder • New York • London

Published by Lexington Books
An imprint of The Rowman & Littlefield Publishing Group, Inc.
4501 Forbes Boulevard, Suite 200, Lanham, Maryland 20706
www.rowman.com

86-90 Paul Street, London EC2A 4NE

Copyright © 2022 by The Rowman & Littlefield Publishing Group, Inc.

All rights reserved. No part of this book may be reproduced in any form or by any electronic or mechanical means, including information storage and retrieval systems, without written permission from the publisher, except by a reviewer who may quote passages in a review.

British Library Cataloguing in Publication Information Available

Library of Congress Cataloging-in-Publication Data Available

ISBN 978-1-7936-4831-0 (cloth)
ISBN 978-1-7936-4833-4 (pbk.)
ISBN 978-1-7936-4832-7 (electronic)

Contents

Introduction: Adaptations of Mental and Cognitive
Disability in Popular Media   1
Whitney Hardin and Julia E. Kiernan

PART I: IMAGINING AND BROADENING NARRATIVES OF DISABILITY   15

1 The Prosthetic Self: Drag and Disability in the Figure of RuPaul   17
   John W. Gulledge

2 Adapting Medical Reports into Narrative Film: Autism,
   Eugenics, and Savagery in Truffaut's *L'Enfant sauvage*
   (*The Wild Child*, 1970)   35
   Joy C. Schaefer

3 Remaking the Image of Autism: Why and How Comics
   Should Reboot Autistic Representation   55
   Robert Rozema

4 An Atypical Interaction with a Typical World: Viewing
   Coming-of-Age through the Lens of Disability Studies
   in Robia Rashid's *Atypical*   71
   Anamika Purohit

5 "But can we agree that he's unwell?": Narrative Resistance
   in *Legion*'s Approach to Mental Disability   89
   Julia E. Kiernan

| 6 | Diagnosing Mental and Moral Disability in Post-9/11 Popular American Film Narrative
Carol Donelan | 103 |

PART II: RENEGOTIATING AND RESISTING NARRATIVES OF DISABILITY — **121**

7	"A document in madness?" Disability Erasure in Contemporary Rewrites of Ophelia *Lindsay Adams Kennedy*	123
8	"You're All about 'Crazy'": Rendering the Visibility of Trauma in *Alias* and *Jessica Jones* *Whitney Hardin*	141
9	Subspaces Run through Your Head: *Scott Pilgrim*, Intertextuality, and Visualizing the Traumatized Mind *Guy Spriggs*	157
10	Minding the Gap: Adaptation of and Mental Disability in *Quiet Life* (1990, 1995) *Rea Amit*	173
11	Adapting Autism in Telenovelas: Venevisión's *La Mujer Perfecta* and the Trace of *Esmeralda* *Martín Ponti*	187
12	Female Representations of Autism and Disability in Telenovelas: *La Mujer Perfecta* *Andrea Urrutia Gómez*	205

Index — 221

About the Contributors — 225

Introduction
Adaptations of Mental and Cognitive Disability in Popular Media

Whitney Hardin and Julia E. Kiernan

In July 2020, Netflix announced that the first season of *Ratched* would be available in mid-September. Developed by Ryan Murphy and starring Sarah Paulson, *Ratched* tells the story of Nurse Mildred Ratched, a character from Ken Kesey's 1962 novel, *One Flew Over the Cuckoo's Nest*. Head nurse at the psychiatric hospital that forms the setting of the novel, Ratched is an imposing, impenetrable, and pitiless figure, the authoritarian foil for Kesey's protagonist, Randle Patrick McMurphy. Although Kesey's novel takes place in the 1960s, *Ratched* opens in 1947, providing Mildred Ratched with an origin story, and giving viewers a look at who she was before the events of the novel. Because of this, *Ratched* functions on multiple levels: as an adaptation of Kesey's novel; as an adaptation of the 1975 film starring Jack Nicholson, which is itself an adaptation; and as a reboot of the "Cuckoo's Nest" universe, one that extends that universe's boundaries by providing a key character with background and motivation missing in earlier renditions.

Ratched was received with enthusiastic interest, hitting the number one spot in the Nielsen streaming charts the weekend it opened (Porter 2020). Reviews were mixed, however; while some praised the show's use of color and beautiful set pieces, critics found the show empty, confusing, and even insulting. Some complaints relied on comparisons to the earlier texts, with *Ratched*'s titular nurse unfavorably compared to her counterparts from the novel and film. But critics were also troubled by the show's representation of mental health and the psychiatric system. One reviewer criticized the show's treatment of Charlotte, a patient with dissociative identity disorder, calling it "the most insulting rendition [. . .] I have seen in a very long time" and adding that "it's deeply uncomfortable to watch such a caricature of a mentally ill woman, especially one who becomes violent in ways that mischaracterizes these very real experiences" (Bastién 2020). A review in *Vanity Fair* agrees, calling Charlotte "a caricature for the worst kind of assumptions about mental health" and lamenting that "her character is reduced to her disorder, becoming a vehicle for unspeakable violence" (Saraiya). Similarly, critics argue that the show minimizes the "very real and very harrowing history of mental hospitals in America" (Bastién 2020), depicting "the brutality and humans rights violations" the mentally ill have been subjected to in ways that feel "uncomfortably close to mere exploitation, making a spectacle of atrocities that don't deserve to be treated as spectacle" (Holmes 2020). These criticisms can't be divorced from *Ratched*'s status as an adaptation; critics expected a more nuanced (even a more ethical) treatment of mental health from the show—one that would reflect current thinking.

The existence, popularity, and reception of pop culture texts such as *Ratched* are at the core of this collection, which brings together the scholarly fields of adaptation studies and disability studies, using a popular media lens, to emphasize the ways that remakes, reboots, and adaptations navigate social representations of mental disability and mental health. Contributing chapters respond to the epigraphs in their emphasis upon difference, particularly mental difference, and the ways that narratives of disability are framed not only by worldviews but also by the mediums which structure and inform them. Historically, mental difference has been framed almost exclusively by deficiency, a framework that persists today even as a greater understanding of neurodiversity has begun to normalize the variety of ways we think, feel, socialize, and learn. In discourse about and representations of mental disability and mental health, however, "'broken brains' 'chemical imbalances' and 'disordered neuronal pathways'" consistently appear as "metaphorical frames that link mental difference to our bodies, our brains and our genes" (Lewis 2017, 1).

Moreover, given that "mass media is one of the public's primary sources of information about disorders such as bipolar, schizophrenia, and depression" (Fawcett 2015), it is crucial that scholars of both adaptation and disability studies are attentive to how mental difference is represented. As the example of *Ratched* indicates, film, television, literature, and other forms of popular media regularly encourage and propagate outdated models of disability. For instance, although nearly 20 percent of the U.S. population experiences some kind of mental health condition, a study of popular films and television series from 2016 and 2017 found that these conditions appear in only 1.7 percent of characters in film and 7 percent of characters in television (Smith et al. 2019, 1). Half of the films surveyed and a quarter of the television shows did not represent mental difference at all, and when they did characterizations were disproportionately white, male, and heterosexual (Smith et al. 2019). More troublingly, characters with mental difference are often portrayed as prone to violence, or have their condition minimized through humor. In other words, mental difference is often invisible in popular media, and when it does appear, it does so in ways that distort the humanity and diversity of the disabled community.

In looking at representations of mental difference, this collection's focus is on the ways that adaptations (including remakes, reboots, and other examples of remixed narratives) can shape and shift the social contexts and narratives we use to define disability. The movement of narratives across media in adaptation, or within media but across time and space in the case of remakes and reboots, is a common tactic for revitalization, allowing storytellers to breathe new life into tired narratives, remedying past inaccuracies, and making them accessible and relevant for contemporary audiences. Thus, adaptation provides a useful tool for examining the constraints or opportunities different media impose on or afford narratives, or for measuring shifts in ideology as narratives move across cultures or through time.

In order to situate this work, we begin with a review of adaptation theory, followed by relevant literature from the field of disability studies. We then offer a contextualization of these approaches via a narrative framework, closing the introduction with a summary of chapter content and organization.

ADAPTATION

Adaptation is often viewed as an act of translation, a process by which a text is reproduced within or across media and genres, while retaining a recognizable core. Because of this relationship to origin texts, adaptations often operate in contested territory and are frequently subject to charges of inaccuracy or inferiority. These, often unfavorable, comparisons are unavoidable, because even in the most faithful adaptations, "transposition to another medium, or even moving within the same one, always means change" (Hutcheon 2012, 16). While this could be seen as a limitation, it is also one of the strengths of adaptation, as each adaptation brings new levels of insight, emphasis, and nuance that can extend the origin text.

Transmedia adaptations, which are one focus of this collection, are those that occur across media and regularly rely on a reimagining of characters and narratives. While transmedia adaptation allows for constant (and potentially infinite) shifts across media, genre, and contexts there are a number of challenges and opportunities that arise when a narrative shifts from one medium to another. As mentioned above, to call something an adaptation is to "openly announce its overt relationship to another work or works" (Hutcheon 2012, 6); this relationship implies that central to any adaptation is some level of perceived faithfulness to the origin text. At the same time, each medium imposes its own, sometimes very different, constraints on a narrative, with the result that "adaptation is [more than] an act of appropriation or salvaging" it is also "a double process of interpreting and then creating something new" (Hutcheon 2012, 20). Consequently, many scholars of adaptation studies dismiss the importance of fidelity to the origin text, with Frederic Jameson (2011) arguing that in order for an adaptation to be of good quality in its new medium it will necessarily be "utterly different from, utterly unfaithful to, its original" (218). Others call attention to the way that *all* texts operate within cultural and textual networks, and that, consequently, all texts contain at least an inkling of adaptation. John Bryant (2013) identifies what he calls the fluid text, "any work that exists in multiple versions where the primary cause of those versions is some form of revision." While some revisions are corrective in nature (such as those an editor or publisher might make), Bryant asks us to view adaptation as a kind of cultural revision, one where adaptors function as "collaborators in the making of the *work* in its totality" (emphasis in original). In this view, adaptation isn't simply the movement of narrative from a single origin text to a new, derivative, text but a sophisticated, multilevel process, one in which each revision enriches the totality of the work.

Chapters in this collection are positioned across the spectrum of these scholarly approaches, emphasizing the different shapes of adaptation, and the ways that adaptations operate as multilevel processes. As a result, chapters provide insight into the ways that adaptations are taken up so that "they actualize or concretize ideas; they make simplifying selections, but also amplify and extrapolate; they make analogies; they critique or show their respect, and so on" (Hutcheon 2012, 3). Contributors examine the ways that texts can operate in a network of references, as sites of renegotiation and resistance to not only narrative fidelity but also the social implications of these narrative shifts. While some chapters deal overtly with the implications of moving narratives across media, others address the historicity and constraints of repositioning narratives of mental illness and disability within a contemporary lens.

DISABILITY

The field of disability studies can be thought of as growing out of disability rights activism. Consequently, much of the scholarship in disability studies "distinguishes between *impairment*—the individual limitation linked to a medically based problem that impairs one or more basic life functions— and *disability*—the individual limitation produced by society's failure to accommodate to the impairment" (Squier 2008, emphasis in original). This approach, known as the social model of disability, positions disability as not only solely about individual limitations but also about the social and cultural significance of bodies—disability studies calls attention to the way all bodies are socially constructed. As Rosemarie Garland-Thomson explains

> disability has four aspects: first, it is a system for interpreting bodily variations; second, it is a relation between bodies and their environments; third, it is a set of practices that produce both the able-bodied and the disabled; fourth, it is a way of describing the inherent instability of the embodied self. (quoted in Ellis 2016, 74)

By underlining this instability, "disability offers a challenge to the representation of the body" allowing the "disabled body [to] provide insight into the fact that all bodies are socially constructed—that social attitudes and institutions determine, far greater than biological fact, the representation of the body's reality" (Siebers 2008, 54). To understand disability is to understand what it means to be embodied and to live and work with other embodied beings.

As a result of this attention to the social construction of bodies, disability studies scholars position their research as central to all categories of human difference, a claim that is only recently gaining acceptance. Historically, "the label of 'disability' has functioned as an accusation more often than an assessment," and discrimination against women, the poor, members of Black and LGBTQ+ communities, and others has often been justified by framing these groups as disabled in some fashion (Ferguson and Nusbaum 2012, 73). Perhaps more than any other category of difference, disability has been used to divide *us* from *them* and to legitimize paternalistic and discriminatory practices. Nonetheless, while categories of difference such as class, gender, race, and sexual orientation are commonly seen as "representative of the human condition," disability has yet to achieve this broad recognition (Davis 2006, xv).

Until recently, there has also been a lack of attention to mental disability even within the field of disability studies; early work in the field focused primarily on physical (and specifically visible) disability, and this "emphasis on the body and not the mind, create[d] fissures through which attention to the mentally disabled easily f[ell]" (Prendergast 2001, 46). Such critiques have pushed research to broaden its scope and recent years have seen increased scholarly attention to "unseen" disabilities: chronic illness, sensory impairment, and mental and intellectual disability. The concept of neurodiversity has also altered how we understand mental disabilities such as ADD/ADHD, autism, Tourette's syndrome, obsessive-compulsive disorder, dyslexia, and others. Neurodiversity frames an individual's neurocognitive function as either neurotypical (the so-called "normal" functioning) or neurodivergent, while recognizing that the neurotypical brain is not inherent superior—it is either more common or more in line with standards that are as much contextual and social as they are medical, if not more so. Neurodiversity doesn't reject the notion of disability, but it resists efforts to see neurological differences as deficits, maintaining that the neurodivergent are "not broken or incomplete versions" of the neurotypical (Bailin 2019). In accordance with the social model of disability, neurodiversity recognizes that the difficulties faced by disabled people are contextual—for example, "living in a society designed for non-autistic people contributes to, and exacerbates, many of the daily living challenges that autistic people experience" (Robertson 2010). At the same time, neurodiversity pushes back against the social model of disability, seeing neurological difference as simply part of being human and seeking to reject or redefine the idea of impairment itself (McWade et al. 2015). Neurodiversity also helps to bridge the gap between disability and mental health, as it doesn't limit itself to disabilities like those listed above, but encompasses mental health conditions such as depression and anxiety as well.

This collection takes a broad approach to disability studies. Although its primary focus is on mental and intellectual disability, contributing chapters also address mental health conditions. Although the mentally ill are often legally classified as disabled, and both the mentally ill and the disabled endure similar forms of discrimination, the two groups are not identical. For instance, while we recognize that mad studies and disability studies are different fields, we believe there is much to be gained by increased collaboration between these two areas.

NARRATIVE, DISABILITY, AND ADAPTATION

Narrative functions within this collection as a framework for examining the ways that popular media exerts rhetorical power, allowing for deeper understandings of the ways that disability is experienced by differently situated individuals, and revealing relationships with broader social narratives that attempt to push definitions of disability onto them. Far from being mere stories, narratives are the primary means through which "human beings make sense of our identities and the social spheres in which we exist," an ongoing process of self-construction that we engage in both "to ourselves and to others" (Jacobs and Dolmage 2012, 72). The stories we tell and those told about us—and about people we recognize as being like us—have significant sociocultural impacts. Narrative approaches, then, can and must provide insight into the construction and power of discourse about disability and the disabled.

For instance, Catherine Prendergast (2001) has noted that the *DSM IV* (the *Diagnostic and Statistical Manual of Mental Disorders* published by the American Psychiatric Association) "has been viewed by many as an illness-constructing document of incredible rhetorical power," a master narrative serving as "the psychiatric profession's main vehicle for maintaining dominance over other mental health disciplines, firmly entrenching the biomedical model of mental disorder" (48). The influence of biomedical narratives like those of the *DSM IV* are problematic, not least of all because of the way they suppress individual experiences of disability and cultural contributions to the construction of disability. Rhetorical scholars James Wilson and Cynthia Lewiecki-Wilson (2001) argue that "what it means to be disabled, indeed the very conditions of a disability, are crucially determined by the society in which one lives," as well as by factors such as race, class, and gender, concluding that "disability is not a universal category but a strategic name marking diverse differences" (10). It is not only simply this marking of difference that is important to this collection but also the ways that narratives can, should, have, and have not shifted in efforts to humanize and, therefore, legitimize the experiences of those who embody a spectrum of mental health conditions.

Unfortunately, however, hegemonic narratives about disability have traditionally been seated in deficit. Couser (2005) identifies five rhetorics that dominate these narratives: triumph, horror, spiritual compensation, nostalgia, and emancipation; moreover, as Jacobs and Dolmage explain

> the rhetoric of triumph demands that people with disabilities overcome or compensate for their disability; horror renders disability abject and terrifying; spiritual compensation implies that disability is a punishment for a moral failing; the memoir of nostalgia longs for the time before the author became disabled. Finally, the rhetoric of emancipation, while not leading to the overcoming of disability, instead removes 'physical, social and cultural obstacles' for people with disabilities. (2012, 76)

The ubiquity of these rhetorics makes it difficult for stories about disability to be told that don't embrace one or more of these frames, particularly given their sociocultural dominance across narratives of disability.

A primary purpose of this collection, then, is to examine and counter these outdated narrative approaches, and offer a rethinking of disability that moves away from biomedical deficit narratives, and limiting options like those described by Couser. Chapters in this collection embrace James Wilson and Cynthia Lewiecki-Wilson's (2001) argument toward "the broadest possible definition of disability" and "the right of the disability community to debate, contest, and change their preferred definitions of disability" (10), in positioning engagement with mental difference as "shaped by the kinds of worldviews we bring to bear on the question and the kinds of narrative communities we choose to join" (Lewis 2017, 5). A "deep ethics" approach to disability, one which allows not only for different narratives but a multiplicity of narratives, is central to this collection because such an approach moves away from a linear baseline toward holistic ideologies of difference, which allow for "one narrative of the self for one situation and another narrative for another situation" (Lewis 2001, 5). This approach is socially meaningful in that it neither eliminates nor validates narratives (of triumph or nostalgia, etc.), but presents them as elements of a wider narrative, enabling other narratives to be told instead of or alongside them. For narratives of mental disability, adaptation also provides an opportunity to more openly address and complicate questions of mental and cognitive health. We argue that contemporary media has a responsibility to consider and (potentially) take advantage of these opportunities as they recycle, rehash, and remix increasingly dated and obsolete narratives of disability.

CHAPTER ARRANGEMENT

To achieve the ends described above, this collection examines how contemporary media has succeeded (and failed) to shift away from deficit-based biomedical models that disempower characters through expectations of definitive diagnosis and recovery. Included chapters examine the ways that reboots, remakes, and adaptations present narratives and characters' experiences as palatable, relatable, and acceptable, particularly in light of audiences who embody increased knowledge, acceptance, and normalization of mental and cognitive disability.

Contributors build upon previous representations and examinations of disability in popular media through examining mental difference via shared themes that include ethical imperatives/responsibility, moral identity, neuroscience/neurodiversity, spatiality, invisible disability, and misrepresentation. However, it is the scope of disciplinary voices, with scholarly perspectives from various disciplines of the humanities and social sciences—anthropology, literary studies, feminist studies, gender studies, disability studies, American studies, Asian studies, adaptation studies, cinema and media studies, television studies, comic studies, and Hispanic studies—that best articulate the ways this collection rethinks, reimagines, renegotiates, and reshapes academic attention to outdated and potentially dangerous narratives of mental disability and mental health. In order to emphasize the ways that adaptations are able to navigate past injustices, authenticate experiences, and take up contemporary societal norms chapters have been organized into two parts: Imagining and Broadening Narratives of Disability, which considers the different shapes of adaptation, and the ways that adaptations operate as multilevel processes, where texts operate in a network of references; and,

Renegotiating and Resisting Narratives of Disability, which considers narrative fidelity and the shifts that occur when an origin text is adapted to across genre and media.

Part I offers analysis from a range of media including comics, streaming services, film, and pay television channels. Contributors in this section offer a variety of approaches to adaptation. The first four authors' position adaptation as multilayered abstraction, not concerned with a one-to-one transfer of a narrative across media, but broad examinations of genre conventions and the expansion of these conventions across social contexts. John W. Gulledge's chapter, "The Prosthetic Self: Drag and Disability in the Figure of RuPaul," reevaluates the adaptive and shifting narratives of atypical identity, with emphasis on the relationships between drag and disability. Gulledge draws attention to the ways that such framing is both complicit in the troubled history of disability representation and provides the potential for disidentification in traditionally normative ontologies and communities. The following chapter, "Medical Records Adapted into Narrative Film: Autism and Savagery in Truffaut's *L'Enfant sauvage* (*The Wild Child*, 1970)," Joy C. Schaefer also unpacks historical representations of disability and neurodiversity, but does so through bringing together the scholarly fields of postcolonial and disability studies. Schaefer argues that these approaches, in the contexts of autism and film studies, can shed light on the ability to assimilate mental illness to the dominant culture, which impacts how viewers judge and value human life. Similarly, Robert Rozema's chapter, "Remaking the Image of Autism: Why and How Comics Should Reboot Autistic Representation," examines how the comic medium can (and should) represent autism more authentically. Arguing for the rejection of detrimental visual and verbal stereotypes as well as the promotion of social, not pathological, model of autisms, Rozema offers examples of ways that comics can authentically and ethically represent autistic experiences. Anamika Purohit's chapter, "An Atypical Interaction with a Typical World: Viewing Coming-of-Age through the Lens of Disability Studies in Robia Rashid's *Atypical*," juxtaposes audience perceptions of traditional coming-of-age narratives against *Atypical*'s reimagining of this genre via an autistic lens. Central to this chapter, like many in this collection (e.g., Adams, Kiernan, and Spriggs), is attention to spatiality as a means of identity construction, particularly in terms of built environments and lived spaces. The closing two chapters in part I offer multilayered analysis of adaptation, framing their approach via transmedia adaptations across specific contexts. Chapter 5, "'But can we agree that he's unwell?': Narrative Resistance in *Legion*'s Approach to Mental Disability," authored by Julia Kiernan attends to the layered rhetorical processes of adaptation, offering an understanding of relationships between language and power in order to draw attention to the ways that mental illness has been represented across a constellation of *Legion* narratives. This chapter interrogates how shifting contextualizations of an origin text can resist prevailing discourses of mental illness, and works against the compartmentalization and reduction of disability to expected narratives of diagnosis and recovery. The final chapter in this section, "Diagnosing Mental and Moral Disability in Post-9/11 Popular American Film Narrative," authored by Carol Donelan emphasizes how novel-to-film adaptation, through its use of conflict and sound style in particular, utilizes the trope of mental disability to (re)negotiate American understandings and interactions with moral disability, which serves to problematize the relationship between viewing and diagnosis.

Part II also offers examinations across a range of media including books, film, graphic novels, streaming services, and telenovelas where contributors position adaptation as multilayered; however, this section pays specific attention to fidelity and renegotiation of origin texts, particularly the ways that recent transmedia adaptations work to resist outdated narratives of mental disability and, instead, bolster contemporary social norms. The first chapter "'A document in madness?' Disability Erasure in Contemporary Rewrites of Ophelia," written by Lindsay Adams Kennedy explores popular culture adaptations of Ophelia and their lack of engagement with her disability. Adams argues that artists have an ethical responsibility when handling narratives of disability, and uses feminist and disability studies frames to encourage the adoption of new narratives for Ophelia that move away from ableist presumptions. Whitney Hardin's chapter "You're All about 'Crazy': Rendering the Visibility of Trauma in *Alias* and *Jessica Jones*," like that of Adams, focuses on a female protagonist; however, unlike Adams this chapter brings together the fields of trauma and disability students to examine the ways that representations of PTSD in these texts both accept and disrupt narratives of normalization and acceptance of female trauma in superhero narratives. Chapter 9, authored by Guy Spriggs, "Subspaces Run through Your Head: *Scott Pilgrim*, Referentiality, and Visualizing the Traumatized Mind," examines the origin text and adaptation of the character of Scott Pilgram, originally a graphic novel and subsequently reimagined into film. Like Gulledge and Adams, much of the focus of Spriggs's chapter is spatiality. This contribution, however, analyzes how visual style effectively dramatizes the impact of trauma, as well as mechanisms for addressing mental illness via visual style and world-building, which work to create a thoughtful portrayal of the depth and inescapability of mental illness. "Minding the Gap: Adaptation of and Mental Disability in *Quiet Life* (1990, 1995)" by Rea Amit focuses on fidelity (and lack thereof) between the depiction of mental disability in the Japanese novel *A Quiet Life* and its cinematic adaptation, emphasizing how sources of influence around mental disability have the potential for media convergence and arguing that being mindful of these disparities supports viewing reevaluations of what it means to be mentally disabled. The final two chapters of this collection focus on the genre of the telenovela. In chapter 11, "Adapting Autism in Telenovelas: Venevisión's *La Mujer Perfecta* And The Trace Of *Esmeralda*," Martín Ponti provides a survey of the ways that telenovelas have occupied a central role on Latin American television, focusing on how the process and analysis of adapted works can allow for the direct transposition of one work into another. Analyzing the Venezuelan telenovela *La Mujer Perfecta*, Ponti uses a disability lens to examine recurring themes common to telenovela narratives, such as overcoming social and class differences, love triangles, and the reworking of Cinderella-fairy tales motifs. Finally, Andrea Urrutia Gómez in "Female representations of Autism and disability in telenovelas: *La Mujer Perfecta*" also engages with *La Mujer Perfecta*, but uses a neurological and feminist lens to unpack the limits of socially tolerated gender identities. Gómez examines the negative social and cultural impacts of ignoring advances in disability research popular media.

Ultimately, in regard to disability studies and mental disability more specifically, this collection positions adaptation as a theoretical framework that can potentially address narrative injustices in origin texts—not just replicating or erasing flawed representations of difference but also confronting them head-on. Given the long tradition of using narratives of disability as a tool for creating and maintaining hierarchies of difference, adaptations of such flawed origin texts serve as a vehicle for measuring social progress. Recognizing that "narrative choices" are "not simply rational or medical choices," but "also ethical choices" (Lewis 2017, 1) this collection argues that contemporary media has a responsibility to consider and (potentially) take advantage of these opportunities as they recycle, rehash, and remix narratives. In examining the way popular media narratives have engaged—successfully or unsuccessfully—with historically normative representations of mental health and disability this collection works to offer "a world in which disability is central, in which the experience of disability is not solely or primarily about loss, lack, charity, pity, vengeance, overcoming, or anger" (Jacobs and Dolmage 2018, 366); a world where disability is characterized by agency and autonomy.

WORKS CITED

Bailin, Aiyana. "Clearing Up Some Misconceptions about Neurodiversity." *Scientific American*, 6 June 2019, blogs.scientificamerican.com/observations/clearing-up-some-misconceptions-about-neurodiversity/.

Bastién, Angelica Jade. "*Ratched* is the Worst Thing That Could Have Happened to Nurse Ratched." *Vulture*, 18 Sept. 2020, vulture.com/article/ratched-netflix-review.html. Accessed 15 Nov. 2020.

Bryant, John. "Textual identity and adaptive revision: Editing adaptation as a fluid text." *Adaptation Studies: New Challenges, New Directions*, edited by Jørgen Bruhn, Anne Gjelsvik and Eirik Frisvold Hanssen. Kindle ed., Bloomsbury Academic, 2013.

Couser, G. Thomas. "Disability, life narrative, and representation." *PMLA/ Publications of the Modern Language Association of America* 120, no. 2 (2005): 602–6.

Davis, Lennard J. "Introduction." *The Disability Studies Reader*, edited by Lennard J. Davis, 2nd edition. Routledge, 2006, xv–xviii.

Ellis, Katie. *Disability and Popular Culture: Focusing Passion, Creating Community and Expressing Defiance*. Routledge, 2016.

Fawcett, Kristin. "How Mental Illness is Misrepresented in the Media." *U.S. News*, 16 April 2015, health.usnews.com/health-news/health-wellness/articles/2015/04 /16/how-mental-illness-is-misrepresented-in-the-media. Accessed 15 Nov. 2020.

Ferguson, Philip M., and Emily Nusbaum. "Disability studies: What is it and what difference does it make?." *Research and Practice for Persons with Severe Disabilities* 37.2 (2012): 70–80.

Holmes, Linda. "'Ratched' Is Pretty, But Very Silly." *NPR*, 18 Sept. 2020, npr.org /2020/09/18/913629938/ratched-is-pretty-but-very-silly. Accessed 15 Nov. 2020.

Hutcheon, Linda. *A Theory of Adaptation*. Routledge, 2012.

Jacobs, Dale, and Jay Dolmage. "Difficult articulations: Comics autobiography, trauma, and disability." *The Future of Text and Image: Collected Essays on Literary and Visual Conjunctures*, edited by Ofra Amihay, Lauren Walsh, WJT Mitchell, and Marianne Hirsch. Cambridge Scholars, 2012, 67–89.

Jacobs, Dale, and Jay Dolmage. "Accessible articulations: Comics and disability rhetorics in Hawkeye# 19." *Inks: The Journal of the Comics Studies Society* 2.3 (2018): 353–68.

Jameson, Frederic. "Adaptation as a philosophical problem." *True to the Spirit: Film Adaptation and the Question of Fidelity*, edited by Colin MacCabe, Kathleen Murray, and Rick Warner. Oxford University Press, 2011, 215–34.

Lewis, Bradley. "A deep ethics for mental difference and disability: The 'case' of Vincent van Gogh." *Medical Humanities* 43.3 (2017): 172–76.

McWade, Brigit, Damian Milton, and Peter Beresford. "Mad studies and neurodiversity: A dialogue." *Disability & Society* 30.2 (2015): 305–9.

Murray, Simone, and Alexis Weedon. "Beyond medium specificity: Adaptations, cross-media practices and branded entertainments." *Convergence: The International Journal of Research into New Media Technologies* 17.1 (2011): 3–5.

Mullaney, Clare. "Disability Studies: Foundations and Key Concepts." https://daily .jstor.org/reading-list-disability-studies/.

Porter, Rick. "'Ratched' Debuts at No. 1 in Nielsen Streaming Rankings." *Hollywood Reporter*, 16 Oct. 2020, hollywoodreporter.com/live-feed/ratched-debuts-at-no-1- in-nielsen-streaming-rankings. Accessed 15 Nov. 2020.

Prendergast, Catherine. "On the rhetorics of mental disability." *Embodied Rhetorics: Disability in Language and Culture*, edited by James C Wilson and Cynthia Lewiecki-Wilson. Southern Illinois University Press, 2001, 45–60.

Proctor, William. "Regeneration & rebirth: Anatomy of the franchise reboot." *Scope: An Online Journal of Film and Television Studies* 22 (2012): 1–19.

Pryal, Katie Rose Guest. "The creativity mystique and the rhetoric of mood disorders." *Disability Studies Quarterly* 31.3 (2011).

Robertson, Scott Michael. "Neurodiversity, quality of life, and autistic adults: Shifting research and professional focuses onto real-life challenges." *Disability Studies Quarterly* 30.1 (2010) https://dsq-sds.org/article/view/1069/1234.

Saraiya, Sonia. "Netflix's *Ratched* is Wretched." *Vanity Fair*, 15 Sept. 2020, vanityfair.com/hollywood/2020/09/ratched-review-netflix-sarah-paulson-ryan-murphy. Accessed 15 Nov. 2020.

Scolari, Carlos Alberto. "Transmedia storytelling: Implicit consumers, narrative worlds, and branding in contemporary media production." *International Journal of Communication* 3 (2009): 586–606.

Siebers, Tobin. *Disability Theory*. University of Michigan Press, 2008.

Smith, Dr. Stacy L., et al. "Mental Health Conditions in Film & TV: Portrayals that Dehumanize and Trivialize Characters." USC Annenberg Inclusion Initiative and American Foundation for Suicide Prevention. May 2019.

Squier, Susan M. "So long as they grow out of it: Comics, the discourse of developmental normalcy, and disability." *Journal of Medical Humanities* 29.2 (2008): 71–88.

Whelehan, Imelda. "The contemporary dilemmas." *Adaptations from Text to Screen, Screen to Text*, edited by Deborah Cartmell and Imelda Whelehan. Routledge, (1999): 3–20.

Wilson, James C., and Cynthia Lewiecki-Wilson. "Disability, rhetoric, and the body." *Embodied Rhetorics: Disability in Language and Culture*, edited by James C Wilson and Cynthia Lewiecki-Wilson. Southern Illinois University Press, 2001, 1–24.

Part I

IMAGINING AND BROADENING NARRATIVES OF DISABILITY

Chapter 1

The Prosthetic Self

Drag and Disability in the Figure of RuPaul

John W. Gulledge

Until 1973, the American Psychiatric Association (APA) considered homosexuality a pathology, classifying it in the first edition of the *Diagnostic and Statistical Manual* (*DSM*) (1952), as a "sociopathic personality disturbance." The second edition (1968) dampened the language but still constructed it as a "deviation." The popular psychiatrist Edmund Bergler described the "condition," in 1956, as thus:

> I have no bias against homosexuals; for me they are sick people requiring medical help. . . . Still, though I have no bias, I would say: Homosexuals are essentially disagreeable people, regardless of their pleasant or unpleasant outward manner . . . [their] shell is a mixture of superciliousness, fake aggression, and whimpering. Like all psychic masochists, they are subservient when confronted with a stronger person, merciless when in power, unscrupulous about trampling on a weaker person. (28–29)

Bergler's characterization is rather typical of psychology and psychiatry throughout most of the twentieth century, painting atypical sexuality and desires as a manner of defect, disorder, and disturbance. The use of a term like "masochist" is a rhetorical signal which steeps same-sex desires in the underground subculture of BDSM, another "sexual disorder" that still exists in the most recent *DSM-5*, though is somewhat curbed by the need for the condition to cause "shame, guilt, or anxiety." As might be expected, the metanarrative of sexual deviance and atypical gender behaviors as mental disorders is one that has had a great influence over the way we tell stories about LGBTQ+ communities, even when those stories are meant to challenge and/or counter the status quo.

One of the earliest gay rights advocates, Karl Heinrich Ulrichs, wrote that criminalizing same-sex relationships between men was wrong because some men were born an *urning*, which is to say, a biological man with a woman's soul trapped within their body (LeVay 1996, 12–13). For the mid-nineteenth century, when Ulrichs was writing, this was far more radical and progressive than it may seem to us today, if not because it conflates sexual desire with gender identity, then because it clings to the problem of dualism. Like sexual masochism and sadism, "Transvestic Disorder" and "Gender Dysphoria" are both still present in the *DSM-5* as mental disorders. What is important to note, however, is that the APA addresses gender identity and gender expression as different phenomena, noting that the former "refers to one's psychological sense of gender, [and the latter] refers to the way in which one presents to the world in a gendered way" ("What is Gender Dysphoria?"). For instance, the *DSM-5* is explicit that "gender non-conformity is not in itself a mental disorder"; therefore, the distinctions drawn both explicitly and implicitly construct varying and uneven paths to gender identity and expression. What's more, four of the *DSM-5*'s six diagnostic elements for Gender Dysphoria depend on the assessment of the person's "strong" desires. Even in the most updated and arguably most LGBTQ+-friendly version of the manual, the "significant distress and impairment in social, occupational, or other important areas of functioning" depend upon some "incongruent" desire in the person (APA 2013).

I begin with a brief discussion of the *DSM* precisely because of its historical and contemporary prominence in understanding mental disability and illness. There is still controversy in psychiatry surrounding the overlapping of these two lived-experiences, and the *DSM* reflects this contested ground. The charges to keep mental illness and cognitive disability distinct are often persuasive and admirable—surely, life with a functional impairment, for example, is not the same as life with same-sex desires, regardless of what edition of the *DSM* we are looking at. The calls to expand and "feel out" the textures of their overlap are equally compelling, however, because both disability and illness are best understood in the context of an individual's lived experience. They each attempt to constitute a mind-body that is interstitial, apart from the "norm." In this sense, neurodiversity is an especially useful term both for political advocacy and theoretical insights because it "is a concept that avoids the trappings of diagnostic language that distinguishes between healthy and unhealthy" (Dyck and Russell 2020, 171). It is an expansive and amenable category, encompassing the neurotypical and neurodivergent in equal measure, not as opposing states of mental life, but rather as signposts on a continuum. In fact, there have been recent conversations in the field of psychiatry to move toward "neurodiversity" in describing conditions like autism. "Disability requires acceptance of difference and diversity, and societal 'reasonable adjustment,'" Simon Baron-Cohen has recently argued, "whilst disorder is usually taken to require cure or treatment" (Baron-Cohen 2017, 1). To be sure, there exists a tension between the political and social rights to full citizenship, which includes medical assistance and treatment, and the unmistakable stigmatization embedded in a medical model of disability. I have no definitive stake in this contest here, seeing both topologies (mental illness, disability) as potentially descriptive rather than prescriptive (or indeed, diagnostic). In this chapter, however, I deliberately welcome their overlap as a promising rubric for reevaluating the adaptive and shifting narratives of atypical identity, even in considering a text like the *DSM* which presents itself as a definitive and durable authority but is ultimately a woven, rebooted, and discursive construction.

In what follows, I trace the personal and professional biography of RuPaul Charles, arguably the most famous drag queen in modern history, to suggest an underexplored relationship between drag and disability, which may revolve around a notion of queer expression and prosthetic performances of the self (McMillan 2015). In the first section, I focus on RuPaul's biography—his personal and professional identity as a constellation of recycled variability. The second section considers narrative prosthesis within a disability studies framework and as a means of rebooting forms of identification for "atypical" minds and bodies. In the final section, I attend more closely to the functions of re-accentuation in a performance of such prosthetic figurations. RuPaul, then, serves as a "network of references" where traditionally neurodivergent narratives are recycled, repackaged, and retold through the slippery genre of drag performance. For a figure like RuPaul Charles, and indeed most drag performers in the United States, gender expression is not so distinct from gender identity, as one leads to the other as a kind of heuristic and template for a performance of the self. What I hope to show in this chapter is how we might find in a popular figure like RuPaul unasked questions and new insights about the performance of identity, the medium of the mind/body in that performance, and its remarkable proficiency in adaptation—what I want to read as a program of prosthesis. I'll end the chapter with a brief discussion about what new questions arise from such an inquiry and what I see as a potentially robust coalition between disability and studies of genre and adaptation.

RUPAUL CHARLES

In his 1995 autobiography, RuPaul begins with his motivation for the project: "I wrote this book because I wanted to reveal my soul to the world" (RuPaul 1995, vii). It is striking that a performer whose career is based in "shapeshifting" and over-the-top personalities would strive for such soul-bearing in his debut biography, aptly titled *Letting It All Hang Out*, but, as he confesses in the opening pages, "[he] particularly wanted to do this because, as a drag queen, people generally see [him] as some kind of thing or freak with a sex fetish" (RuPaul 1995, vii). For RuPaul, drag has always been about enterprise, to him no different than a nurse or businessman preparing for work in the morning. Among many things, RuPaul's observations in these opening lines are a reminder that the narrative hold of medicine and social norms is a firm and lasting one. The *DSM* had softened the pathologizing language more than twenty years before RuPaul wrote about his early life, and yet the seeds of stigma remain. Importantly, RuPaul is of a somewhat waning generation, born out of the liberation politics of the 1970s and 1980s, which today may appear at times conservative. That is to suggest, RuPaul's life and career are filled with controversy and what some may call "cringe" moments—incidents that he has often brushed aside and/or redeployed in his ever-adapting ways.

The way RuPaul tells his life is remarkable, always in a tint of memoir. He considers himself an outsider as much now as he felt as a child growing up in San Diego, California, and then Atlanta, Georgia, where he moved with his sister when he was a teen. His feelings of isolation and, at times, alienation, led to a fascination with pop music, television, and iconic Hollywood stars like Barbara Streisand and Diana Ross. He became a student of pop culture, learning to rearrange and synthesize its tropes, genres, and leading figures the way a poet might effortlessly stitch together a line of Shakespeare, a stanza by Hughes, and the one-line graffiti art just down the street. His talent, apart from charismatic performance, has always been the ability of reference. For instance, in the autobiography, he reminisces about watching a commercial with Edie Adams advertising Tiparillo cigars when he was only about five or six:

> She would do big Broadway-style production numbers in gorgeous evening gowns, dripping with fur, and surrounded by male dancers. The commercial would always end with her saying, "Why don't you come up and see me some time?" I had no idea that she had stolen the line from Mae West, but I loved it all the same. (RuPaul 1995, 18)

More recently, RuPaul characterized his drag persona as being "developed out of [his] study of pop culture and how to create a caricature someone could draw on a page and be recognizable." He continues with the perfect "recipe" of sorts for doing just that:

> I took two parts Cher, three parts Diana Ross, a dash of Dolly Parton, and a little bit of David Bowie and James Brown [. . .] and a smattering of Bugs Bunny! That's how my public persona came to be. (RuPaul 2019)

Decades later, and he is still thinking about how his performances and personae might be drawn on the page; in other words, how his remix of popular icons and references might be further extended and represented anew by an artist.

RuPaul begins to articulate this hybrid vision of himself in a 2019 conversation with Judge Judy, stating, "I love when cultures and words get mashed up. . . . Drag reminds people that all artifice is temporary—that all structures are just temporary, and the only thing that stays real is the energy" (Judy 2019). This "mashing up" of cultural influence and icons began early in his life. He describes his childhood as not unhappy, but no fairy tale either, and recounts an experience when he was about ten years old that speaks to his lifelong skill at seeing reflections of his own life in popular movies and television. "When I saw [*The Prince of Tides*]," he explains,

> I started crying uncontrollably, and not silently. It was embarrassing because I literally could not control myself. The movies triggered these feelings that just gushed out of me. As children we bury a lot of our feelings deep inside and learn to become experts at hiding out emotions behind masks. Much later in life some catalyst, some event, will bring them all back, and they will all pour out, even stuff we forgot was there. (RuPaul 1995, 21–22)

RuPaul's early observations share similar threads with the many autobiographical accounts of people with posttraumatic stress (PTS) and anxiety. It likewise speaks to the role narrative has in our shared exploration of personal identity, as well as that of our communities. Seeing his life in *The Prince of Tides*, then, was a paradoxically textured moment of both the pain and sorrow of circumstance and the joy that comes with self-exploration and awareness; it was, to be short and perhaps too simple, a moment of *catharsis*. This term is apt to help frame the work of adaptation in identity and performance because of its deep roots in a tradition of mimesis. Stigma, for instance, is a collection of narrative, networked and reproduced in its cultural transmission. In recounting his life, RuPaul draws out the overlap of stigma, sexuality, and mental illness. The one time his father ever spoke directly to RuPaul about his sexuality, for example, he warned: "This lifestyle—you'll be very lonely" (RuPaul 1995, 213). By reforging affective relationships to stories, to memory, to the self, and to others, into simulated experiences of feeling, the exercise of emotions is never simply an exorcism of them. Through his revisions, RuPaul rearranges his own life story while adapting others—even if totally fictional—to augment and make sense of whomever and whatever he is in a given time and place. As RuPaul tells it, the emotional valence of said arrangement simultaneously affects his adaptive maneuvers and come to reveal an effect of the interwoven narrative.

Today, RuPual's approach to such emotions is somewhat more ambivalent, but still retains the sentiment that what's at work is a re-presentation of the "common," popular sense. "My advice to someone who feels alone," he says in a 2019 interview,

> first off, feelings are not facts; what you feel is an indicator but it's not the truth. The Truth is that we are not separated from one another. We are actually one thing. But your perception and ego makes you think we are two different things, that you are over there and I'm over here, but we are actually one thing together. (RuPaul 2019)

And yet, he sees feelings of alienation as very material and, indeed, quite real: "I feel most like an outsider every day of my life. I've come to peace with feeling like an outsider. I know it's a condition of my brain; it's actually not the truth because everybody feels like an outsider" (RuPaul 2019). On the one hand, RuPaul's autobiographical accounts seem to resist, if not at times reject, his experiences with difference. There is always nestled and lurking the specter of some normative disciplinarian at work in the way he constructs his own narrative. And yet, on the other hand, there is a confession and celebration of that material and mental difference. As this volume attests, neurodiversity is an expansive and collective bridge, a network of cognitive and mental possibility, rather than some gangplank with pointed and exclusionary aims. RuPaul's ambiguity in repackaging his own self-constitution is but an expression of that boundless possibility. Like the constantly rebooted and adapted narrative/fragment, identity is a fluid, often messy affair. "In practice, it is in crisis," Amir Ben Porat observes, and at the level of signification, "The symbolic experiences of identity [. . .] is highly instrumental: it indicates sameness *and* otherness" (Porat 2010, 287). The contest is one of contradictory impulses whereby we adapt to our social and cultural environment while simultaneously adapting *away from* or *out of* those norms to express a unique individuality.

Questions of identity are always unwieldy and contested, of course, and to approach such questions through an adaptive, often controversial figure like RuPaul invites *aporia* rather than unties the knot. Just as Judith Butler's observations in the late 1990s remind us that "cultural values emerge as the result of an inscription of the body, understood as a medium" (Butler 1989, 604), RuPaul maintains the body as a canvas for expression and re-presentation of *personality*: "My identity changes hourly, by the second, and I'm not married to any single one. I'm a shape-shifter. What I've taken away is that those who can adapt will survive" (RuPaul 2018). Two years later, and RuPaul doubles down on this "recipe for success," claiming that "in this life, if you can stay flexible, you have a really good chance of navigating a really rich experience for yourself on this planet" (RuPaul 2020). To this adaptive performance made visible by the body, I should like to add the mind, which is historically, if erroneously, taken to be the seat of the self, and is not divorced from Butler's process of inscription. Figures like RuPaul, however, have made a life and career specifically out of mocking the inscribed, articulated identity-markers that have come to be filial monikers for political and community mobilization. "Some people are a little put off by [drag] because they suspect we're making fun of them, their identity. The truth is we are," he says unapologetically (RuPaul 2018). Elsewhere, he's been more direct about his understanding of the current model of identity politics in the United States, as when he called the entire framework a "lie" and uses the matrix as an analogy to identity-fluidity:

> You know, the matrix says, "Pick an identity and stick with it. Because I want to sell you some beer and shampoo and I need you to stick with what you are so I'll know how to market it to you." Drag is the opposite. Drag says, "Identity is a joke." (Volkert 2016)

Given RuPaul's relatively recent hit reality television series, *RuPaul's Drag Race (RPDR)*, and his own flourishing status as a celebrity, it might be difficult to grasp how something that is now so seemingly mainstream can be, as he argues, the "antithesis" to the neoliberal, capitalist machinery ("the Matrix") he's spent his life rejecting and terrorizing. *RPDR* has now been aired on multiple networks and streaming services, had more than ten seasons, and is parent to a list of adaptations and spinoffs that grows in number every year. The show itself is a ripe case study for questions of the power (and responsibility) popular media wields in rebooting and adapting to cultural and audience expectations.

Although such a study would be worthwhile and generative to the questions posed throughout this chapter, what I choose to focus on is RuPaul himself as a site of competing, mutable, and ultimately adaptive narrativizations of difference. Through a constant breach of the status quo, followed by the crisis it creates in understanding one's "community," and which ends in redress, resolution, and eventual reintegration, RuPaul suggests to us that within an unusual popular medium, like say, a celebrity drag queen, we may be privy to an ongoing "social drama" which is told to us in the ever-adaptive performance strategies of remix, or what I want to suggest as "re-accentuation." In performance theory, re-accentuation is a strategy by which particular qualities of a pretext are foregrounded in performance. As Richard Schechner (2017) outlines,

> No event can exactly copy another event. Not only the behavior itself—nuances of mood, tone of voice, body language, and so on, but also the specific occasion

and context make each instance unique. . . . The uniqueness of an event does not depend on its materiality solely but also on its interactivity—and the interactivity is always in flux. (30)

For identities and categories often at the periphery, this is likewise a strategy of self-constitution.

Therefore, RuPaul's comfort and familiarity with society's "freaks" and "monsters" is not only personal but also a kind of manifesto of the self—like the chameleon, already alien-like with the ability to change hue to sometimes blend in and other times contrast with its environment and an expansive field of vision which may simultaneously look behind and ahead, left and right. Although, the external presentation is not the primary source of this identity, nor is it divorced from the mental and emotional life of that same-self. RuPaul emphasizes instead an "emotional transformation," which is found in the moment of performance after the ritual of getting "into" drag. Monét X Change, a drag contestant on *RuPaul's Drag Race* (Season 10, All Stars 4), describes it as the "heart of the show": "there's something about putting on a wig and a frock for the first time that makes you access parts of your personality that you did not know that were there" (Ifeanyi 2020). This relationship between drag and mental life has not been explored in great detail, owing, in part, to drag's historical position in the cultural periphery. This oversight is made more urgent, given that, as is often the case with members of LGBTQ+ communities, many drag performers (RuPaul included), struggle with mental illness, stigma, and alienation. It seems to me that drag, with its queer, disruptive program of burlesque, reveals a performance strategy of adaptation borne out of necessary innovations and resourcefulness in the face of such mental and social circumstance. To put a finer edge on it: in confronting the stigmatizing and disorienting narratives about nonstandard, queer, crip bodies and minds, drag destabilizes and mocks rather than attempting to rehabilitate and recuperate from such epistemological dizziness. This should not appear as a disavowal of the material, however, nor is it a swearing off the exterior aesthetic project that is drag. As RuPaul puts it, "the medium is the message" and for him, self-expression is joined with self-love, the message he assures us his life and career have been devoted to (RuPaul 1995, 118).

In this construction, I follow the work of José Esteban Muñoz, whose theory of disidentification suggests the many ways minoritarian communities might strategically conform to dominant ideologies while also resisting those same norms and expectations. By way of political and aesthetic appropriation of normative cultural productions, drag is a technique of disidentification where exclusionary narratives are reworked for new world-building imaginings. In the frictions and textures of such negotiations, a sense of identity, both for the individual and for the community, is borne out. Like Katie R.

Horowitz, I am disinclined to see a wide chasm between the material conditions of identity and its socially constructed and scripted aspects. As she explains,

> In contradistinction to discursive ontologies that counterpose performativity with embodied experience, innate with acquired identity markers, reality with pretense, I believe, that such ontologies unnecessarily restrict our ability to make any but the narrowest claims about the relationship between individual and cultural identities. (2013, 323)

NARRATIVE PROSTHESIS AND/AS IDENTITY

Drawing on RuPaul's rich biography and professional work, I will now turn to the larger theoretical implications of "the prosthetic self," an identity formed around the incorporation and remixing of variation and reference. In a recent autobiography that reads more like a "self-help" guide, RuPaul offers up a slew of aphorisms on life, identity, love, and success. Less personal than the 1995 autobiography, *Guru* (2018) does give a glimpse into a more formal philosophy on topics that have marked his life and career. For instance, he recounts what it is like to catch a glimpse of himself in the mirror, affirming in his way, the intimate relationship between the corporeal and the cognitive. He muses,

> Wow, is that really me? I've never quite gotten used to seeing myself in the mirror, in drag or out of drag. "Who am I?" Always creates a deafening silence in the soul. I believe the depth of that silence is the answer. Where do *you* begin and end? Who are you? What are you? I still feel like The Boy Who Fell to Earth, fell into his body, and is experiencing humanity, having fun with it. (RuPaul 2018, 22, emphasis in original)

In the end, it's a story of questions, or rather a series of narrative prompts which beg creative re-invention. There's an implied beginning and end and a spatial sense of setting ("Fell to Earth . . . to his body"). The shift from first person ("Who am I?") to second person ("Who are you?") might suggest the already present act of de-facement in autobiographical composition.

Increasingly referred to as "life writing" today, autobiographical accounts swell in generic (and therefore, ontological) tension—at once preoccupied with what Paul de Man (1979) describes as "their thematic insistence on the subject, on the proper name, on memory, [. . .] and on the doubleness of specularity, [and] equally eager to escape from the coercions of this system" (922). For de Man,

> The specular structure has been displaced but not overcome, and we reenter a system of tropes at the very moment we claim to escape from it. The study of autobiography is caught in this double motion, the necessity to escape from the tropology of the subject and the equally inevitable reinscription of this necessity within a specular model of cognition. (1979, 923)

Indeed, when taken as a form of de-facement, autobiography is already a reboot that, by definition, suspends reality and fantasy, recycles both truth and lies, and remixes fact with fiction. Prosthesis, both as an abstract concept and as a material technology, operates in a similar fashion. (So, too, does drag and performance more broadly.) RuPaul's many reincarnations attest to how a self—or *the* self, since RuPaul claims we are all the same—moves in and out of fantasy. Similarly, David Mitchell and Sharon Snyder explore the enduring relationship between literary discourse and its prosthetic features as well as its own prosthetic function in the field-defining book *Narrative Prosthesis*. Like the double-edge of drag, where it might reify heteronormative narratives as it struggles to resist and breach the status quo, prosthesis can have contradictory effects on an audience. "Whereas an actual prosthesis is always somewhat discomforting," Mitchell and Snyder observe, "a textual prosthesis alleviates discomfort by removing the unsightly from view. . . . The erasure of disability via a 'quick fix' of an impaired physicality or intellect removes an audience's need for concern or continuing vigilance" (2014, 8). To be clear, drag is already in some sense an act of prosthesis, and that they should carry the similar risk of reifying, even comforting, that which they might also resist or reject, serves as a reminder that identity is not autonomous nor is it always a reflection of pure authorial command. This lesson, as commonplace as it is in need of reminder, is one we might continue to explore when allying adaptation studies and mental and cognitive disability. Neurodivergence has much to instruct us regarding future iterations of identity: the happily but not always peacefully rejoined "body-mind" (as the human being) is itself already an adaptation wherein sometimes discrete and competing discourses are remixed into something new.

RuPaul's self-proclaimed deployment of *personae* in the spirit of queer and punk culture has always been a point of contention among his audience, especially those who identify as such. If narrative prosthesis arises, as Mitchell and Snyder suggest, from "a narrative issue to resolve or correct [. . .] a deviance marked as improper to a social context," then we might adapt such a framework for what I refer to as the "prosthetic self" (Mitchell and Snyder 2014, 53). RuPaul's anecdote about the mirror supports such a motion not simply because it flaunts an ableist metaphor or treats the mirror as an extension/assistance, but precisely because the moment of self-realization is thwarted—where exactly does the (prosthetic) self begin and end? What does it mean to feel out of place, alien to one's environment and to one's body? The context of the mirror incident is an unusual, but not impossible, example of autobiographical performance. In this case, RuPaul is not only the performer and his life not simply the content of the performance act, but he is also the spectator. Relating performer, performance, and audience is at the core of a dramatic and/or theatrical event, and like the troubled genre of autobiography, it becomes clear that these roles are not three distinct pillars, but rather an interdependent network of reference. As one might expect from any type of prosthesis, its technological function is assumed to be programmatic, and to be sure, this is how Mitchell and Snyder imagine narrative prosthesis to operate as well. Though minor, I find this characterization more limiting than descriptive. I propose we think of narrative prosthesis instead as a kind of *techne*, the Greek term which marries craft and art. Like rhetoric, which is also described as a *techne*, prosthesis is not only a program of practice and craft but also likewise an aesthetic category of artistic invention and creativity. What I want to suggest here is that the prosthetic self, which is undeniably devoted to tropes and programmatic scripts, mediates and mixes cultural reference so as to reveal the inherently mutable, artificial dimensions of life. In other words, the prosthetic self is a hybrid form, a medium of revelation like the Latin *monstrum* (monster/omen) which signs a shadowed futurity by recycling and adapting familiar, though often exclusionary and problematic, cultural cues. As devoted as it may seem at times, this assemblage is not without infidelity and maintains, I think, an equally stout commitment to oddity, queerness, and difference. RuPaul describes something similar when he writes,

> Transformation, adaptability, alchemy, and re-creating of self are the words I live by. Birth and death and rebirth are constant themes in life. Staying flexible, both figuratively and literally, is what being vital is all about. Seeing myself from outside myself helps. . . . The crucifixion at the end of the first act is meaningless without the resurrection in the second act. (2018, 148)

Even in describing a part of his life philosophy, he recycles and adapts a Biblical story, which incorporates the cultural reference into his own imagination of self as well as his discursive construction of that self. Simultaneously, however, it unsettles that narrative, since he, a gay drag queen, is positioned as analogous to Christ. What's more, the adapted reference is reframed as a two-act play; by melding dramatic structure with religious historiography, RuPaul engages in world-building, as it were, rewriting a historical and spiritual record into a one-man play. Through this engagement with disidentification, he performs as both an anthology of dominant culture and as its worst nightmare. Simply, he is student and steward who, in keeping, shows room for revision and artistic adaptation.

The connections seem endless. RuPaul's questions and narrativizations in both instances are forms of speculation. From the Latin *speculatus*, meaning to spy or observe, and connected to the *speculum*, or "looking glass," his experience of speculation is one wherein his identity roils and flees from fixity; he spies a figure that is not only himself but also *not* not himself. Though a talent of his, he seems surprised by the constant translation of himself and, in turn, finds pleasure in the interpretive role of a reader. Writing himself anew is akin to re-reading himself, a skill that is considered "fundamental" in drag culture. Reading in this sense, however, is an in-group practice of critique, sometimes referred to as "shade." "Shade comes from reading," explains Dorian Corey in the groundbreaking documentary, *Paris Is Burning* (1990), "[and] reading is the real art form of insult" (Livingston). Though based in insult, the practice is one of humor, play, and ultimately, a kind of kinship. As Corey explains further,

> When you are all of the same thing, then you have to go to the fine point. . . . If I'm a black queen, and you're a black queen, we can't call each other black queens. That's not a read, that is just a fact. So, we talk about your ridiculous shape, your saggy face, your tacky clothes. (Livingston)

Notice that the emphasis is not on "fact," but rather on a mode of interpretation, revision, and invention. Reading is an act of prosthesis, then, one where adaptation is the fulcrum for understanding one's self as both part of and separate from a community—from a network of reference, for that matter. Reading is also performative, reliant on a shared sense of citation and scripting without totally erasing any expression of individuation.

Another, more recent project of RuPaul's fits well within this frame of reference. Released toward the beginning of 2020, *AJ and the Queen* riffs on all kinds of genres and tropes, never shy of its heavy-handed program of appropriation. The story puts Ruby Red, a drag queen who was duped and robbed by her former boyfriend, on a cross-country tour with AJ, a preteen whose parents are absent and has been trying to survive in New York City all on her own. One critic noted soon after its release: "Watching AJ and the Queen feels akin to pulling a VHS from the comedy rack at a Blockbuster in 1996" (Kornhaber 2020). The nostalgia of each episode is unmistakable but equally reimagined, adapted, and reread. It begins with an attitude that RuPaul has diffused throughout his professional career;

> On a TV in an RV, Oprah speaks. "You have to start with beginning to love yourself," she says. "You hear a lot of that in the '80s. And what does that

mean?" Oprah's guru guest, a feathered blonde in a blazer, replies that it means that you should stop beating up on yourself. "When you begin to love who you are, then you can love your neighbor, because you love yourself," the woman says. "See, I don't think we can really love our neighbor until we do love ourselves." (Kornhaber 2020)

The layering of sentiment and affect, not to mention of a kind of philosophical outlook, is legible at first blush. Ruby Red is a remake of RuPaul, both of whom are adaptations of an Oprah-like figure. If "You're born naked[, and] the rest is drag" is RuPaul's most famous catchline, his second most famous is "If you can't love yourself, how in the hell can you love anyone else?" At all turns, the individual is placed in contact with the communal; sociality and individuality are not binaries for RuPaul's artistic vision. And it is this vision, I argue, that is realized through a method of performance.

PERFORMANCE ACCENTUATION AND/ AS MEDIA ADAPTATION

For a realized "self" embedded in a technique of prosthesis, the significance of performance cannot be overstated. Although we might read finished "products" of the self, or its media, in this vein, we risk missing its ongoing, always-in-formation aspects. Although such peculiar, agile facets inevitably remain out of total reach, it is through a study of its performative nature that this chapter argues we may come nearest. Following Paul Edwards, I define a "performance text" as "the orchestrated, 'woven' ensemble of materials and effects that an audience 'reads'" (2006, 240). To be sure, reader reception has been fashionable in both literary and performance studies for some time now. What an audience understands as spontaneity, for instance, is just as critical as the performer's repetition and preparation in rehearsal. The creation of a *sense* of spontaneity, or "free improvisation," might depend upon a "habituated, automatic response," paradoxically forged in practice. Adaptation in performance has been described as a product of "pre-text," any preestablished dramatic circumstance (or "orchestrated, woven ensemble of materials and effects"), and thus cannot establish on its own any sense of a "finished" performance text. The approach is more easily applied to a traditional theater setting, where there is a literal play-text, an obvious element of a performance's "pre-text." What the medium of drag asks of performance studies, however, is more suggestive and speculative. The "pre-text" is itself already an amalgamation of stitched and repurposed citation material—this part is not so different to aesthetic, theater performance—but its status as pre*established* is dubious in the sense that the performance text depends upon the usurpation and/or revision of a rehearsed, habitual script. And yet, it's not "free improvisation" either. My approach to the adaptations of drag and neurodivergence, particularly in narrative and performance, relies upon a theory of re-accentuation.

In 1974, Augusto Boal lamented the rise of what he labeled "the finished theatre," a reflection of the bourgeois demand for images of a "completed, finished world" (142). As discussed earlier, drag performance intimates radical futurity while reifying conservative ideology; it is not an either/or. A site of queer, divergent, and, therefore, unfinished expression, drag reflects back a world *in-the-making*. Even as it may recycle and reboot modes of cultural oppression, drag is a program of re-accentuation whereby the deviant and disorderly, for example, are reread as beautiful and generative. Re-accentuation considers the elements of a performance as plastic, easily manipulated and adapted to new contexts. Bakhtin defines re-accentuation similarly in his discussion of the novel form, noting how "the novel parodies other genres (precisely in their role as genres); it exposes the conventionality of their forms and their language; it squeezes out some genres and incorporates others into its own peculiar structure, reformulating and re-accentuating them" (Bakhtin 2010, 5). Read this way, I propose to identify drag with the early, often radical nature of the novel: it presents as ever-new, but to achieve that level of novelty, it must constantly resurface and manipulate other social and cultural productions. It has been argued that drag unveils and critiques the artificial nature of gender and sexuality; it has also been argued that drag reinforces heteronormative binaries, which are often narrativized as essential aspects of the human experience. The ambiguity that drag suggests to us in this regard depends upon re-accentuation. What I mean by this is not at all controversial: context in performance makes all the differences, it would seem. Oliver Norman puts this succinctly when he writes, "drag is about our culture's vision of femininity or gender and drag plays with that in the bars and clubs" (2019, 120). "RuPaul's aim," Norman continues, "is to tell people that men are not born but made: the clothes don't make the man and neither does the penis!" (2019, 122). The position is frustrating in its ambiguity, but it does suggest something more complex about the relationship between a performed identity (through costuming and behavior, for instance) and the material conditions of one's body and mind. In sussing out this relationship, we may turn again to disidentification.

Disidentification is ultimately a strategy for survival, and the drag queens who grace *RPDR* speak to the connection between their performance and mental health regularly. In fact, the show has made it a prominent component of each episode, cohesively marking it a part of RuPaul's brand of queer self-love. Either in conversation with one another or in private confessionals, contestants reveal their histories with depression, anxiety, homelessness, addiction, and trauma. They actively negotiate questions surrounding their sexuality, gender, race, and ability in an attempt to make sense of the roles and scripts they are performing, both on and off the stage. The show's emphasis on this reboots a familiar story of queer survival, whereby the "deviant outsider" may find oneself within the narratives, images, and cultural references they are ostensibly exiled from. The recent novel *Drag Teen*, by Jeffrey Self, for example, references *RPDR* as well as the classic movie *To Wong Foo, Thanks for Everything! Julie Newmar* (1995)—in which RuPaul had a cameo. In those popular representations, the novel's protagonist finds narrative inspiration for his own story: "[They] knew how to cope with their inner strands of self-doubt and sew those strands into something fabulous. Usually a dress" (Self 2016, 78). Rather than the message "It Gets Better," which still dominates much of the discourse targeting LGBTQ+ teens, the message of drag is to take an active role in projecting that better world and imagined self into being. For instance, Matthew Lent, who was on season 7 of *RPDR*, describes his experience in creating his drag persona, Pearl, as "this character that [he] would draw just 'cause it distracted me from the horrible things that I felt were going on around me, and one day, I just painted her *on* me" (emphasis mine). Like RuPaul's earlier reflections that his persona arose out of a desire to be easily and readily "drawn," Pearl's anecdote reminds us that re-accentuation has material dimensions. On the one hand, the adaptation colorfully translates interiority into aesthetic enterprise, making legible mental and cognitive difference just as it shapes that variation anew; while on the other hand, what may be perceived or narrated as "disorderly" is rendered "in order," spontaneously remade by the arrangement and "read" within its new context.

AJ and the Queen displays a similar constitutive program, registered in the disabled character Louis. When Robert ("Ruby") notices a large, uneaten cake waiting on the table, he asks Louis who it is for. Because Louis is a diabetic and Robert "do[esn't] eat cake," the following exchange is riddled with comedy and exposition:

Louis: Oh, I guess it's for me, then.
Robert: You're diabetic.
Louis: A diabetic person can eat anything anyone else can eat. They just have to be more careful about it. Now, that's a quote from WebMD, so you know it's true.
Robert: Uh-huh. Interesting you can read all that, you being blind and all.
Louis: Don't put limits on me!

I argue that *AJ and the Queen* already begins to make connections between disability and health/illness that have gone largely ignored in critical disability studies. Louis's comment about his chronic illness echos and recycles the same language often used in disability narratives. One way to read this is as a commentary of "overcoming," a narrative that admittedly has plagued disability representation, particularly when those narratives are told by a nondisabled author. But I propose to read this moment as a response to the stigmatizing assumptions—the very narrativized building blocks of disability—wherein Louis purposefully conflates his diabetes and his blindness. The paradigm he conveys is already an adaptive one, and by way of recontextualizing his disability, Louis foregrounds a strategy of re-accentuation. What's more, because this exchange occurs while Louis, a queer black man in NYC, is in full drag, I cannot help but be reminded of the *DSM* and the many ways nonnormativity and stigma form an ever-shifting lattice of disability.

CONCLUSION

Drag performance, and in particular, the affordances of reinvention that come with it, is simultaneously fortifying and an opportunity for vulnerability. A helpful framework for this type of performance comes from Uri McMillan's phenomenal work in *Embodied Avatars: Genealogies of Black Feminist Art and Performance*. Through daring modes of embodied performance, McMillan traces women performers who maneuver their way toward a liberated subjectivity through improvisation and disruptive performances of objecthood. Of particular use here is the theory of "prosthetic performance," which accounts for the "protean ploys including both repurposed objects . . . and the embodied behaviors" that might be performed toward strategic ends—and indeed, for survival (McMillan 2015, 75). In drag culture, which is rooted in queer anti-heteronormativity, the "disordered" self is reimagined into a hybrid figure where orderly parts are stitched together, even if those parts are not socially expected to "fit." The result is not necessarily a self-in-order, and in fact, drag queens thrive on adapting and exaggerating the parts of society that elicit gawking onlookers, as we have discovered in RuPaul's biography as well as through the character of Louis. Instead, the figure is more like the "less-encumbered other" of McMillan's avatars, where objecthood remains a compromised position but represents movement toward freedom: for Robert, it is nothing short of a "saving."

"The Prosthetic Self" begins to help bridge performed identity with the lived realities of mental difference. Whether this difference is marked by material circumstance or stigma (or as is often the case, both), the strategies and resilience of marginalized communities signal novel ways of re-reading and remixing the narratives that might story a life.

WORKS CITED

Association, American Psychiatric. *Diagnostic and Statistical Manual of Mental Disorders (Dsm-5®)*. American Psychiatric Pub, 2013.
Bakhtin, Mikhail Mikhaĭlovich. *The Dialogic Imagination*. University of Texas Press, 2010.
Baron-Cohen, Simon. "Editorial Perspective: Neurodiversity–a revolutionary concept for autism and psychiatry." *Child Psychol Psychiatry* 58.6 (2017): 744–47.
Bergler, Edmund. *Homosexuality: Disease or Way of Life*. Hill & Wang, 1956.
Boal, Augusto. "Theatre of the oppressed." Theatre Communications Group, 1985.
Butler, Judith. "Foucault and the Paradox of Bodily Inscriptions." (1989): 601–7.
De Man, Paul. 1979. "Autobiography as De-facement." *MLN* 94 no. 5 (1979): 919–30.
Dolmage, Jay Timothy. *Disability Rhetoric*. Syracuse University Press, 2014.
Dyck, Erika, and Ginny Russell. "Challenging Psychiatric Classification: Healthy Autistic Diversity and the Neurodiversity Movement." In *Healthy Minds in the Twentieth Century*, pp. 167–87. Palgrave Macmillan, Cham, 2020.
Edwards, Paul C. "Staging Paradox: The Local Art of Adaptation." In *Sage Handbook of Performance Studies*, pp. 227–51. Sage, 2006.
Horowitz, Katie R. "The Trouble With "Queerness": Drag and the Making of Two Cultures." *Signs: Journal of Women in Culture and Society* 38, no. 2 (2013): 303–26.
Ifeanyi, K. C. "Trixie Mattel and Monet X Change Reveal the Transformative Power of 'RuPaul's Secret Celebrity Drag Race." *Fast Company*, April 24, 2020.
Judy, Judge. "Justice is Served: A Conversation Between RuPaul and Judge Judy." Interview with *Interview Magazine*, August 19, 2019.
Kornhaber, Spencer. "AJ and the Queen Says Drag Will Make America Okay Again." *The Atlantic*, 2020.
LeVay, Simon. *Queer Science: The Use and Abuse of Research into Homosexuality*. MIT Press, 1996.
McMillan, Uri. *Embodied Avatars*. NYU Press, 2015.
Mitchell, David, and Sharon Snyder. "Narrative Prosthesis." *The Disability Studies Reader* 4 (2013): 222–35.
Muñoz, José Esteban. *Disidentifications*. University of Minnesota Press, 2013.
Norman, Oliver. "And the Rest is Drag?" *Rupaul's Drag Race and Philosophy*, eds. Hendrik Kempt and Megan Volpert. Open Court Publishing, 2019.
Porat, Amir Ben. "Football Fandom: A Bounded Identification." *Soccer & Society* 11, no. 3 (2010): 277–90.
RuPaul. *Lettin it All Hang Out*. Hyperion Books, 1995.
RuPaul. *Guru*. HarperCollins, 2018.
RuPaul. "RuPaul, Curtis Sittenfeld and More on Identity." Interview with *The Wall Street Journal*, March 26, 2018. https://www.wsj.com/articles/rupaul-curtis-sittenfeld-and-more-on-identity-1522071601#comments_sector.
RuPaul. "RuPaul Answers Increasingly Personal Questions." Interview with *Vanity Fair*, November 20, 2019. https://www.youtube.com/watch?v=72AAlCa1Nko.

RuPaul. "RuPaul's Recipe for Success? Love Yourself and Stay Flexible." Interview with Terry Gross, *NPR,* March 10, 2020. https://www.npr.org/transcripts/813970591.

Schechner, Richard. *Performance Studies: An Introduction.* Routledge, 2017.

Self, Jeffery. *Drag Teen.* Scholastic Inc., 2016.

Ulrichs, Karl Heinrich. *The Riddle of "Man-Manly Love."* Prometheus Books, 1994.

Volkert, Zachary. "RuPaul's Drag Race' Will Die Before It Goes Mainstream, Says Show Creator." *The Inquisitor,* May 14, 2016.

Chapter 2

Adapting Medical Reports into Narrative Film

Autism, Eugenics, and Savagery in Truffaut's L'Enfant sauvage (The Wild Child, 1970)

Joy C. Schaefer

Like postcolonial studies, disability studies teach us that the ability to assimilate to the dominant culture is *not* how we should judge the value of human life. I use this common theoretical thread to examine French New Wave critic-turned-filmmaker François Truffaut's tenth feature-length film, *L'Enfant sauvage* (*The Wild Child*, 1970), an exceptionally early representation of autism in the history of narrative cinema. The film adapts several historical and medical texts concerning the "wild boy of Aveyron," a feral child found in a Southern French forest in 1798 when he was twelve years old. Truffaut's primary source text was Dr. Jean-Marc Itard's *Memoire and Report on Victor of Aveyron* (1806), which includes two of Itard's reports, the first sent to the Academy of Medicine in 1801 and the second to the French Minister of the Interior in 1806 asking for continued funding for the boy's guardian, Mme. Guérin. Truffaut also did extensive research on autistic children before directing the film. Some of the common autistic characteristics we see "the wild boy of Aveyron" portray in the film include difficulty with social interactions and language acquisition, flat affect, and stimming (self-stimulation, or repetitive movements that help to focus and calm oneself, easing a heightened sensitivity to more anxiety-producing environmental stimulation). In these ways, the film is important in terms of the representational history of autism and neurodiversity.

Equally important for both disability studies and postcolonial studies—and whether or not Truffaut intended it—the film's autistic child works as a metaphor for the "savage" colonial subject who is in need of the benevolent colonizer to teach him how to be "civilized." This representation is what

Mark Sherry (2007) warns against—the dangers of abusing the "rhetorical connections" that exist between disability and postcolonialism (21). Yet, it is precisely the film's problematic representation of disability as metaphor that becomes interesting for disability studies. In *Cultural Locations of Disability*, Sharon L. Snyder and David T. Mitchell (2010) claim that our current theories of eugenics ignore disability and impairment as socially mediated categories of human difference because they "exclusively reference 'race' as the social locus of ascribed insufficiency, while leaving disability as the default category of 'real' human incapacity" (111). This warning renders *L'Enfant sauvage* a complicated case study, as its conflation of ethnicity and disability leaves the uninformed spectator to wonder from which social locus the wild child's "insufficiency" stems.

The film takes place less than a decade after the French Revolution of 1789. It begins with a woman "discovering" the twelve-year-old nude boy—played by Jean-Pierre Cargol, a dark-skinned Romani boy from the outskirts of Montpellier. The fictional boy runs around on all fours, bites people who try to touch him, and is unable to speak due (presumably) to lack of human contact. He is taken to Paris where he is exposed to the public as a spectacle, much like the organizers of the World's Fair would soon do to people of color from the East and Global South beginning in the late 1800s. Truffaut's film shortens this part of the boy's journey, focusing instead on the relationship among the boy, Dr. Jean-Marc Gastard Itard (played by Truffaut himself), and Itard's housekeeper and Victor's future guardian, Mme. Guérin (played by Françoise Seigner). In Paris, at the National Institute for Deaf-Mutes, the most celebrated psychiatrist of the time, Philippe Pinel (Jean Dasté), thinks the boy is an irrecuperable "idiot," while his young colleague Itard (Truffaut) thinks he has the ability to become a "normal" child with proper education. Itard takes him to his suburban home where he begins to educate him, naming his pupil-patient Victor because of his strong response to the sound "O." Sometimes Itard takes these lessons too far, provoking temper tantrums in Victor, and Mme. Guérin is consistently there to offer the boy comfort and unconditional love when this occurs. Near the film's end, Victor disappears for a long time but comes back on his own after discovering that he's lost many of his survival skills. The film ends much like Truffaut's semiautobiographical French New Wave film, *Les Quatre cents coups* (*The 400 Blows*, 1959): the rebel child returns the camera's ageist and ableist gaze.

With co-writer Jean Gruault, Truffaut adapted Itard's *Memoire and Report on Victor of Aveyron* into daily diary entries, enacted in the film as a voice-over read by Truffaut in the role of Itard. Through this focus on Itard's medicalizing voiceover, Truffaut's adaptation ends up doubling down on the ableism and the racism of post-Revolution medicine; other factors that contribute to this ableist representation include two key preproduction choices and several formal choices. In terms of preproduction, Truffaut cast the brown-skinned Cargol as the historically white Victor, allowing the white Truffaut, who plays Itard, to become the boy's "white savior": Truffaut/Itard thinks Victor can and should change with a "proper education," and he teaches Victor behaviors that will help him assimilate to dominant French culture. Second, Truffaut's choice of shooting location—from urban institution to rural setting—buttresses the film's ability to conflate disability and savagery by surrounding the boy with symbols of nature, rendering him visually "primitive" in contrast to the well-educated Itard, who is consistently associated with "science." In terms of formal choices, the film repeatedly renders Victor an inscrutable object by visually framing him as more of an animal or a medical specimen than a human. These elements echo the creation of colonialist spectacle, transforming the boy into an object of the imperialist gaze. Finally, the film's narrative focus on Itard's medicalizing voiceover highlights his role as white savior.

Autobiographical examinations of *L'Enfant sauvage* are numerous because Truffaut himself plays the doctor who attempts to cure the child (e.g., Allen 1985; Codell 2006). While several scholars have analyzed the film with the knowledge of Truffaut's interest in representing autism (Andrew 2013; Gillain 2013) or language difficulty (McCance 2008), or even within the context of a decolonizing France (Codell 2006), I have found none who consider both disability and colonialism together—nor the film's overt racialization of the "wild boy" via Truffaut's casting of Cargol. In what follows, I use the method of close formal scene analysis to argue that the film metaphorizes the neurodiverse child as the colonial subject. In addition, due to Truffaut's adaptive choices, the film evokes the ways in which colonial attitudes reinforced ableist attitudes (and vice versa) at the beginning of what Snyder and Mitchell (2010) term the "Eugenic Atlantic" period—when racial and disability eugenics dovetailed at the end of the eighteenth century. Despite French decolonization and Truffaut's involvement in the movement, the film reveals a troubling conflation between the disabled child and the colonial subject.

STIMMING AS EVIDENCE

Before diving into Truffaut's adaptive preproduction choices, this section aims to firmly establish our film's character, Victor, as autistic—both through the film's representation of him, as well as via Truffaut's intention for the character.

In *L'Enfant sauvage*'s opening sequence, we are introduced to the "wild child" through the eyes of an elderly woman who is mushroom hunting in the Aveyron Forest in the South of France. She sees rustling in the trees, an image of nature before human civilization, and what appears to be a frightened animal begins to grunt in a high pitch and violently kick up leaves and dirt from the ground. The woman drops her mushroom basket and runs away down the hill; we cut back to the "animal" as the camera follows him running on his hands and feet through the trees. A three-quarter shot zooms into a medium shot to reveal a dark-skinned boy with long, matted hair and a filthy face who grabs the basket and shoves several mushrooms into his mouth at once. He then makes his way to a stream to drink water and finally climbs up a tree and sits on a branch near the top where he rests, basking in the sunlight. There, he holds his hair and begins to rock back and forth at a steady tempo as the camera pans out amidst the chirping of birds; the scene finally fades in an iris shot. Already in this opening sequence, we learn several things about the boy's tendencies, as well as his relationship to nature and civilization. First, we have evidence of his tendency toward stimming. As Anne Gillain (2013) writes, "The self-cradling of the wild boy at the end of this sequence is characteristic of young autistic children" (209). Second, we know the boy is "wild" enough to climb trees with ease and is comfortable walking on all fours.

The opening sequence's representation of stimming should be contextualized in light of the film's other representations of this autistic tendency and Truffaut's study of autism. In addition to reading Itard's work on Victor, Truffaut collected books and articles on autistic children as he prepared to direct the film, and he also viewed films of autistic children and used their traits when creating his titular character (Truffaut 1987, 114). Found in the F. Truffaut files at the Archives of the BiFi (Cinémathèque Française Bibliothèque du Film, Paris), these include a French translation of autism studies pioneer Dr. Lorna Wing's "Autistic Children" (1968), which describes the behavior (including "abnormal movements") and educational needs of autistic children; and a French translation of a speech by Dr. Bernard Rinland, "A New Perspective in the Treatment of Children with Mental Illness," given in 1965 at the National Society for Autistic Children in Washington, D.C. (all translations from the French are my own unless otherwise noted). Also drawing on archival research, Dudley Andrew (2013) has shown that Truffaut was influenced by leftist activist and filmmaker Fernand Deligny's documentary work on autistic children. In 1968, Deligny wrote to Truffaut about his newest autistic subject, Janmari, describing in detail his autistic characteristics and relating him to Mowgli of *The Jungle Book*, likening him to "a young orangutan." Truffaut was enthusiastic about the letter and sent his associate Suzanne Schiffman to Cevennes to take notes and photos of Janmari, who provided an "ideal model" for Truffaut's subject (Andrew 2013, 231).

We find Truffaut's knowledge of autism throughout the film, but the way he frames his autistic subject is problematic: when Victor stims, the camera shows him via a long shot instead of a close-up. The close-up shot is more likely to evoke a viewer's emotion and connect us to the character because we are able to see their facial expressions and emotions, thus allowing us to sympathize with them. Conversely, long shots tend to distance us from understanding or connecting to the character's emotions. In the case of *L'Enfant sauvage*, the formal choice of showing us the "wild boy" through long shots cements him as just that—a specimen to be rationally studied (as "defective") rather than emotionally understood (as human). For example, when Victor escapes the carriage to Paris, a long shot shows him flapping his arms up and down into river water; instead of a close-up on his face to show his confusion during travel, Truffaut again offers us a long shot of the stimming boy whose instinct pulls him back to nature. At the Institute for Deaf-Mutes, where a worker displays him to Parisian visitors, Victor moves his head and shoulders around in a haphazard circle as he sits on the bed as object of the ableist gaze; here, we see the spectators in a medium shot while the boy's body remains entirely visible to the camera—except for the gazing bodies that cover him.

Long shots throughout the film also display Victor as he stims while connecting with nature—again cementing the autistic child as an inscrutable specimen to be studied. These shots illustrate Stuart Murray's (2008) explanation of the public's fascination with, and misunderstanding of, autism. In *Representing Autism*, Murray states,

> Autism appears as a peculiarly silent and pernicious version of this disruption [of the majority, non-disabled, worldview], an object difficult to identify and too problematic in its range (from the non-verbal to the garrulous, from severe sensory and environmental experiences to small character "eccentricities") to regulate precisely. (2008, 4)

The film thus presages our contemporary media landscape: representations of autistic people abound that reveal a fascination with a disability that "elude[s] comprehension" and thus is thought to be unable to be "corrected" (2008, 4).

The long shots of Victor stimming in nature offer a stark contrast to the close-up shots we see of Itard's hand as he writes his notes on the boy's progression (with Itard's patronizing voiceover on the audio track), as well as the close-ups on Itard's stoic face throughout the film. Even a three-quarter shot reveals Itard as the protagonist with whom we should sympathize while distancing us from Victor: in an early scene, the doctor teaches Victor how to walk upright; all we see of Victor is the lower half of his torso, his arms, and his legs (see figure 2.1). While the camera consistently humanizes the rationalist doctor and prioritizes his story, it distances the audience from its

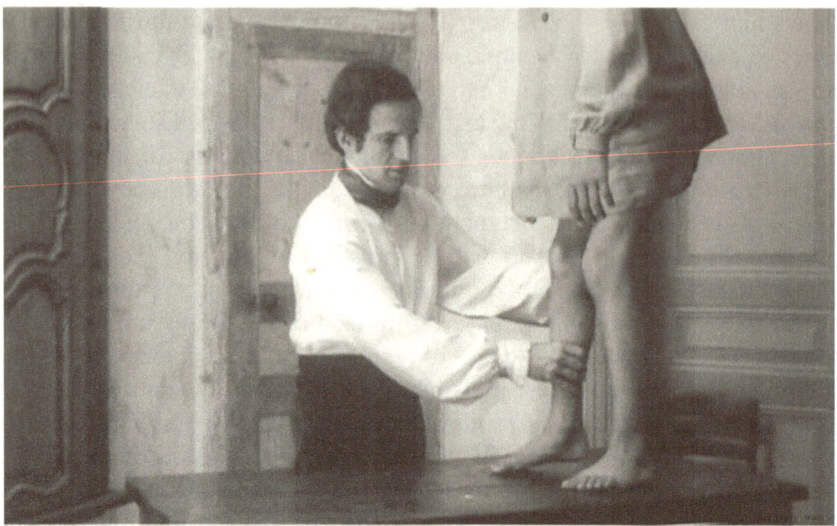

Figure 2.1 A Three-Quarter Shot of Victor's (Cargol) First Upright Steps Focuses on Itard (Truffaut) Rather Than Our Titular Character, Whose Face We Cannot See. *Source*: *L'Enfant sauvage*, Les Films du Carrosse, 1970.

disabled patient, especially when that patient becomes too "uncivilized" due to his tendency to stim.

CASTING EUGENICS

The cinematic Victor becomes a symbolic nexus of the "Eugenic Atlantic" period through Truffaut's adaptive choice to represent him as an autistic boy of color. Kateřina Kolářová (2019) writes that "disability is always both entangled in symbolic racializations and serving dynamic constructions of the East-West dichotomies" (161). Not only does *L'Enfant sauvage* showcase Victor's autism as a deficiency via distancing long shots; equally important, it presents the autistic boy as racialized. This is because Truffaut and his assistant chose a dark-skinned Romani boy to play the "wild child" even though several reports that Truffaut collected described the boy as ethnically Caucasian. This is significant when we consider that the film was produced just after the end of the second colonial empire, which began with the conquest of Algeria in 1830 and ended when colonized subjects pushed the French out during the Algerian War of Independence from French colonial rule (1954–1962). The film thus locates the intertwining of racism and ableism at two critical points in French (and global) history: the film represents the period after the Revolution of 1789, the nascent eugenics period, and it was produced only a year after the events of May and June 1968, France's nationwide upheaval of protests and strikes that were heavily influenced by the decolonial movement in France and Algeria (Ross 2008).

In her book *Tout Truffaut*, Gillain (2019) analyzes *L'Enfant sauvage* through the literal lens of the window and the dichotomy of universes between which it sits: "child/adult, nature/culture [. . .] house/forest, inside/outside, tree/staircase, writing/body" (121). These binaries, she argues, structure the film and lend meaning to its narrative, with the window acting as "a place of communication between these two universes, [. . .] at once a promise of harmony and a call to escape for the savage" (122). While useful, Gillain fails to mention that these binaries are historically situated within French colonialist ideologies and contemporary stereotypes of—and discriminations against— people of color in France. As Edward Said established in *Orientalism* (1978), Western imperialistic discourse has for centuries constructed people of "the East" (e.g., the Middle East, Africa, and Asia) as exotic, irrational, incomprehensible, primitive, innately connected to nature, and ruled by instinct—a discourse that in many ways mirrors ableist discourses regarding disabled and impaired bodies. Orientalism thus renders the rational, secular, white Western man as the universal "normal" subject, while ableist discourse constructs the able-bodied, able-minded, neurotypical person as the norm.

The film's conflation of Victor's disability with primitive instinct illustrates a historical slippage between race and disability. Roger Shattuck (1980) explains in *The Forbidden Experiment* that

> Truffaut imagined a whole repertory of animal-like movements, some of them derived from the behavior of autistic children. In the film the boy at the beginning is almost on all fours and gradually becomes erect. Like a cat, he continues to rub against and touch many of the objects in his environment. (210)

As the films' first scene ends, Victor rocks steadily back and forth as the camera pans out amidst the chirping of birds, conflating the stimming child with the magic and mysteriousness of nature. Here and elsewhere in the film, the disabled body becomes a metaphor for nature, man's prelinguistic state—similar to the representation of racialized people during (and after) colonization.

In this context, it is important that Cargol, who plays Victor, is Romani (better known by the racial slur "Gypsy," which originated in the sixteenth century when Europeans thought Romani people had come from Egypt). Romani is an ethnicity, culture, and language originating in India that was particularly vulnerable during the Holocaust. Cargol was living in a *cité* (low-income housing projects—or the suburban "ghetto") in the outskirts of Montpellier when he was "discovered" by Truffaut's assistant. Contrasting

Truffaut's method of casting to Werner Herzog's for *Kaspar Hauser* (1974), Andrew (2013) claims that "the Gypsy [*sic*] boy chosen to portray Victor was not essential" (238). Yet, Truffaut's adaptive choice to cast a Romani boy to play Victor is important, especially considering that several of the reports Truffaut collected described the boy as white. For example, excerpts from the reports of biology professor Pierre Joseph Bonnaterre, the first scientist to study Victor, describe him as having "fine, white skin; a round face; black, sunken eyes, brown hair; a long, pointed nose; an average mouth; rounded chin; an agreeable physiognomy and gracious smile; in short, from the outside, nothing distinguishes him from others." With writings like these in Truffaut's own *L'Enfant sauvage* file (BiFi Archives), it seems odd that he would choose a boy of color to play his pupil. Truffaut had returned to his casting method for his second film, *Les Mistons* (*The Mischief Makers*, 1957). He states,

> I directed five boys from Nîmes, of whom one or two really had something savage about them. [. . .] I sent my assistant to watch when school let out, at Arles, Nimes, Marseilles, etc. It was in a street in Montpellier that she noticed, questioned, and photographed among others a little gypsy [*sic*] boy, Jean-Pierre Cargol. Jean-Pierre, the little gypsy [*sic*] who I finally chose to play the role, is a very handsome child, but I think he really does look as if he just came out of the woods. (Truffaut 1987, 115)

Perhaps without realizing it, his casting and direction of Cargol allows the "wild child" to mirror France's constructed image of the people of its former colonies: dark, different, savage, and inscrutable.

Ian Hancock (1985), scholar of Romani culture and language, writes that "Somehow Gypsies aren't considered real people; the word is usually written without a proper noun's initial capital letter, as though it referred to a category like 'hippie' or 'beatnik'" (16). Indeed, more than half of the film reviews found in the BiFi that mention the ethnic background of Cargol use the French word's lower-case spelling: "gitan" instead of "Gitan." *Canard Enchaîné*'s review, with its repetition of the word "little," explicitly links savagery to Romani culture: "The role of the little savage is played by a little gypsy [*sic*]" (D. 1970). The most famous Romani character in French literature, Esmeralda in Victor Hugo's *The Hunchback of Notre Dame* (1831), largely aligns with Hancock's (1987) analysis of the Western representation of Romani people in children's literature: Romani characters are inserted into a text to serve a specific narrative purpose as "liar and thief of property or (especially) of non-Gypsy children" and as "witch or caster of spells" (47; see also Kilbane 2008). This negative portrayal of Romani people helped legitimize their oppressors' actions against them. The Nazi Regime murdered over 90,000 Romani people (Margalit 2002, 53–54). Marie-Christine Hubert (1997) has shown that between 6,000 and 6,500 "nomads," most of whom were *tsiganes* (gypsies, [*sic*]) that had been in France for several generations, were kept in 30 different internment camps in France between 1940 and 1946 with the help of French collaborationist government Vichy. Henri Rousso (1991) writes that "Vichy's antisemitism, which had concrete, official ramifications in law and justice, was inspired not by Nazism but by French antisemitic traditions" (7). Neither did Vichy need encouragement from German Nazi ideology or authority to dehumanize Romani people—there was an established set of anti-Romani beliefs and practices in France well before German influence (see Hubert and Filhol 2009).

This context is important for *L'Enfant sauvage* because it represents the beginning of a historical period that Snyder and Mitchell (2010) deem the "Eugenic Atlantic"—a transnational site where beliefs about racial and biological inferiority joined forces for a period of one hundred fifty years (100–1). They explain that eugenics became a transatlantic pseudo-science shared and (re)produced among the fields of social work, public policy, science, and psychiatry in the United States, France, Canada, and Great Britain—even before German eugenicists began using it as an ideology to justify murdering disabled bodies in psychiatric institutions and, later, Jewish people, Romani people, and other nonnormative people in concentration camps during the Holocaust. Drawing on Paul Gilroy's (1993) notion of the "Black Atlantic"—the transatlantic movement of Black cultural production—Snyder and Mitchell (2010) locate the beginning of the Eugenic Atlantic in the late 1700s, when "beliefs that informed racial and disability eugenics as peculiarly Western modes of intolerance toward biologically based differences explicitly dovetailed" (112). They define eugenics as the "science of racial purification and the elimination of human 'defects'" (2010, 100–1)—presumed biological inferiorities in terms of physical or mental impairment. Important for our film, they explain that the "wild boy" was the historical starting point of eugenics:

> The context for eugenics first took shape in France. In 1797 the capture in rural France of a "savage" or "wild boy" [. . .] led to his involuntary incarceration. During the period of his confinement the "wild boy" was objectified as a specimen of exhibition. French researchers pursued numerous efforts to "train" him out of his "prelinguistic" silence. (2010, 113)

Snyder and Mitchell (2010) explain that eugenics stemmed from these early theories and practices, and the ideology included training people with cognitive and physical differences, confinement practices, sterilization, intelligence testing (a move from focusing on apparent disability to measuring nonapparent "inferiority"), and restriction of marriage, reproduction, work, neighborhoods, and immigration (112–13). They maintain that the Eugenic Atlantic, as a diasporic discourse of disability, constructed disabled persons as pariahs and "defectives," and they theorize that disability studies must contest the assumption that "normalization [is] the adjudicator of human value" (103–5). *L'Enfant sauvage* evokes the nascent Eugenic Atlantic period in its representation of a white-French doctor who treats, trains, confines, and attempts to normalize an autistic child and "cure" him of his "defects" (e.g., stimming). Equally troubling, Truffaut's adaptive choice to cast Cargol in the role of Victor allows him to depict the child as a "savage" boy of color in need of these theories, judgments, treatments, and punishments.

SHOOTING IN NATURE

Truffaut's adaptive location choice for the majority of the film—out of the institution and into the suburbs—buttresses the film's conflation between disability and savagery. The provincial location allows Itard to educate Victor in a calm, idyllic space, linking Victor with nature and placing him in opposition to Parisian urbanity, civilization, and Itard's cultivated connection to science. For instance, one scene shows Itard drawing a hammer, scissors, and key on a chalkboard. Victor successfully places the objects under the appropriate drawings, a training method known as the "Sicard Method," named after Abbé Sicard, director of the Institute for Deaf-Mutes who would eventually be responsible for evaluating the historical Victor's condition. A gentle, high-pitched flute begins to play—a recurring extradiegetic melody that signals progression—as Itard says, "good job, Victor, that was very good." He hands Victor his prize, a glass of water, and encourages him to drink. Itard is framed by an anatomical diagram of a human skull hanging on the wall behind him, which mirrors the shape of Truffaut's head and is consistently aligned with him throughout the film, visually associating Itard with culture and science (Codell 2006, 117). Yet, the poster is also reminiscent of eugenicist images created to evaluate and compare the shape and size of human skulls to produce racialized hierarchies of intelligence (see figure 2.2).

While Itard is framed by a symbol of "civilization," Victor is framed by the open side of a two-paneled window as he calmly sips his water. Itard's voiceover states,

> He stands near the window looking out over the countryside, as if in this moment this *child of nature* had sought to reunite the two blessings to survive his loss of freedom—a drink of pure water and the sight of sunlight on the countryside. (Emphasis mine)

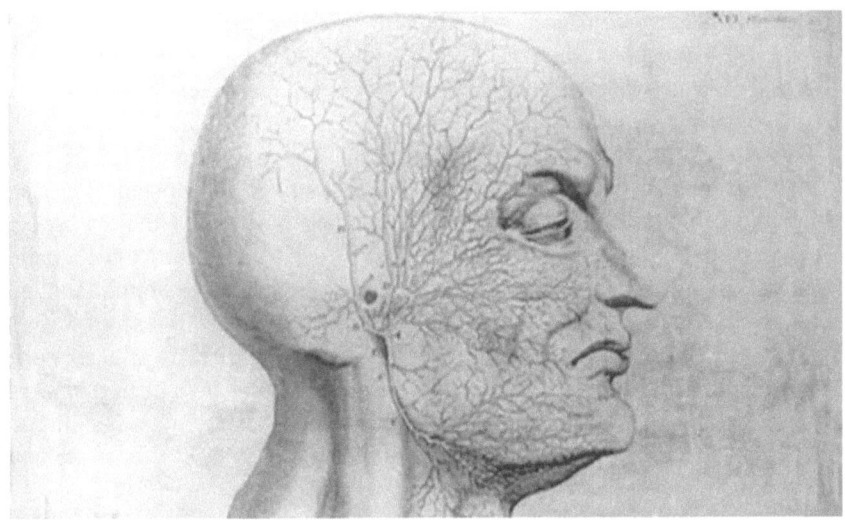

Figure 2.2 An Image Reminiscent of Eugenicist Pseudo-Science Lurks in Itard's Office.
Source: *L'Enfant sauvage*, Les Films du Carrosse, 1970.

We cut to pigeons on top of a barn, panning down to a long shot of Victor cutting wood. Given the image's consistent conflation of Victor with nature in these scenes, Itard's paternalistic voiceover becomes redundant and even patronizing; it reifies the boy's connection to nature on the audio track even while we have a clear image of the boy's affinity for nature on the image track.

In a scene that follows, Itard takes Victor for a long walk in the countryside as the extradiegetic soundtrack of Vivaldi's upbeat and joyous "Concerto for Mandolin" plays. After several long shots of Itard and Victor walking along playfully together, with Victor wearing Itard's top hat, we see the boy running around, sometimes on all fours, in the rain via a static long shot. Victor opens his mouth several times to catch the drops and we cut to a close-up shot of Itard, his head mirroring one of his medical posters. This scene clearly juxtaposes Victor, who relishes being in nature, revealed to us via a distancing long shot, and the cultivated doctor, shown via a humanizing close-up shot, who is associated with science. These key scenes in the middle of the film highlight its representation of the binary oppositions of civilized/savage and the association of these concepts with Itard the doctor versus Victor the autistic child.

When we do see close-up shots of Victor, it is usually when he is indoors and in the process of "becoming more human"—for instance, when Mme. Guerin cuts his hair; when he begins to cry; or when he attempts to connect to his teacher. An hour into the film, Itard receives news that

Citizen Pinel has convinced the administration that the idiot children he observed at Bicêtre Asylum share traits with the wild boy of Aveyron, and therefore Victor will never learn how to socialize, and nothing can be hoped for by continuing his education.

Itard rushes off to Paris in a horse-drawn carriage to persuade Parisian authorities of the usefulness of Victor's education but returns home worried. He enters the boy's bedroom and sits on his bed. Victor takes Itard's hand and places it over several parts of his face in a moment of communication. Itard says to the boy, "That's your way of talking." We end the scene with a close-up of Victor's face under Itard's hand. The scene directly after this one reveals another close-up on Victor's face, but only after he's been punished with a few moments in the closet and, due to this treatment, he begins to cry—again revealing his progress in becoming more (visibly) sensitive and thus more "human" (see figure 2.3).

We again see Victor's face in a close-up shot after a language acquisition exercise for which he is blindfolded and, upon failing several times—each time with a cheeky adolescent smirk—Itard uses a pointing stick to tap his hand with force. Gillain (2019) notes the "cruelty of the exercise that consists of blinding a child devoid of language. Itard deprived him of his major sense of relating to the world" (124). Itard says to Victor, "I'm wasting my time with you [. . .] I'm discouraged and disappointed." Then Itard's voiceover takes over:

> Had I known his limits I would have thought he understood. I had barely spoken when the tears started streaming from under his blindfold. [. . .] I condemned the curiosity of the men who wrenched him away from his innocent and happy life.

Figure 2.3   To His Doctor's (Truffaut) Satisfaction, Victor (Cargol) Begins to Leave His Flat Affect Behind. *Source*: *L'Enfant sauvage*, Les Films du Carrosse, 1970.

The scene ends with a close-up on Victor's blindfolded, tear-stained face. These close-up shots on Victor allow the spectator to sympathize with him when he appears "human" by showing affect—crying and communicating with another human—much more easily than when we are offered long shots of the boy as stimming spectacle as he connects with nature. Moreover, the long shots construct Victor's stimming as abnormal, in need of fixing, savage, and even scary—rather than allowing this common autistic tendency the humanizing effect of the close-up.

After the failed blindfold lesson, Itard thinks Victor has run away and goes out into the trees to search for him. Itard's voiceover narrates, "I heard rustling above my head." Itard looks up into one of the trees that surround him to find Victor sitting on a high branch. This scene mirrors the sequence of events at the film's end. When Itard cannot take Victor on their daily walks due to being ill, the boy's frustration leads him to jump out of the window. Just as in the previous scene in which the boy runs away from Itard's home—as well as when we first meet Victor in the woods in Aveyron—we hear and see leaves rustling. This sound and image of Victor-as-nature is contrasted with a striking medium shot of Itard and the recurring image of the anatomical poster of the skull (see figure 2.2); while Itard's face and torso remain in the dark, candlelight illuminates the poster that symbolizes cultivation, indicating Itard's presumed failure at civilizing the boy. We see Victor attempt to steal a hen from a neighbor before he finally comes back to Itard's home. Itard tells him, "This is your home. You're no longer a savage, even if you're not yet a man." As Mme. Guérin guides Victor up the stairs to his bedroom so he can rest, Itard looks up at him. "Later we'll resume our lessons," he says to Victor, his pupil, who returns the doctor's gaze with a rebellious gaze of his own.

We could read Victor's return of the gaze as a form of the child's power (Codell 2006, 107). However, an iris shot frames him before fading the screen to black and ending the film, again placing Victor in the position of a disabled and racialized medical specimen. Codell writes that, throughout the film, the iris shot "captures Victor in his stages of development, his past joys (the rain), his important lessons, and his frustrations. But the iris also expands and closes in on Victor, mirroring his confinement" (2006, 113). While Truffaut as Itard remains human in his final close-up, the iris shot—meant to return us to a former time in cinema history and reminiscent of D. W. Griffith's racist film *The Birth of a Nation* (1915)—once again renders Victor inhuman. Further, the casting of Cargol creates an image of a racialized pupil who has yet to be truly "saved" or "cured" by his master's teachings.

The final iris fade-out echoes an iris fade-out shot that occurs midway through the film, again highlighting the nature/civilization dichotomy that Truffaut's adaptive choice regarding setting and shooting location buttresses.

Figure 2.4 Victor of Aveyron (Jean-Pierre Cargol) Receives the Patronizing Touch of Itard and the Medicalizing Iris Shot of Truffaut. Source: *L'Enfant sauvage*, Les Films du Carrosse, 1970.

We see Victor tapping on the windowsill as he looks outside, framed by the window and greenery. Mme. Guérin calls out the name "Victor" for the first time and he swiftly turns around to claim it as his own. She and Itard approach the boy excitedly as the doctor places his hands on him and an iris shot closes in on the boy, who appears confused. This close-up shot, which indicates that the boy is becoming more "human" by accepting a name, quickly turns into a cinematic microscope: we see the boy through a circular lens as a doctor might examine a specimen. Victor becomes a passive object as he receives the patronizing touch of Itard and the medicalizing iris shot of Truffaut (see figure 2.4).

WHITE SAVIOR

With the casting of a Romani boy in *L'Enfant sauvage*, Truffaut's cinematic Itard becomes a "white savior"—a white character who purportedly saves a person of color from the "backward" aspects of their own culture. In *The White Savior Film*, Matthew Hughey (2014) examines dozens of based-on-a-true-story Hollywood films, arguing that each film "provides a roadmap for the navigation of race relations" in "subtle and friendly terms" (15–16). Hughey explains that the white savior film works to "repair the myth of the great white father figure whose benevolent paternalism over people of color is the way things not only have been but should be" (19). Looking at *L'Enfant sauvage* through the lens of this narrative genre, it becomes clear that Truffaut's adaptive choices position Itard as the benevolent father figure to Victor, the "noble savage,"

> the nonwhite characters [who] are often framed as worth saving because of their custody of unexplainable magical or spiritual quality that is valued but not fully understood by the logic and materialism of the white savior. By saving the people of color, the white savior takes possession of the primordial morality, making him- or herself more complete as a person, all under the guise of rescuing and protecting nonwhite others. (Hughey 2014, 64)

A key scene near the end of the film represents Victor's noble savagery. After the scene in which Victor is blindfolded and reprimanded for his failure to learn, we cut to Victor swaying back and forth on his knees under the moonlight. We see medium and close-up shots of Itard through the lens of the window as he looks down upon the "wild child." The countershot—a long shot—then reveals the boy from the aerial point of view of Itard's medicalizing gaze as he watches him stim under the moon. Gillain's (2013) close analysis of this scene describes problems inherent to the white savior narrative—but, again, without critiquing them:

> Bathing the wild child's body with its natural light, [the moon] seems to communicate to him a happiness of which Itard has lost the secret. [. . .] The symbiotic relationship between the child and the elements is contrasted against the symbolic mastery achieved by Itard through writing. Whereas the one lacks language, the other lacks immediate contact with the world. [. . .] The doctor's words give a voice to the wild child, and they come to confer an order, coherence, and meaning to his experience. (217)

Here, Gillain implies that Victor's magical oneness with nature can only be fully experienced and made coherent with the help of his savior's words. The lack of engagement with the racial and colonial politics of this representation uncritically celebrates Truffaut as the civilizing, brilliant *auteur* filmmaker—rather than considering Victor's experience as an autistic child as important in its own right. Gillain (2019) further claims that the moon scene "returns us to the origins of our being-in-the-world" through "its penchant for non-verbal communication," and that the "jubilation of the savage speaks to us" (127). Her claims depict autism as primitive, exotic, and mystical. Moreover, her analysis does not take into account the experience of the autistic child, nor does it speak to the film's conflation among stimming, racialized savage, and colonial subject. Instead, it centers on the feelings of the white neurotypical spectator.

By the end of our film, Victor has "progressed" somewhat according to Itard, but he most certainly has not achieved assimilation—and the historical Victor would die at the age of forty under Mme. Guérin's care. However, these medical "failures" in terms of Victor's ability to assimilate to dominant culture do not render his life without value—even though enlightenment "science" proposed otherwise. Enlightenment ideals maintained that human bodies could be categorized based on "innate" characteristics. Like people of color, disabled people were judged on biological, rather than cultural, inferiority—the *inability* to assimilate to the dominant culture. Snyder and Mitchell (2010) state, "This immutable quality attributed to races through biological traits serves as the primary locus for an analysis of human disqualification shared by racial Others and people with disabilities" (110). As several scholars point out, Victor in our film represents a post-Revolution *tabula rasa* (blank slate) out of which Itard can sculpt "a civilized being" (Andrew 2013, 238), much like the historical Victor of Aveyron was perceived and treated (see, for example, Yousef 2001). French sociologists Patrick Simon and Sylvia Zappi (2003) suggest that

> to benefit from rights [in France], minorities are summoned to transform themselves into an ideal citizen, to fit into certain codes and norms. [. . .] This idea of the "universal" [. . .] obligates the citizen to adopt very precise cultural codes to benefit from the laws and rights that are supposed to apply to all people regardless of sex, origin, religion, sexual orientation, health condition. (2003, 6)

They maintain that "French Republican universalism works to create and justify a system of domination—founded on an idea of the superiority of certain values and of those who embody them—over Others who are presumed as in need of enlightening" (2003, 7; see also Ville and Ravaud 2007). In their explanation of universalism, we can see Itard and his project of "enlightenment" for Victor. This normalization process becomes infused with discursive neocolonial power given the film's conflation of autism with savagery.

The film even exhibits material neocolonial power when we consider that Truffaut, as Itard, is directing a Romani boy to enact savagery—again reminding us of the colonial subjects of the World's Fairs who were compensated to perform their cultures for the consumption of the white Orientalist gaze. Truffaut-as-Itard is also directing Cargol-as-Victor to experience intense training methods and punishments. While many of Itard's training methods represented in the film are humane (e.g., the "Sicard Method"), other methods are violent. In one of the most discussed scenes of the film, Itard tries to teach Victor a sense of justice. Itard's voiceover proclaims, "I must do an 'abominable' thing: lock him in the closet after he successfully completes one of my assignments to test his sense of justice." When Victor bites his doctor, Itard says, "you're right to rebel." The voiceover says, "His bite filled my soul with joy. [. . .] By provoking the sentiment [of injustice] I had elevated the savage man to the stature of a moral being by the most noble of his attributes." While this monologue has obvious ties to the civilizing discourse of French colonizers (i.e., "I had elevated the savage man"), the film form directly after this event is perhaps even more telling: from outside the provincial home, the camera offers us a long shot of Victor, who looks calmly out the window that frames him; slowly, the camera closes in on the window as the gentle flute music plays. Here, Victor's contemplative shot becomes less a celebration of his success and more a celebration of Itard's success at normalizing him; after all, we still have no close-up shot of Victor's face when he's at rest after his success. His body is once again one small portion of a long shot that allows nature to encompass him.

CONCLUSION

Truffaut was deeply concerned with disability rights in France at the time of filming *L'Enfant sauvage*. In an interview in *Cri du Monde*, he explains that

> we can find connections between [my film] and the problem of being handicapped, which authorities barely pay attention to, except during election time. Afterwards, they quickly forget. Politicians can sleep in peace: they will never see martyred and handicapped children take to the streets to protest! (P.A. 1970)

While Truffaut's intent in adapting Itard's medical reports into a narrative film was sympathetic, *L'Enfant sauvage* illustrates the ongoing colonial association of people of color with savagery. In doing so, it also represents the historical moment when racial and disability eugenics dovetailed at the end of the eighteenth century. In Truffaut's film, Victor of Aveyron—both autistic and of color—becomes a symbolic nexus of the "Eugenic Atlantic" period. The film's context, form, and narrative illustrate a strong desire to cure and "civilize" a child that may not want or need curing. Moreover, the civilizer is played by a white-French man, Truffaut, while Truffaut cast a dark-skinned Romani boy as Victor, despite Truffaut's knowledge that the historical Victor was white. In its representation of autism only a year after May 1968, a key moment in postcolonial French history, *L'Enfant sauvage* reveals that colonialism and ableism are mutually imbricated historical methods of normalization that span centuries.

The context of the cinematic adaptation's production in 1969 marked the emergence of postcolonial discourses that questioned the Enlightenment foundations of Victor's assimilationist "education." However, the film's representation of this questioning merely reiterates binaries that are historically informed by colonialist ideologies: body/mind, primitive/educated, dark-skinned/light-skinned, "idiot"/doctor. Truffaut's *L'Enfant sauvage* "makes no attempt to enter the boy's inner world" (Andrew 2013, 237). Contemporary autism studies scholarship theorizes that people within autistic cultures should have the opportunity to define themselves and their experiences (Strauss 2013). What the current moment calls for are representations of autistic people created by autistic cultures.

A previous version of this chapter appeared in the first issue of *Ought: The Journal of Autistic Culture*. Thank you to Robert Rozema, editor-in-chief of *Ought*, for helping to inspire this work.

WORKS CITED

Allen, Don. *Finally Truffaut*. London: Secker & Warburg, 1985.
Andrew, Dudley. "Every Teacher Needs a Truant: Bazin and *l'Enfant sauvage*." In *A Companion to François Truffaut*, edited by Dudley Andrew and Anne Gillain, 221–41. Malden, MA: John Wiley & Sons, 2013.
Codell, Julie F. "Playing Doctor: François Truffaut's '*L'Enfant Sauvage*' and the *Auteur*/Autobiographer as Impersonator." *Biography* 29 (2006): 101–22.
D., M. "L'Enfant sauvage." *Canard Enchaîné* (Paris, France), March 11, 1970. (Available in the F. Truffaut files, BiFi, Paris)
Gillain, Anne. *François Truffaut: The Lost Secret*. Bloomington, IN: Indiana University Press, 2013.
Gillain, Anne. *Tout Truffaut: 23 Films Pour Comprendre l'Homme et le Cinéaste*. Paris: Armand Colin, 2019.
Gilroy, Paul. *The Black Atlantic: Modernity and Double Consciousness*. Cambridge, MA: Harvard University Press, 1993.
Griffith, D. W., dir. *The Birth of a Nation*. Los Angeles, CA, U.S.: David W. Griffith Corp., 1915.
Hancock, Ian. "Gypsies: A People Forgotten." *Humanist* 45, no. 5 (1985): 12–16.
Hancock, Ian. "The Origin and Function of the Gypsy Image in Children's Literature." *The Lion and the Unicorn* 11, no. 1 (1987): 47–59.
Herzog, Werner, dir. *Kaspar Hauser*. West Germany: Werner Herzog Filmproduktion, 1974.
Hubert, Marie-Christine. "Les Tsiganes en France, 1939–1946: Assignation à Résidence, Internement, Déportation." PhD diss., Paris 10, 1997.
Hubert, Marie-Christine, and Emmanuel Filhol. *Les Tsiganes en France, 1939–1946*. Paris: Perrin, 2009.
Hughey, Matthew. *The White Savior Film: Content, Critics, and Consumption*. Philadelphia, PA: Temple University Press, 2014.
Hugo, Victor. *Notre-dame de Paris*. Paris: Gosselin, 1831.

Kilbane, Aimee. "Theater of the Underworld: Spectacle and Subculture in Hugo's *Notre-Dame de Paris*." In *'Gypsies' in European Literature and Culture: Studies in European Culture and History*, edited by Valentina Glajar and Domnica Radulesco, 217–34. New York: Palgrave Macmillan, 2008.

Kolářová, Kateřina. "Mediating Syndromes of Postcommunism: Disability, Sex, Race, and Labor." In Focus: Cripping Cinema & Media Studies. *JCMS: Journal of Cinema and Media Studies* 58, no. 4 (2019): 156–62.

Margalit, Gilad. *Germany and its Gypsies: A Post-Auschwitz Ordeal*. Madison, WI: University of Wisconsin Press, 2002.

McCance, Dawne. "The Wild Child." *Revue Canadienne d'Études Cinématographiques / Canadian Journal of Film Studies* 17, no. 1 (2008): 69–80.

Murray, Stuart. *Representing Autism: Culture, Narrative, Fascination*. Liverpool, England: Liverpool University Press, 2008.

P.A., J. "François Truffaut et 'l'Enfant Sauvage'." *Cri du Monde*, Jan. 30 (Available in the F. Truffaut files, BiFi, Paris), 1970.

Ross, Kristin. *May '68 and its Afterlives*. Chicago, IL: University of Chicago Press, 2008.

Rousso, Henri. *The Vichy Syndrome: History and Memory in France since 1944*, translated by Arthur Goldhammer. Cambridge, MA: Harvard University Press, 1991.

Said, Edward. *Orientalism*. New York: Vintage, 1978.

Shattuck, Roger. *The Forbidden Experiment: The Story of the Wild boy of Aveyron*. New York: Farrar Straus Giroux, 1980.

Sherry, Mark. "(Post)colonising Disability." *Wagadu* 4 (2007): 10–22.

Simon, Patrick, and Sylvia Zappi. "La Lutte Contre les Discriminations: La Fin de l'Assimilation à la Française?" *Mouvements* 3 (2003): 171–76.

Snyder, Sharon L., and David T. Mitchell. *Cultural Locations of Disability*. Chicago, IL: University of Chicago Press, 2010.

Strauss, Joseph N. "Autism as Culture." In *The Disability Studies Reader*, edited by Lennard J. Davis, 460–84. New York: Taylor and Francis, 2013.

Truffaut, François, dir. *Les Mistons*. Paris, France: Les Films du Carrosse, 1957.

Truffaut, François, dir. *Les Quatre Cents Coups*. Paris, France: Les Films du Carrosse, 1959.

Truffaut, François, dir. *L'Enfant sauvage*. Paris, France: Les Films du Carrosse (Available in the F. Truffaut files, BiFi, Paris), 1970.

Truffaut, François. *Truffaut by Truffaut*, translated by Robert Erich Wolf. New York: Harry N. Abrams, 1987.

Ville, Isabelle, and Jean-François Ravaud. "French Disability Studies: Differences and Similarities." *Scandinavian Journal of Disability Research* 9, no. 3–4 (2007): 138–45.

Wing, Lorna. "Les Enfants Autistes." L'Association au Service des Inadaptés Ayant des Troubles de la Personnalité. Paris: Sceaux (Available in the F. Truffaut files, BiFi, Paris), 1968.

Yousef, Nancy. "Savage or Solitary? The Wild Child and Rousseau's Man of Nature." *Journal of the History of Ideas* 62, no. 2 (2001): 245–63.

Chapter 3

Remaking the Image of Autism

Why and How Comics Should Reboot Autistic Representation

Robert Rozema

An adaptation, by definition, is a new treatment of an artistic work, usually involving a fresh medium or a changed format, as in a film adaptation of a best-selling novel. With this narrow definition in mind, a handful of recent works featuring autistic characters qualify as adaptations—and these include the BBC series *Sherlock* (2010–2017), a reimagining of the famous detective stories of Arthur Conan Doyle; the 2011 film *Extremely Loud and Incredibly Close*, based on the 2005 novel by Jonathan Safran Foer; and the recent stage version of *The Curious Incident of the Dog in the Night-Time*, which premiered in London's Royal National Theater in 2012 and has since featured on Broadway and elsewhere. More broadly, however, an adaptation can be understood as a modified version of an original, even a close reproduction with only minor alterations. In this sense, the great majority of works with autistic characters—who now feature in fiction, film, and television—can be considered adaptations, since they have largely reproduced, with little variation, a stereotypical image of autism that owes more to popular fiction such as *Curious Incident* than to the reality of autistic experience.

Autistic adaptations of this sort have permeated almost every storytelling medium, but they remain rare in comics. The few depictions of autistic people that do exist in mainstream comics have, regrettably, also replicated a limiting, limited version of the disability. In my view, this constitutes a critical failure, given the potential that comics have to remake the image of autism. As this chapter argues, this reconstructive power lies in the highly visual nature of comics themselves.

I begin by focusing on a recent comic, the neo-noir series *Postal* by Matt Hawkins, Bryan Hill, and Isaac Goodhart (Image Comics 2015–2019), which features an autistic protagonist named Mark Shiffron. In my analysis, *Postal* exemplifies the problematic reproduction of negative, even exploitative images of autism. I contrast literal images from *Postal* to the construct of autism created by dominant cultural narratives, which rely on a closed set of readily deployable tropes that have come to signal and signify autism. As a point of contrast, I then discuss *The Song Collector* (2020) an ongoing web comic by the autistic artist Rebecca Burgess. In doing so, I build on the foundational scholarship of Stuart Murray (2008), Sonya Loftis (2015), and James McGrath (2017), who have critiqued depictions of autistic adults in scientific discourse, literature, and popular culture, though notably, not in comics. Examining a specific neurocognitive condition within comics is necessarily a cross-disciplinary endeavor, so I also draw on disability theory, comics criticism, visual aesthetics, and the growing body of scholarship that exists at the intersection of these fields. In doing so, I hope to show the critical importance of autistic representations in comics, arguing that stories about autism—good or bad, misleading or illuminating—are central to the way we know autism.

THE IMAGE OF AUTISM IN *POSTAL*

Though our current culture is replete with instances of autistic representation (Kurchak 2021), this was not always the case. Undoubtedly, Dustin Hoffman's Raymond Babbitt in 1988's *Rain Man* set the mold for representing autism in fiction for nearly two decades. Hoffman's depiction reflects an earlier, classic understanding of autism—one based on Leo Kanner's model that conceived of the disability as a severe impairment (Silberman 2015). In the film, Raymond is socially isolated, has limited, echolalic language, and lives in an institution—all signs of a debilitating condition. If there is a single, iconic image of autism from *Rain Man*, it is likely the picture of Raymond and his brother Charlie descending the casino escalator, wearing matching Italian suits, preparing to count cards at the blackjack table. More recently, however, a new image of autism has emerged, reflecting the prominence of Asperger syndrome, a milder version of autism first included as a separate diagnosis in the *DSM-4* in 1994. Today, the dominant cultural image of autism is an Aspergian composite. Unlike the single iconic image of Raymond on the escalator, the new image of autism is a collection of physical attributes, social behaviors, special interests, and speech patterns that signal and signify "autistic."

Different iterations of the newer, Aspergian image have appeared in novels, young adult literature, television, and film, almost always as a high-functioning white male, often a child or an adolescent, who possesses spectacular facility in science, technology, or mathematics (McGrath 2017). If Raymond Babbitt personifies classic autism, then the contemporary autistic character Christopher Boone (*The Curious Incident of the Dog in the Night-Time*) embodies the new, Aspergian composite. Asperger's cultural legacy endures as proliferations of fictional Christopher Boone look-alikes—characters such as Oskar Schell (*Extremely Loud and Incredibly Close*), Sheldon Cooper (*Big Bang Theory*), and Sam Gardner (*Atypical*). The Aspergian character endures even as the reputation of Asperger the man declines: Asperger syndrome is fading from current clinical discourse, removed as a clinical diagnosis from the *DSM-5* in 2013, and recent research has unequivocally linked Asperger to the Nazi euthanasia program (Czech 2018; Sheffer 2018). But the Aspergian image of autism seems immune to these mitigating factors. If anything, it remains stubbornly self-replicating: the more versions of Christopher Boone appear, the more we are imprinted with a particular brand of autism, and the more we come to expect future autistic characters to act, think, and communicate like Christopher.

To date, mainstream comics have featured far fewer autistic characters than other forms of popular media, but when they do appear—in a few superhero comics such as *The Fantastic Four* or *Aquaman*, for instance—they tend to be based on the Aspergian composite (Rozema 2019). *Postal* is just the latest example of this trend. As a highly successful and second-longest running comic series featuring an explicitly identified autistic main character (following Keiko Tobe's manga *With the Light*), it merits critical attention. As a story told in a predominantly visual medium, it also bears an added responsibility for representing autism truthfully, even within the context of fiction. By my count, *Postal: The Complete Collection* contains just over 800 frames with whole or partial images of Mark Shiffron, its autistic main character. Collectively and individually, these images constitute representations and should be evaluated accordingly. My assessment relies on the evaluative criteria outlined by media theorist W. J. T. Mitchell in *Picture Theory*:

> The good or true representation is "responsible" to what it represents and to whom it represents it. "Responsible representation" is a definition for truth, both as an epistemological question (the accuracy and faithfulness of a description or a picture to what it represents) and as an ethical contract (the notion that the representor is "responsible for" the truth of a representation and responsible to the audience or recipient of the representation). (1994, 421)

To understand how *Postal*'s pictorial representation of autism fails to be a "good or true representation" in Mitchell's standards, it is first necessary to examine its narrative, however briefly. *Postal* tells the story of Mark Shiffron, an autistic, white male postal officer who lives in the small town of Eden,

Wyoming. Eden is not just another town, though: it is inhabited entirely by ex-criminals given a second chance if they abide by Eden's draconian justice system, which imposes capital punishment on any and all lawbreakers. Mark, who identifies as having Asperger syndrome in the first issue, is also Eden's self-appointed detective, using his position with the postal service, along with his heightened senses and exceptional memory, to uncover criminal plots and report them to his mother, Eden's mayor. The plot of the series revolves around the return of Mark's exiled father, a sadistic killer, to Eden, and the ongoing attempts of the FBI to destroy the town.

From the first issue of the series, when Mark introduces himself, he embodies stereotypes about autistic individuals already well-established in existing fiction. To begin, his interest in solving Eden's crimes places him in a long line of Aspergian detectives, beginning with Sherlock Holmes, who is identified as having Asperger syndrome in the recent BBC adaptation, *Sherlock* (Episode 2.2, 2012). Contemporary literature also has no shortage of autistic characters who idolize Holmes, including *Curious Incident's* Christopher Boone, who channels Sherlock Holmes and goes "detecting" to determine who murdered the neighbor's dog (2004, 52); Ted, the hero of the 2007 intermediate novel *The London Eye Mystery* by Siobhan Dowd; Colin Fischer, the protagonist of the eponymous 2012 young adult novel by Ashley Miller and Zach Stentz; and a wide range of others in fiction, film, and television. These literary representations have real-world consequences. Sonya Loftis, who has examined the autistic detective trope in depth, notes that "suddenly, it is not autistic people who are the interpretative template for the literary character; instead, the public perception of the literary character may reshape and inform how autism is defined as a social construct" (2015, 25). In noir film and fiction, the detective plays a prominent role, so *Postal* is ostensibly adhering to the conventions of this well-known genre. At the same time, by choosing to make the detective autistic, the writers are, more subtly and perhaps unknowingly, satisfying neurotypical cultural expectations surrounding autistic individuals. With their impassivity, calculating minds, and keen eye for detail, the stereotype suggests, autistics make for natural detectives.

Despite their use of this trope, *Postal* writers Bryan Hill and Matt Hawkins do employ language associated with neurodiversity, at least initially. When a hostile town citizen calls Mark a "retard" early in the story, for instance, Mark's narrative text boxes express his view on his neurological difference: "He's incorrect. I'm not retarded. I have Asperger's syndrome. It's not a disability. It's a difference" (2020, 4). Mark's rebuttal seems to preface a story that would resist pathologizing autism, but it soon gives way to a far more typical characterization of autism. In the pages immediately following Mark's rejection of the word "disability," we see him exemplify all of the usual impairments in sensory processing, social interaction, social communication, and social imagination derived from a medical model of autism. His routine is absolutely rigid: each day, he sorts mail at the post office, completes his route, and eats lunch at the diner where his love interest, Maggie, waits tables. Through narrative boxes, Mark discloses that he cannot eat food that is touching, a well-worn trope in autism narratives (5); that he has difficulty with theory of mind, admitting "I have a problem with empathy" (6); and that he imposes rules on his speech, rehearsing something three times before saying it aloud, particularly when speaking to Maggie: "I want her to have sex with me. . . . I say that in my head three times. Then I decided not to say it aloud" (7). It is feasible that Mark both values his neurological differences and recognizes the challenges brought about by his Asperger syndrome. But while this internal conflict might generate a more interesting and authentic autistic character, *Postal* misses this opportunity, providing only fleeting glimpses into Mark's psyche.

While the overarching narrative of *Postal* warrants further critical attention, I am most interested in evaluating the literal image of autism presented by the comic, and less in its literary qualities—its adherence to detective genre conventions, its noir setting, or religious themes, for instance. My focus on the image of autism, however, does not exclude the linguistic content of the comic. By definition, of course, comics combine two modalities, images and words, into a sequential narrative consisting of panels and pages. Examining the image of autism in comics means understanding words and images as what Mitchell calls *imagetext*, or "composite, synthetic works (or concepts) that combine image and text" (1994, 89). Mitchell also posits that comics are "literal manifestations" (2018, 39) of imagetext. By extension, we might say that individual comic panels, extracted from their narrative context, constitute smaller imagetexts, frozen in time and space.

Single comic panels provide especially compelling illustrations of autistic representation, and I scrutinize two from the first two issues of *Postal* here. Removed from their temporal and spatial contexts, these single panels act as stilled and distilled depictions of autistic subjects. In this regard, such representations act as what McGrath calls "mirrors" (2017, 72), a particularly pertinent visual metaphor for describing comic images. While fictional characters and events are often said to mirror the lives of readers, McGrath argues that depictions of autism often do the opposite, reflecting what neurotypical experiences are *not*, thus determining the clearly demarcated boundaries of their own neurotypicality. "Autism, then, is not a mirror of neurotypical behaviours," McGrath explains, "But autism is a mirror of neurotypical *expectations* [emphasis in original]" (72). In figure 3.1, which shows Mark working at Eden's Post Office, we see this kind of mirror image. Viewing it, neurotypical readers define and recognize their own neurotypicality more completely: the gaze (not) staring back at them is not their own.

Figure 3.1 Mark at the Post Office: Multiple Autism Signifiers. *Source*: Hawkins, Matt, Bryan Hill, and Isaac Goodhart. *Postal: The Complete Collection*. Image Comics, 2020. p. 4.

This single panel in figure 3.1, in fact, demonstrates message abundancy (Gibbons 2003) in the number of autistic signifiers it includes. Mark's first narrative text box reveals a pedantic mindset and a fondness for numbers; the second and third show that he favors truncated, utilitarian syntax that echoes computer language. The picture of the panel is also replete with signifiers. Mark's gaze is averted, so he seems to avoid direct eye contact with the viewer. His face is expressionless and inscrutable, his posture rigid. He stands against a backdrop of mailbox slots, and the visual grid behind him suggests both structure and confinement. The picture illustrates the textual idea that Mark's job is to put "everything in its right place," but this aphorism is also intended to describe autistic repetition and routine. Indeed, the maxim recurs two pages later when Mark arrives at the diner at noon—to the second (6). McGrath might also draw attention to the presence of a "neurotypically authored metaphor . . . invoke[ing] autism as something it is actually not" (2017, 86). Metaphorically, the panel implies that having Asperger syndrome is akin to being a mail carrier, an occupation that demands machine-like exactitude and a high tolerance for routine. Proverbially, too, mail carriers cannot be deterred by rain or snow or heat or gloom of night. The mail arrives like clockwork, to invoke another metaphor, just as Mark himself shows up to the diner precisely at noon each day.

All of this amounts to an Aspergian stereotype, an image of autism that looks all too familiar to many autistic readers. To underscore the power of this particular image, it is helpful to turn to another graphic work that addresses stereotyping—not of the neurodivergent but of the racial other. In

Gene Yang's *American Born Chinese* (2006), the character Chin-Kee embodies nearly every negative stereotype about the Chinese: he wears traditional Chinese dress and hairstyle and has yellow skin, squinty eyes, and large buck teeth that allude to anti-Asian propaganda. His name itself is a racist slur. Chin-Kee is present in the story as a foil to the main character, Jin, who hates his Chinese heritage. Jin, whose desire to become American transforms him into a white boy named Danny, is tormented by Chin-Kee's yearly visits, until he finally learns to accept his Chinese identity, prompting Chin-Kee to reveal himself as the mythological Monkey King. The relationship between the "American" Danny and the stereotyped Chin-Kee is, in my view, analogous to that between the neurotypical reader of *Postal* and its autistic other, Mark. Just as Jin/Danny sees Chin-Kee as everything he wishes to reject in his quest to be American, an act of othering that depends on grotesque caricature, so too neurotypical readers view the stereotypical autistic figure in opposition to themselves. In *American Born Chinese*, however, Yang employs the stereotype knowingly, using Chin-Kee to address the identity crisis that Chinese and other immigrants endure under the pressures to assimilate. The image of Chin-Kee is ultimately self-destructive or iconoclastic, a manifestation of the stereotype threat (Steele and Aronson 1995) that Jin feels. *Postal*, in contrast, presents a stereotypical image of autism as realistic or iconic: this is what autism looks like and is.

If the panel in figure 3.1 replicates well-established stereotypes about autism (and specifically, Asperger syndrome) through abundant verbal, visual, and verbal-visual signifiers, then a second panel from the comic (figure 3.2) deserves scrutiny for a different reason. It shows another image of autism that has grown disturbingly prevalent in recent years: the violent autistic. As Loftis (2015) notes, this image emerged in conjunction with the 2012 Sandy Hook school massacre, which was carried out by Adam Lanza, who had Asperger syndrome. Mainstream media linked Lanza's violence to his autism, and at least one subsequent review of medical literature drew a tentative connection between neurodevelopmental disorders, head injuries, and serial killers (Allely et al. 2014). The image of the violent autistic was reinforced in the wake of the Charleston church mass shooting, as the media speculated that Dylan Roof was autistic, a diagnosis he apparently resisted, despite being described as a "geyser of autistic symptoms" by his lead attorney (quoted in Tripp 2017). In light of the repeated associations between autism and violence, no matter how uncertain such associations might be, it seems insensitive, at best, to present an image of another autistic shooter.

The panel occupies a full page and concludes the second issue of *Postal*. Narratively, the panel marks an erratic shift in Mark's behavior, as he abruptly turns on Maggie, whom he has discovered works as an FBI mole. The next issue reveals that the gun is not loaded, but the image nevertheless

Figure 3.2 The Violent Autistic: Mark Goes Postal. *Source*: Hawkins, Matt, Bryan Hill, and Isaac Goodhart. *Postal: The Complete Collection*. Image Comics, 2020. p. 42.

reinforces the stereotype of the cold-blooded autistic killer. Mark's visage is flat and stern, betraying no emotion, and he stoically holds the shotgun, even as Maggie is caught completely off guard, dropping her dishrag in surprise and falling to the floor. More importantly, we see the encounter from Maggie's neurotypical perspective, and it is clear she is afraid of what Mark might do. The oblique angles of her/our viewpoint evoke unease and anxiety. Mark stands at a forty-five-degree angle to the background of the diner, its ceiling, windows, and checkerboard floor rendered in disorienting diagonal lines (McCloud 1993, 125). In contrast to the placidity of Mark's first appearance (figure 3.1), this Mark is unhinged and dangerous.

The panel also alludes to another, very specific kind of violence: "going postal," an idiom that surely occurred to *Postal* writers Bryan Hill and Matt Hawkins. The OED records that the phrase "going postal" entered the language in 1993, following multiple incidents in which disgruntled U.S. postal workers shot and killed their colleagues. In the image, Mark's occupation as a U.S. postal worker is prominently displayed. He is in uniform and his mailbag is slung over his shoulder, its familiar logo in full view. The inclusion of these markers is suspicious, considering that it is late afternoon (the sky is yellow and the diner is closed) and that Mark, like Maggie, should be finishing work for the day. Mark's mailbag is nevertheless full, and he remains in uniform, though previous panels show him favoring a gray hoodie when off duty. Regardless of authorial intent, this panel overlays one harmful stereotype with another, as the violent autistic and the murderous postal worker converge. Returning to the metaphor suggested by the first panel—being autistic is like being a mail carrier—this image doubles down on the conceit.

I am not objecting to the presence of violence itself in *Postal*: since the Golden Age, comics have featured gruesome violence of all sorts, particularly in the crime, horror, and superhero genres. The infamous 1950s comics critic Frederick Wertham (1954) was right about this much. Eden is a blood-soaked town, and the story includes lynchings, filicide, summary executions, human sacrifice, amputations, and many other horrific acts, all drawn in graphic detail. And it is important to note that Mark is both a perpetrator of violence and a victim of it, even surviving being hanged by his father in the third issue. But the depiction of autistic violence in figure 3.2 belies the reality experienced by autistics, whom research indicates are more likely to be targets of violence than instigators. In her study of autism and violence, McGuire (2016) theorizes that mainstream culture's pathologizing of autism—that is, understanding it as a discrete disability to be cured rather than as a condition integral to identity—gives neurotypicals allowance to commit violence against autistic children, adolescents, and adults. McGuire shows how the medical, media, and legal systems have legitimized this "war on autism" through sympathetic treatment of parents who have murdered their "difficult" autistic children. The image of Mark further justifies violence against autistic individuals, just as the image of the dangerous black male, on an endless loop in the news and entertainment media, justifies preemptive killings by police officers and vigilantes.

Nor does the narrative arc of *Postal* solve the problem of the violent autistic. Instead, Mark becomes increasingly committed to bloodshed as a means to defend Eden against his father, the intrusions of the FBI, a white supremacist gang, drug runners, and others. Ultimately, Mark takes his mother's place as mayor after defeating his father in the all-out war that ends the series. In an epilogue issue entitled *Postal: Mark*, he muses on his newfound power:

> They used to call me names. Retard. Misfit. Outcast. Freak. I have Asperger's syndrome and people made fun of me because I was different. I was weird to them. Now they *fear me* [emphasis in original]. They still whisper names behind my back, but now the words are different. Tyrant, monster, bully, despot . . . violence is the only road to peace. (2020, 4–5)

Returning to Mitchell's criteria for a "good and true" representation, it is clear that the narrative as a whole, and more importantly, the pictorial representations of autism within this narrative are not "accurate and faithful" depictions. Instead, they portray a highly otherized autism, pathologizing the disability and exploiting cultural anxiety over violent autistics. Of course, *Postal* is a work of fiction—a highly stylized, heightened version of reality. And Mitchell, in a complicated turn, also suggests "irresponsible" representations are necessary for art: "The lie, the fiction, the false oath, the error . . . the playful, irresponsible representation . . . all these are not only possible within the polity of representational responsibilities, they are its necessary supplement" (1994, 421). But in a culture saturated by misrepresentations of autism, from the merely implausible (*The Accountant*) to the highly offensive (*Atypical*), it is crucial to call out problematic portrayals when they occur. As Sonya Loftis reminds us,

> Cultural stories—whether told by the news media, the literature taught in classrooms, or a television sitcom—matter. They influence the way we think about people with autism, the way we think about disabled people as a cultural minority group, and the way our society regards, values, or disvalues anyone who is different. (2015, 2)

Postal, of course, matters too.

REMAKING THE IMAGE OF AUTISM: AWARENESS, AUTHENTICITY, AND EMPATHY IN *THE SONG COLLECTOR*

Gene Yang's deconstruction of the Chinese-American stereotype in *American Born Chinese* makes it possible to imagine a comic in which an autistic author or character knowingly confronts and undermines prevailing stereotypes about autism, rather than reproducing them, as *Postal* does, for the neurotypical reader. Such a work would also fulfill what Mitchell describes as the "ethical contract" (*Picture Theory* 1994, 421) between creator and intended recipients—and specifically, the autistic audience—by treating autistic characters empathetically. I might also suggest that autistic authorship is a key provision of the contract, at least until autistic representation moves beyond its tokenistic, reductivist phase.

The work of one autistic comics author, Rebecca Burgess, already meets these criteria. Burgess is most recognized for her short strip "Understanding the Spectrum," which was originally published in 2016 for Autism Acceptance Week but has since featured in dozens of other publications, including medical books. Her recent work includes *How to Be Ace: A Memoir of Growing Up Asexual* (2020), a graphic autobiography that examines the intersection of neurological and sexual difference; and *The Song Collector* (2020—), an unfinished web comic. This latter work, still in progress, nevertheless exemplifies how comics can remake the image of autism, and it is the focus of the remainder of this chapter.

Set in Cambridge in 1913, *The Song Collector* tells the story of an autistic academic, Theodore, whose research involves documenting English folk music from around the countryside. The narrative begins when Theodore is paired with a new research assistant, Shryva, a young woman of color, who is brought on board to ease the social connections required by the project. As Theodore's project manager, Henry, gently puts it: "You [Theodore] don't always understand people . . . right away. But your travel schedule is tight. We think it might take you some time to adjust to working with strangers" (2020, 8). Theodore reluctantly agrees, and the remainder of the first chapter shows the couple driving to English towns in search of folk music and musicians. By the end of the first chapter, the unlikely couple have managed to record a group of folk musicians from Long Bennington playing "The Wild Rover."

From the beginning, *The Song Collector* slyly subverts the narrative tropes that typify autism narratives. The historical setting of the comic predates the medical diagnosis of autism, so unlike most autism narratives, the comic does not need explanatory exposition or medical terminology. This circumvention allows Theodore to be described in more personal, humane terms: he is a little "unusual," according to Henry, but "not difficult" (2020, 3). Although he is another high-functioning white male, Theodore appears to work in the Anthropology Department at Cambridge, breaking another stereotype about autistic prevalence in the hard sciences or STEM disciplines (McGrath 2017). And while Theodore definitely qualifies as what Simon Baron-Cohen calls a "systemizer" or a person whose intellect is well-suited for scientific inquiry and organization (2020, 60), his relationship with music is decidedly personal and emotional. As he confesses to Shryva at the end of chapter 1 in a flashback to his turbulent childhood, music "makes me feel safe." It seems more than a coincidence that Theodore works in the humanities at Cambridge, now the seat of autism research in the UK, and the academic bully pulpit of Simon Baron-Cohen, who has published multiple works, including his most recent monograph *The Pattern Seekers* (2020), that seek to prove how autistic talents are particularly suited to the hard sciences. In his tweeds and round spectacles, Theodore is every bit the Cambridge academic, but one who is in love with sentimental folk music—and not numbers.

When Theodore's autistic behaviors surface in the story, they are depicted knowingly and with a dose of self-deprecation. In an early panel, for instance,

Theodore shouts, "I don't need a co-worker! I assure you I'm absolutely a people person!" as he encroaches Henry's personal space, planting his hands on Henry's desk, and using too much volume for an indoor conversation (8). In another scene at the end of the first chapter, Theodore insists on his usual night-time routine, including being able to sleep in the hotel bed next to the window. After Shryva objects, the subsequent panels (figure 3.3) show Theodore nervously tapping his knuckles, an obsessive stimming behavior that emerges in stressful situations. As the panel sequence illustrates, Burgess uses motion lines to illustrate Theodore's stimming. Within an autistic context, the motion line, a basic component of visual language (Eisner 1985; McCloud 1993; Cohn 2020) takes on a new meaning, in essence becoming a stim line. In addition, the close-ups of Theodore's hands in the second and third panels show Burgess paying attention to autistic traits in ways that never occur in *Postal*. Stimming is shown to be important, an integral part of Theodore's identity, and closely tied to his emotional state. One autistic reader with the handle NerdyKid noticed Burgess' emphasis on stimming, commenting "I see those happy stims, Theodore!"

The simplest explanation of Burgess' more carefully drawn image of autism in *The Song Collector* is, of course, that her own autism lends her work an undeniable authenticity, an awareness (self-awareness, in fact) of what to look for and what to reveal in her depictions of autistic characters. This cannot be said for Bryan Hill, the creator of *Postal*, who said in a 2018 interview that he "found a bunch of YouTubers that were also on the Asperger's spectrum [*sic*] monologuing about what their lives were like. So I reached out and said hey, I'm working on the story and I want to be authentic and not turn your perspective, your experience into a gimmick" (as quoted in O'Keefe 2018). Substituting this kind of piecemeal consulting for

Figure 3.3 Theodore Stimming in *The Song Collector*. *Source*: Burgess, Rebecca. *The Song Collector*. 2020. Tapas. https://tapas.io/episode/788084.

actual experience, McGrath notes, leads to stereotypical, composite characters (2017, 82), as I hope my analysis of *Postal* has made clear. In contrast, Burgess' personal experiences inform her stereotype-defying autistic characters. In an email, she noted that she "slipped under the radar" until adulthood, her autism diagnosis coming comparably late. "I was older because I didn't fit more obvious stereotypes. So I do intentionally make comics with autistic characters that are creative, emotional/empathic and enjoying relationships in spite of social difficulties" (2021).

Ultimately, *The Song Collector* presents an empathetically rendered image of autism. In addition to surrounding Theodore with supportive characters, Burgess draws Theodore in a way that encourages autistic and neurotypical readers—the "recipient[s] of the representation" for Mitchell—to identify with Theodore. Stylistically, her cartooning is more abstract and universal (figure 3.4), and this illustration technique may allow readers to see themselves as the character, as McCloud has famously theorized (1993, 31–37).

Cohn (2020) also cites neurocognitive studies examining whether autistic children understand the emotional expressions on cartoon faces better than those on photographs of human faces. The findings of one study (Rosset et al. 2008) are complicated, but it is clear that autistic individuals are interested

Figure 3.4 A Compilation of Theodore's Emotional Expressions in *The Song Collector*.
Source: Burgess, Rebecca. *The Song Collector*. 2020. Tapas. https://tapas.io/episode/788084.

in cartoons, and that the reduced complexity of cartoon faces may allow for easier configural face processing among autistics—in essence, inferencing the entirety of a face based on a limited set of facial features (eyes, nose, mouth). I have speculated elsewhere (Rozema 2015) that manga may owe its popularity among autistics, at least in part, to its consistently drawn, simple faces and exaggerated emotional expressions.

As figure 3.4 illustrates, Theodore experiences a wide range of emotional states: from top left to bottom right, these include impatience, uncertainty, bliss, panic, remorse, excitement, disapproval, timidity, and smugness. Theodore's many facial expressions, drawn in Burgess's loose, expressive lines, often accompanied by stim lines or squiggles, and set against bright blocks of color, remake the image of the cold and distant Aspergian that appears—endlessly—in *Postal*. Of course, neurotypical and autistic readers alike will warm to Theodore, who is like them both. As McGrath suggests, narratives about autism can contribute to the "double empathy problem" first described by Milton (2012), who argued that although autistics are typically faulted for not understanding neurotypicals, neurotypicals have been equally guilty of lacking empathy for autistics. In this equation, *Postal* seems part of the problem and *The Song Collector* part of the solution.

In Rebecca Burgess' work—and in the work of other independent autistic comics creators such as Robert Wollstein (*Boundless* 2019) and Dave Kot (*Face Value* 2013)—images of autism are being actively remade into better, more truthful representations of autistic people. As this chapter has argued, this recasting is necessary, both aesthetically and ethically, to challenge the ubiquity of the Aspergian image—a stereotype that has been widely "adapted" across narrative media, including comics, with very little alteration. Comics are not the only medium that can refashion the representation of autism, but its dependence on images makes it the most suitable for this purpose.

WORKS CITED

Baron-Cohen, Simon. *The Pattern Seekers: How Autism Drives Human Invention*. Basic Books, 2020.
Burgess, Rebecca. "Comics." Email, 2021.
Burgess, Rebecca. *How to be ACE: A Memoir of Growing Up Asexual*. Jessica Kingsley Publishers, 2020.
Burgess, Rebecca. *The Song Collector*. Tapas, 2020. https://tapas.io/episode/788084.
Czech, Herwig. "Hans Asperger, National Socialism, and Race Hygiene in Nazi-era Vienna." *Molecular Autism* 9, no. 1 (2018): 1–43.
Cohn, Neil. *Who Understands Comics?: Questioning the Universality of Visual Language Comprehension*. Bloomsbury Publishing, 2020.
Dowd, Siobhan. *The London Eye Mystery*. David Fickling Books, 2007.

Gibbons, Pauline. "Mediating Language Learning: Teacher Interactions with ESL Students in a Content-based Classroom." *TESOL Quarterly* 37, no. 2 (2003): 247–73.

Haddon, Mark. *The Curious Incident of the Dog in the Night-Time*. Vintage Contemporary, 2004.

Hawkins, Matt, Bryan Hill, and Isaac Goodhart. *Postal: The Complete Collection*. Image Comics, 2020.

Kot, David, and Angela Kot. *Face Value Comics*. Face Value Comics, 2013. https://facevaluecomics.wordpress.com/order-comics/.

Kurchak, Sarah. "*Atypical* Fell Short as Both Autistic Representation and Entertainment. At Least It Was Eclipsed During Its Own Time." *Time*. July 16, 2021. https://time.com/6080754/atypical-autism-representation.

Loftis, Sonya Freeman. *Imagining Autism: Fiction and Stereotypes on the Spectrum*. Indiana University Press, 2015.

McGrath, James. *Naming of Adult Autism: Identity, Ambiguity and Culture*. Rowman & Littlefield, 2017.

McGuire, Anne. *War on Autism: On the Cultural Logic of Normative Violence*. University of Michigan Press, 2016.

Miller, Ashley, and Zach Stentz. *Colin Fischer*. Penguin, 2012.

Milton, Damian EM. "On the Ontological Status of Autism: The 'Double Empathy Problem'." *Disability & Society* 27, no. 6 (2012): 883–87.

Mitchell, W. J. Thomas. *Picture Theory*. University of Chicago Press, 1994.

Mitchell, William John Thomas. *Image Science: Iconology, Visual Culture, and Media Aesthetics*. University of Chicago Press, 2015.

Murray, Stuart. *Representing Autism: Culture, Narrative, Fascination*. Liverpool University Press, 2008.

NerdyKid. May 25, 2020. Comment on Rebecca Burgess, *The Song Collector*. https://tapas.io/episode/1326103.

O'Keefe, Matthew. "Matt Chats: Bryan Hill Discusses Identity, Researching to Write and Working on DC Comics and TV." *The Beat: The Blog of Comics Culture*. September 18, 2018. https://www.comicsbeat.com/matt-chats-bryan-hill-discusses-identity-researching-to-write-and-working-on-dc-comics-and-tv/.

Rosset, Delphine B., Cecilie Rondan, David Da Fonseca, Andreia Santos, Brigitte Assouline, and Christine Deruelle. "Typical Emotion Processing for Cartoon but not for Real Faces in Children with Autistic Spectrum Disorders." *Journal of Autism and Developmental Disorders* 38, no. 5 (2008): 919–25.

Rozema, Robert. "Waiting for Autistic Superman: On Autistic Representation in Superhero Comics." *Ought: The Journal of Autistic Culture* 1, no. 2 (2020): 5.

Rozema, Robert. "Manga and the Autistic Mind." *English Journal* 105.1 (2015): 60–68.

Sheffer, Edith. *Asperger's Children: The Origins of Autism in Nazi Vienna*. W.W. Norton & Company, 2020.

Sherlock. Series 2, episode 2. "The Hound of the Baskervilles." Mark Gatiss and Paul McGuigan. January 8, 2012. BBC.

Silberman, Steve. *NeuroTribes: The Legacy of Autism and How to Think Smarter About People Who Think Differently*. George Allen & Unwin, 2017.

Steele, Claude, and Joshua Aronson. "Stereotype Threat and the Intellectual Test Performance of African Americans." *Journal of Personality and Social Psychology* 69 (5): 797–811.
Tripp, Drew. "Dylann Roof Likely Has Autism, but Preferred Death Over That Label, Court Records Show." *ABC News*. May 10, 2017. https://abcnews4.com/news/.
Wertham, Frederick. *Seduction of the Innocent*. Rinehart & Company, 1954.
Wollstein, Robert. *Boundless*. 2019. https://www.kickstarter.com/projects/boundlesskickstarter/boundless-a-60-page-epic-comic-series?ref=project_link.
Yang, Gene Luen. *American Born Chinese*. First Second Books, 2006.

Chapter 4

An Atypical Interaction with a Typical World

Viewing Coming-of-Age through the Lens of Disability Studies in Robia Rashid's Atypical

Anamika Purohit

Coming-of-age, as a genre of storytelling, focuses on the arduous journey of an adolescent protagonist who needs to establish a sense of belonging in society. Having its roots in an older literary genre of the *bildungsroman*, or the novel of formation/education, coming-of-age genres are narratives of the growth and development of a young protagonist. They often entail an inspirational journey of overcoming, in which a teenager encounters many hurdles that function as means of negotiating with an adult world. A conventional coming-of-age story is, thus, concerned with the integration of the protagonist into a society that is governed by preestablished norms, dominant narratives, and ideological practices. While *bildungsroman* and coming-of-age predominantly situate the protagonist's conflicts in ideological practices and/or systems of belief, for a young, disabled protagonist[1] coming of age, and the journey toward integration needs to incorporate routine experiences consisting of structural and spatial barriers such as "inadequate public and personal transport, unsuitable housing [. . .] and a lack of up-to-date aids and equipment" (UPIAS, n.d.). These quotidian exclusions not only augment the struggle of a young disabled protagonist toward growth and integration but also foreground the social implications of the experience of disability that is often constructed or heightened in specific sociocultural contexts.

This chapter aims to analyze the first two seasons (with a few references to the third season) of Robia Rashid's *Atypical*, as a reboot of the coming-of-age genre in the paradigm of disability studies. *Atypical*, a web-series that debuted on Netflix in 2017, is about a high school student, Samuel Gardner, or Sam, who has autism, and who states his intention to start dating. The chapter probes into the predominant perceptions of disability in conventional coming-of-age or youth narratives, particularly the rehabilitative paradigm, in Western popular culture. The conventions of rehabilitative coming-of-age are juxtaposed with *Atypical* as a means to propose the latter as a reworking of the genre under the social model of disability. The remainder of this chapter delves into specific nuances of the coming-of-age narrative such as dating, displacement, and conflicts with the ideology of standardization as rearticulated by *Atypical* in the framework of disability studies. In congruence with the objectives of disability studies, this section explores the web-series' emphasis on the spatial, material, and cultural dimensions of disability in a contemporary milieu that requires the protagonist to routinely engage with social institutions and sites of consumption. The engagement between the protagonist and the built environment, in *Atypical*, may be proposed as a means to initiate experimentation into conventions of social institutions, and spatial arrangements thereby implicating society in enabling the protagonist's sense of belonging. In addition to the above, this chapter also explores the analogical dimension of the protagonist's comprehension of the external world as perceived through his autistic imagination.

DISABILITY AND THE GENERIC COORDINATES OF COMING-OF-AGE

This section analyzes the formal features of the conventional coming-of-age genre with specific attention to the concept of rehabilitation. These formal elements are set against *Atypical* to suggest the latter as a reboot of this genre. In a typical coming-of-age story, the characteristic trope of integration often renders the external environment fixed and unyielding in response to the protagonist's resistance. According to Elman (2014), this generic interplay between the volatile phase of adolescence and the supposed rigidity (often articulated as stability) of the external world may be connected to an ideological conception of the teenager as a threat to an established social order, and norms of citizenship in the United States, particularly in the twentieth century. By proposing rationality and steadiness as reflective of the ideal adult subject, Elman (2014) conceives of the teenager as "a figure that serves as a paradigmatic crisis to be overcome in order to achieve the role of adult citizen, a rational and stable subject position . . . in contrast to the unstable and irrational teen" (3). In response to such a collective conception of the teenager, Elman (2014) foregrounds a body of rehabilitative edutainment that emerged in the United States, in the late twentieth century, as a means to provide a solution-driven, diagnostic, or preventive formula to recognizable teenage crises such as parental alcoholism, sexuality, identity crisis, and disability. For Elman (2014), the language of rehabilitation percolated into most forms of youth popular culture including coming-of-age narratives in different media in the United States by the late twentieth century. She mentions television dramas such as Kleiser's *The Boy in the Plastic Bubble* (1976), and books such as McDaniel's *Six Months to Live* (1985), which may both be seen as coming-of-age narratives in the rehabilitative paradigm.

It is significant to note Elman's (2014) criticism against "ableist representations of disability as tragic, undesirable, or inspirational" (5) in rehabilitative coming-of-age narratives. In these narratives, the disabled protagonist may embark on a journey of supposed growth and development consisting of personalized attempts to transcend or overcome his/her disability in order to revert to an "able" body and mind, as it were. As Elman (2014) observes, "rehabilitation rests on ableist notions of embodiment involving the language and activity of 'return'—a return to a state of able-bodied normalcy or stability—through 'personal effort'" (17). Alternatively, in a rehabilitative coming-of-age, the very concept of disability may be suggested as a metaphor for the turbulent period of adolescence: "casting adolescence as a disability and 'coming of age' as a process of 'overcoming' disabling adolescence" (Elman 2014, 20–21). In both the possibilities, according to Elman (2014), the framework of rehabilitation, in contrast to cure and elimination, endorses the ideology of self-help and self-discipline to render disability "an undesirable and transitory obstacle to be surpassed through individual will" (18). Self-help in a rehabilitative coming-of-age, thus, may be proposed as a means to overcome disability figuratively, in instances where it is seen as a metaphor for the temporarily painful phase of teenage, which the protagonist eventually transcends to enter a stable state of adulthood. Alternately, in coming-of-age texts with a disabled protagonist, self-discipline or individual effort is highlighted as a means for the protagonist to achieve an "able" body, and fit into an unyielding, exclusive world.

However, the reliance of rehabilitative coming-of-age on the ideology of self-help to overcome disability, particularly in case of a disabled protagonist, may be seen as contradictory to the social model of disability because such a narrative expects the disabled individual to independently devise a means of integration into society without offering him/her any possibilities for such an inclusion. Shakespeare (2006) emphasizes the significance of society's involvement in the social model's approach to disability, which "demonstrates that the problems disabled people face are the result of social oppression and exclusion, not their individual deficits. This places the moral responsibility on the society to remove the burdens which have been imposed" (217). Additionally, the language of rehabilitation in a traditional coming-of-age may erase the specific historicity of the exclusions faced by disabled individuals to propose disability as a "more general 'obstacle'" (Elman 2014, 19), and suggest that "minor inconveniences experienced by the nondisabled are somehow the same as those experienced by disabled people as they navigate inaccessible environments . . . and social stigma on a daily basis" (Elman 2014, 19). Such a suggestion may be furthered in a conventional coming-of-age by positioning disability as a metaphor for the painful period of adolescence that all individuals (disabled or abled) grapple with, thereby disregarding the material exclusions faced by the disabled people, and the sociopolitical implications of disability. Alternatively, in a coming-of-age featuring a disabled protagonist, the latter may be interpellated into an ableist ideology that not only unjustly places him/her on a comparable footing with nondisabled youngsters but also considers his/her disability a hurdle, which can be controlled or overcome through sustained individual effort.

Zemeckis's *Forrest Gump* (1994) may be seen as an example of the conventional rehabilitative coming-of-age. It is a narrative of the eponymous protagonist, who is disabled, and who recounts his inspirational journey of overcoming all odds to achieve fame, community respect, and filial-familial love. While the film attempts to set Gump apart by highlighting his inability to walk without braces in childhood, and lower IQ in comparison to other children of his age, Gump is also interpellated into the supposedly integrative ideology of rehabilitation, a message iterated by his mother in his childhood: "You're the same as everybody else. You are no different" (Forrest Gump 1994). The proposed integration, however, is illusory, since Gump is continually posited as an outsider to social norms and ideologies that most individuals have imbibed unconsciously. In the film, while American society passes through a number of historical and cultural landmarks paralleling Gump's journey toward adulthood, the responsibility for integration into society is entirely left on him.

By compelling a disabled individual to devise ingenious ways to fit into the dominant ideology of ableism and normalcy, the film fails to suggest inventive possibilities toward inclusion. In fact, Gump's inexplicable victory over his physical impairment becomes a surrogate means for him to be accepted by a rigid world that either ignores or tolerates his lower IQ because of his physical functionality. The audience derives little insight into the exact experience of disability or difference that Gump experiences because of lower IQ, since the film's focus remains on his physical accomplishments. For instance, Gump summarizes his entire college life into five years of playing football and eventually meeting the President of the United States. Moreover, by sanctioning Gump to overcome the difficulties faced by him due to his physical and psychological difference, the film seemingly reprises the rehabilitative norm of using disability metaphorically as a phase that can be overcome to step into a stable, almost-able adulthood.

Despite the discernibly outdated vision of disability in the film, in Western popular culture *Forrest Gump* remains a landmark that exerts influence on the collective imagination of intellectual disability. While scholars such as Murray (2008) critique the film's "prosthetic use of the [autistic] idiot figure" (83), *Forrest Gump* emerges in popular conversations as a "bit of a *punchline*, especially when it comes to its use of mental disability" (emphasis mine, Lopez 2019). Along with Levinson's *Rain Man* (1988), *Forrest Gump*, according to Lopez (2018), remains a preferred representation of intellectual disability particularly for a mainstream (able-bodied) audience; the protagonist of this coming-of-age is "*just disabled enough* to be pitiable, but not so much as to make the audience uncomfortable" (emphasis mine). The rehabilitative tropes in *Forrest Gump*, such as life-affirmation, a spirit of *carpe diem*, and the physical productivity of the disabled protagonist (Lopez 2018) render the film a favored representation of disability "palatable to an able-bodied audience" (Lopez 2018).

Atypical presents a viable contrast to the rehabilitative approach of a mainstream coming-of-age such as *Forrest Gump*. It is imperative to note that as a web-series on Netflix, *Atypical* arrives at resisting mainstream expectations from a coming-of-age featuring a disabled protagonist, for, given the norms of content-delivery via online streaming platforms on smart-devices, the web-series addresses relatively individualized audiences that "have more content to choose from, are able to better control how, when, and what media they choose to attend to, and are increasingly fragmented as media consuming communities" (Coleman 2018, 408). *Atypical*, thus, is not pressurized to adhere to standard requirements of a rehabilitative coming-of-age with a disabled protagonist, who may be "disabled enough to be different from mainstream" (Lopez 2018), but is also supposed to be angelic, charming, or compliant (Lopez 2018) so that "the able-bodied [mainstream] audience watching [his] exploits can embrace [him]" (Lopez 2018) without feeling discomforted or implicated. On the contrary, as a coming-of-age, *Atypical* implicates and interrogates social institutions, spatial arrangements, and individuals Sam Gardner interacts with in his journey toward integration. Instead of compelling Sam to transcend or overcome his condition of autism through self-discipline or individual efforts, social institutions and spaces, such as college, police stations, or coffee-shops are held accountable for their relative ability or inability to create an inclusive environment for the disabled, thereby reiterating the social-model approach of the web-series, in which "it is not the disabled person who is to blame, but society" (Shakespeare 2006, 217). Moreover, in its attempt to foreground Sam's experience of disability, the web-series adopts an insider's view so that "the audience does not look at Sam with worry or fear. Instead, they feel for him and look for the issue to be resolved" (Wolff 2018, 57). For example, in an episode of season 1, Sam is goaded into going on a date to a coffee-shop (Atypical "Antarctica" 2017). The scene in the coffee-shop is shot in such a way that it foregrounds Sam's discomposure. Dull lights and incessant noise, which are regular and overlooked features of coffee-shops, are rendered awkward and discomforting with the help of the frame composition, which on the one hand foregrounds a close-up of Sam's troubled facial expressions, and on the other, confines him to a corner of the frame even as the blurred background remains noisy with people talking and moving about.

As a result, the audience is no longer a voyeur pitying Sam; they are forced to notice the way that a supposedly innocuous spatial arrangement such as a coffee-shop performs spatial and ritualistic exclusivity, iterates standardization, and fails to create avenues for a clientele with varied sensorial responses to external surroundings. Kaweski (2011) explains the sensory integration of students with Autism Spectrum Disorder (ASD), who "struggle to 'modulate' (alter the intensity) of incoming sounds, smell, light, and touch. Some students struggle to filter out unwanted stimuli" (21). In filming this scene as it does, *Atypical* helps the audience experience the confusing stimuli in the coffee-shop along with Sam. It further implicates the audience into quotidian struggles of a protagonist with an intellectual disability instead of glossing over discomforting moments to focus on the life-affirming aspects that a rehabilitative coming-of-age would emphasize. *Atypical*, then, rethinks the conventions of coming-of-age through a disability lens, for the genre is used to not only facilitate the growth of the adolescent protagonist but also initiate a revisionary approach to various spatial arrangements and social institutions that the disabled protagonist interacts with.

Furthermore, *Atypical* rejects a metaphorical view of disability by anchoring Sam's autism in lived experiences and underlines the need to perceive human variation through the movement and interactions of disabled individuals in specific surroundings: "how motion affects perception. The ways that our bodies are configured and the ways that our sensory systems function all affect how we move through space and perceive the world" (Linton 2005, 522). This positioning is central to the conception of disability in the framework of disability studies and challenges the tokenistic promise of inclusion within the ideology of rehabilitation, which "spotlights the disabled . . . but paradoxically, only so that 'they are made to disappear'" (Elman 2014, 18); the society, thereby, need not register the structural, social, and economic inequality that disabled individuals routinely encounter. *Atypical*, in fact, implicates the society and community in the protagonist's growth and integration. By doing so, the web-series not only rethinks the representation of disability in a coming-of-age narrative but also rejects ableist and stereotypical representations of disability that may comfort a mainstream audience but are not authentic in the least.

MATERIALIZING COMING-OF-AGE IN THE SPATIAL, THE ANALOGICAL, AND THE LIVED

This section explores the engagement between disability and external environment as seen in *Atypical* by analyzing coming-of-age rituals such as dating, standardization, and displacement. As mentioned earlier, most conventional coming-of-age narratives position the young protagonist's resistance in confrontation with dominant belief-systems or ideologies. Hader (1996) considers "repeated clashes between the protagonist's needs and desires and the *views* and *judgments* enforced by an unbending social order" (emphasis mine) a significant characteristic of a *bildungsroman*, or a coming-of-age story of a young individual's development. *Atypical*, however, revises this characteristic to predominantly materialize Sam's trajectory of growth in practical engagements with the built environment. It interrogates ideological practices of the adult world by engaging with specific social institutions (and individuals) that contribute to the standardization of these ideological practices. The choice to situate Sam's coming-of-age in lived experiences in specific sites is significant to disability studies, for it suggests a material/spatial and cultural dimension to Sam's experience of disability, as his suffering gets accentuated in certain spatial arrangements. Garland-Thomson (2013) observes on the importance of the material in disability studies: "Disability ... merges the profoundly cultural with the material, as the human variations that cultures have designated as disability have helped shape built and social environments (just as those environments have, in turn, shaped bodies)" (917). Moreover, the focus on spatiality in the web-series assists in exploring the spatial and analogical nuances of Sam's autistic imagination and perception of the adult world. Sam's analogical engagement with norms of the adult world in *Atypical* may be seen as a means to further his growth as he seeks meaning and belonging in an external world—a quest integral to the coming-of-age genre.

Rituals of Dating and Sites of Consumption

When Sam announces his desire to date, his mother worries about his inability to grasp the social cues accompanying dating and relationships and consults his therapist, who suggests the possibility for Sam to learn the social skills appropriate to dating (Atypical "Antarctica" 2017). The web-series, however, establishes an additional need for Sam to engage with unfamiliar locations and sites of consumption that form an important part of dating. As seen in *Atypical*, rituals of dating are often situated in specific spatial arrangements. Dwyer (2000) utilizes Eva Illouz's analysis to explain the connection between sites of consumption and the rituals of romance in the contemporary postmodern era: "Commodities and consumption are not opposed to romance but form a key part of it, its preferred romantic situations being sites of consumption whether gastronomic, cultural or touristic" (13). For Sam in *Atypical*, the plunge into dating requires not only an initiation into appropriate social skills but also the need to execute these skills in unfamiliar spaces, mostly, sites of consumption such as a coffee-shop or a restaurant.

In the same episode, since Sam does not prefer a coffee-shop for a second date he suggests Techtropolis, the technology-and-gadget store where he works part-time, as an alternative (Atypical "Antarctica" 2017). Techtropolis too is a retail store, and thus, a site of consumption; however, Sam creatively maneuvers the proposition by planning his date in the parking area of Techtropolis, and not inside the store. By choosing the parking area of Techtropolis, Sam is able to resist the uniform set of spatial practices expected of a retail store or a coffee-shop, such as the persistent consciousness of sales representatives and customers having conversations, and the requirement for constant consumption of products and services. In the parking lot, on the contrary, the frame composition is rendered tranquil and bereft of interruptions, consisting of street-lights, and a bare background with some greenery. Sam's date in the parking lot highlights his comfort, for he is able to break away from a predetermined set of social practices, and strikes an almost unrehearsed conversation with his date, unlike an earlier experience in the coffee-shop where he was rendered too overwhelmed by the surroundings to apply the social skills that he had researched for the occasion or have an unrehearsed but significant interaction on his own.

The contradiction in the two experiences of Sam's date makes explicit the spatial and cultural coordinates of disability, for Sam's discomfort and suffering seem pronounced in spatial arrangements that disregard the nuances of his autistic condition, such as an increased sensitivity to noise, glaring lights, unfamiliar textures, and smells. Garland-Thomson (2005) defines the concept of disability as a condition of the human body's interaction with the built environment and indicates the need to perceive ability and disability in the light of the external environment that bodies interact with:

> Ability and disability are not so much a matter of the capacities and limitations of bodies but more about what we expect from a body at a particular moment and place. [. . .] We are expected to look, act, and move in certain ways so we'll fit into the built and attitudinal environment. If we don't, we become disabled

[. . .] the changes that occur when body encounters world are what we call disability. (524)

By situating Sam's growth, especially his plunge into romantic relationships, in lived experiences and literal settings, *Atypical* reiterates Sam's experience of disability as a sociocultural construct instead of an individual peculiarity, thereby underlining the material, and cultural framework for perceiving a particular form of impairment as disability. This is crucial to the social model of disability, which proposes critical differences between the concepts of impairment and disability, wherein "the former is individual and private, the latter is structural and public [. . .] the real priority is to accept impairment and to remove disability" (Shakespeare 2006, 216). Sam's interaction with the built environment stresses this distinction, for standardized or commercial spatial arrangements such as the coffee-shop augment his suffering unlike spaces such as the parking lot that do not strictly adhere to a standard layout and code of behavior. Sam's engagement with varied spatial arrangements, thus, becomes crucial to the social model of disability proposed by the show.

Ideology of Standardization

Sam's interactions with individuals in various institutional spaces, as he embarks on the journey to adulthood, function as a means to confront the capitalist-modernist ideology of standardization, which threatens or excludes any format of human variation that does not fit into its predetermined norms. Garland-Thomson (2005) observes on the capitalist-modernist urge toward standardization and uniformity, especially in case of human bodies and embodied experiences, that pressurizes societies to deny or "devalue physical and mental variety" (524) in favor of normative behavior, body comportment, and appearance. This dominant desire for uniformity may further be connected to the concept of rehabilitation, which also emphasizes self-help or self-surveillance in order to restore a "normative" body and mind. Such a personal quest, as discussed earlier, is an integral component of a rehabilitative coming-of-age. *Atypical* presents many instances of confrontation between the protagonist and the institutions or individuals reiterating the ideology of standardization. However, in keeping with the objectives of disability studies, the web-series does not use these confrontational moments to deny or devalue Sam's condition or compel him to alter in accordance with standardized ideological practices, something that is customarily expected of the protagonist of a rehabilitative coming-of-age. In fact, Sam's engagement with different social institutions serves as a means to interrogate standardized ideological practices within that institution that may not be inclusive toward human variation. The ideology of standardization imbibed by specific individuals, especially with regard to the process of embodiment or bodily experiences, is consequently further problematized by the web-series.

An example of an encounter between Sam and the ideology of standardization is seen in season 2, when Sam exits his best friend's house, alone at night, and is inadvertently assumed to be a drug-addict or a criminal by a police officer (Atypical "In the Dragon's Lair" 2018). While a conventional coming-of-age may have isolated Sam expecting him to devise ingenious means of survival in the situation or would have overlooked the episode once the misunderstanding was cleared, *Atypical* uses this instance to interrogate the system of patrolling and interrogation that is not sensitive to a condition such as autism. When Sam's father challenges the police officer's lack of sensitivity to individuals with autism, who may exhibit fear by twitching or not being able to respond in a tense situation, the officer indicates the standard code followed by them, and the need to make quick decisions based on experience (Atypical "The Smudging" 2018). In spite of giving credibility to the officer's point of view, the web-series does not revert to cautioning Sam or educating him to repress his organic responses to tense situations in the external world; instead, the interaction with the officer encourages Sam's primary caretakers to organize a training for the police force in the city to help them understand the nuances of autism. This approach turns toward community networks and social institutions for solutions instead of the disabled individual, an approach that is consistent with Linton's (2005) analogical explanation of disability studies, in which a curled right fist signifies the disabled people, and the open left hand, the society at large: "In disability studies, the lens is turned toward the representational and institutional structures that constitute the left hand to discover what kinds of analyses and interventions can reconstruct the left hand and make for a better fit" (518).

The ideology of standardization is not merely reflected in institutions such as the police station, but is also internalized by the human body that functions under predetermined norms and repetitive disciplinary practices. According to Butler (1988), "Embodiment clearly manifests a set of strategies [. . .] never fully self-styled, for living styles have a history, and that history *conditions* and *limits* possibilities" (emphasis mine, 521). It may be argued that in *Atypical*, the capitalist-modernist ideology of standardization conditions and restricts bodily practices thereby initiating exclusivity into the very genesis of embodiment and norms of physical proximity, something that Sam is incrementally made to grapple with. For instance, in an episode where a date applies customary norms of arousal, consisting of soft-touch and caress, Sam is rendered uncomfortable and restless, pushing his date away (Atypical "Antarctica" 2017). The scene establishes Sam's discomfort toward soft or tender touch. However, the date's inability to fathom Sam's discomfort, as she blames it on his supposedly disturbed state of mind, unveils and problematizes the disciplinary or performative[2] foundation of the act of sexual intimacy, which is expected to be unrestrained, spontaneous, or experimental. As the example indicates, human bodies and the process of embodiment are similarly inscribed by repetitive, standardized, and disciplinary norms; consequently, most youngsters are unable to conceive of or be inclusive toward alternative bodily practices. By providing an insight into Sam's state of mind, *Atypical* helps the audience notice the disconnect between Sam's expectations of sexual intimacy and the exclusive set of standardized practices for sex that have been imbibed by most teenagers unconsciously. As a coming-of-age, however, the web-series enables a gradual initiation of Sam into practices of physical intimacy along with his girlfriend, Paige. Sam and Paige discuss their respective expectations and preferences regarding physical intimacy at different points in their relationship, setting rules that both are comfortable with, and being experimental as required. For example, in season 2, they attempt a casual relationship centered on sexual intimacy only to eventually realize its failure as their companionship begins to grow (Atypical "Penguin Cam and Chill" 2018). Thus, in congruence with disability studies, *Atypical* not only critiques the internalization of standardized norms of embodiment by individuals but also proposes a rethinking of bodily practices in alternative frameworks inspired by the disabled protagonist thereby suggesting a possibility to "expand on the quirkiness of [the] forms [of the disabled] and to cultivate the interesting styles such bodies can produce" (Linton 2005, 521).

In a similar manner, *Atypical* indicates a potential for experimentation with spatial arrangements on the basis of Sam's engagement with these spaces, or "how the bodies [the disabled] have can articulate new art forms" (Linton 2005, 521). An instance of an experimental spatiality is seen when Paige proposes that Sam accompany her to the high school prom (Atypical "The D-Train to Bone Town" 2017). Given the spatial characteristics of the prom venue—disco lights, loud music, and noisy crowd—Sam hesitates. However, since Paige is aware of his condition, she convinces the Parent-Teacher-Association that the prom be reworked creatively as a "silent-night," and that all students wear headphones so that music is only audible on the headphones. The theme of the venue, decided as "The Penguins of Antarctica," renders the setting familiar for Sam, who eventually attends and enjoys the event. This example shows the possibility of initiating creativity and inclusiveness into the otherwise standardized spatial arrangement of a prom dance, defined by loud music, bright lights, and noise.

As a reworked coming-of-age within a social model approach to disability, *Atypical*, thus, brings to crisis the ideology of standardization internalized by the external world the protagonist interacts with—social institutions, individuals, and spatial arrangements. By rendering the external world capable of transformation in engagement with the disabled protagonist, the web-series resists the rehabilitative design in which only the protagonist has to alter to fit into a standardized system. *Atypical*, in fact, provides suggestions for inclusivity of Sam in mainstream activities and experiences, which places responsibility on the society "to enable disabled people to participate" (Shakespeare 2006, 217).

Displacement

Displacement is another characteristic of adulthood that Sam encounters in his journey. Displacement may be a universal obstacle in coming-of-age narratives, however, for Sam, this impediment is intensified since, as an individual with autism, his comfort largely depends on routine and constancy. Shore and Rastelli (2011) explain the significance of routine and structure for individuals with autism, who regularly struggle with

> a confusing jumble of unrelated events, loud and painful sounds, or overly bright lights. . . . In such a situation, the person feels the need to impose an order on the world just to survive and have a feeling of security. (184)

Additionally, due to his autism, Sam has always been displaced (or marginalized) from mainstream society, yet has been protected by his family's timely interventions. His sense of belonging, therefore, has always been tentative and dependent on his efforts in collaboration with his parents, close friends, and therapist.

It is imperative to consider Sam's fascination with penguins and Antarctica here, for this preoccupation, which may be seen as a characteristic of his autistic imagination, also functions as a coping-mechanism used by him in situations that render him displaced, and/or insecure. Shore and Rastelli (2011) note "preoccupation with at least one stereotyped and restricted pattern of interest" (15) as one of the diagnostic criteria for autism, further recapitulated by Sam's therapist in *Atypical*, who considers "intense and obsessive preoccupations" (Atypical "Antarctica" 2017) a common trait of individuals with ASD. In *Atypical*, however, Sam's preoccupation with penguins and Antarctica is not merely a fact associated with autism; this fixation helps the audience unpack his analogical mode of cognition and comprehension of the adult world. Such a mode of perception helps him feel emplaced, and forge a temporary sense of belonging during moments of displacement. For instance, in an example discussed earlier, in order to grapple with the discomfort of romantic physical touch, Sam imaginatively displaces himself from the dorm room of his date and places himself in the cold surrounding of Antarctica (Atypical "Antarctica" 2017). He re-imagines the extreme cold to be akin to a sound or an experience that renders him numb enough to bear the harshness of the moment. Sam's regular and strategic use of material or spatial analogies from Antarctica in uncomfortable situations can be seen as reflective of his desire for belonging in a harsh world that considers him unusual but does not deny or devalue his dissimilarity.

In season 3, after entering Denton University, he uses similar analogies to fathom the complexity of college life and academic expectations. Initially, the unfamiliar world of college, new friends and teachers, and the hectic schedule render him overwhelmed, but he eventually begins to perceive his presence in the tough environment of college in terms of the resilience and perseverance of penguins in severe Antarctic conditions. The analogy assists him in adapting and feeling relatively emplaced at Denton. However, unlike a rehabilitative coming-of-age, *Atypical* refrains from establishing or celebrating the protagonist's heroic triumph over his sense of displacement or alienation. Sam's distinctive journey as a disabled protagonist and his need to rely on others are highlighted at regular intervals. For instance, in college, although Sam initially assumes that he can function without the help of disability services, he is eventually convinced to approach them acknowledging his diverse trajectory in comparison to other students (Atypical "Cocaine Pills and Pony Meat" 2019).

Sam further relies on analogies from Antarctica in situations that demand an emotive response. Displacement in these instances may be perceived in emotive or affective terms. For example, in season 1, when Paige visits Sam's room, and fiddles with different items, he is rendered discomforted and displaced in his own space (Atypical "That's My Sweatshirt" 2017). Later, however, he processes the ideological practice of sharing (the same space) with one's partner analogically with the help of Arctic foxes, who form monogamous pairs and share a den. Sam's desire to utilize instances from the Antarctic animal kingdom to comprehend relationship rituals of the human adult world can be seen as an important method to unpack his distinct mode of expressing emotion or reciprocation, and establishing a feeling of comfort and belonging in a relationship. Kaweski (2011) explains alternative modes of emotive expressions used by adolescents with ASD:

> They are perfectly capable of forming connections with friends and family. The disconnect lies in fully expressing their emotions in a manner easily understood by friends and loved ones. [. . .] When they attempt to join in conversation, they miss the point . . . or switch the focus to their special interest with no transition to inform the listener of a change in conversational direction. (15)

Thus, in *Atypical*, though Sam is frequently discouraged from talking about penguins by his family and close friends, he feels motivated to share facts related to penguins with these very people. The conversations on Antarctica and the penguins, then, maybe seen as a means to express his sense of comfort with a person, or reciprocate feelings; when Sam confesses his affection to Paige for the first time, he gifts her a necklace with a penguin-shaped pendant (Atypical "That's My Sweatshirt" 2017). By foregrounding Sam's fascination with penguins and Antarctica *Atypical* not only underlines a crucial nuance of Sam's autistic imagination but also helps the audience delve into the analogical strategies used by Sam for securing a sense of belonging in the external world, and in relationships that matter to him, thereby reprising an essential element of a coming-of-age narrative.

Another intervention into Sam's displacement in *Atypical* is his intermittent desire to escape when he feels trapped by the adult world. This is predominantly seen in season 2 as Sam is about to graduate from high school. The proposition of being isolated in the supposedly predatory adult world of college renders Sam anxious as he mentions the need for docile animals to form groups in order to survive (Atypical "Little Dude and the Lion" 2018). The trope of a young protagonist feeling threatened by the adult world during crisis or a transitional phase is universally seen in coming-of-age narratives; however, *Atypical* connects this universal trope to Sam's ASD, due to which he has often been marginalized in school. This augments his anxiety, for his chances of having a peer group to survive the transition are rendered low. However, in keeping with the social model approach, *Atypical* revises the conventional coming-of-age characteristic of individualistic confrontations or clashes between the protagonist and the external world during crises to enable a possible reconciliation. Sam is goaded into reconfiguring his sense of community by joining the peer group of high school students with autism convened by the school's career counselor to help them transition from high school to college (Atypical "Little Dude and the Lion" 2018). This choice supports the social model approach of *Atypical*, which, according to Shakespeare (2006) is progressive, and "mandates barrier removal" (216) against the medical model that is reactionary, and "reduces the complex problems of the disabled people to issues of . . . cure or rehabilitation" (216). As a coming-of-age narrative, *Atypical* exhibits Sam's journey toward emplacement through his desire for control and autonomy over his space and surroundings, which emphasize Sam's incremental progression toward independence facilitated through collective effort. In congruence with the social model, *Atypical* does not lose sight of collective participation in enabling the young disabled protagonist's growth and integration even as it continues to underline his alternative trajectory of coming-of-age.

CONCLUSION

This chapter has delved into the generic characteristics of coming-of-age in order to explore *Atypical* as a reworking of this popular genre in the paradigm of disability studies. As a reboot, the web-series assists in surfacing and problematizing traditional conventions of coming-of-age in the rehabilitative paradigm that restrict the possibility of showcasing the journey of growth of a disabled protagonist. This chapter has further examined the spatial and material foundations of different rituals of adulthood such as dating, confrontations with the ideology of standardization, and displacement through which *Atypical* maps Sam's gradual transition from adolescence to adulthood, thereby giving an insight into sociocultural dimensions of disability. Delving into the spatial and analogical facets of Sam's autistic imagination is integral to the analysis of his journey of integration in this chapter; this nuance adds a material layer to his desire for emplacement and helps unpack his alternative response to varied ideologies of adulthood.

Moreover, by exploring varied encounters between Sam and standardized spatial arrangements and social institutions, this chapter has located avenues for inclusivity toward human variation as proposed in *Atypical*, especially in accordance with the practical approach of the social model of disability that "[identifies] social barriers to be removed . . . [in order to be] effective *instrumentally* in the liberation of the disabled people" (emphasis in original, Shakespeare 2006, 217). The chapter, thus, emphasizes the ways in which *Atypical* moves away from the rehabilitative toward the social model approach, a choice especially feasible in case of visual media relayed via streaming platforms, which allows audiences to be individualized and fragmented. By providing a rounded approach to Sam's growth and integration into the adult world, *Atypical* paves the way for similar interventions of disability studies into a variety of conventional narrative forms and genres.

NOTES

1. The identity-first appellation (disabled individual) derives from the social model of disability, which proposes disability as a social condition instead of an individual characteristic. The person-first appellation (individual with disability) emanates from the medical model that renders disability "an individual's personal problem" (Smith 2016) that possibly requires medical intervention. While both the appellations belong to different approaches, thinkers from Disability Studies assert that "using person-first language does not always suggest that the user follows the medical model, or vice versa" (Smith 2016). Moreover, the usage should be based on the concerned

individual's preference. In solidarity with the social model, this chapter uses identity-first appellation. However, in certain specific instances from *Atypical*, person-first appellation may be used.

2. Butler (1999) uses the term "gender performativity" to refer to repetitive, and disciplinary iteration of certain practices, acts or gestures that over a period of time induce docility and conformity to a particular gender identity made intelligible through these very acts/enactments. Performativity is distinguished from performance: the former does not necessarily involve individual volition, has a collective dimension, and is "sustained through corporeal signs and other discursive means" (173).

WORKS CITED

Butler, Judith. "Performative Acts and Gender Constitution: An Essay in Phenomenology and Feminist Theory." *Theatre Journal* 40, no. 4 (1988): 519–31.
Butler, Judith. *Gender Trouble*, Routledge, 1999.
Coleman, Robin R. Means, and Aniko Bodroghkozy. "African Americans and Broadcasting." *A Companion to the History of American Broadcasting*, edited by Aniko Bodroghkozy. Wiley-Blackwell, 2018, 389–412.
Dwyer, Rachel. "All You Want is Money, All You Need is Love: Sex and Romance in Modern India." Cassell, 2000.
Elman, Julie Passanante. *Chronic Youth: Disability, Sexuality, and US Media Cultures of Rehabilitation.* Vol. 4. New York and London: NYU Press, 2014.
Garland-Thomson, Rosemarie. "Disability and Representation." *PMLA/Publications of the Modern Language Association of America* 120, no. 2 (2005): 522–27.
Garland-Thomson, Rosemarie. "Disability Studies: A Field Emerged." *American Quarterly* 65.4 (2013): 915–26.
Hader, Suzanne. "The Bildungsroman Genre: Great Expectations, Aurora Leigh, and Waterland." *Victorian Web* (1996).
Kaweski, Walter. *Teaching Adolescents with Autism: Practical Strategies for the Inclusive Classroom.* Corwin Press, 2011.
Linton, Simi. "What is Disability Studies?." *PMLA/Publications of the Modern Language Association of America* 120, no. 2 (2005): 518–22.
Lopez, Kristen. "Ten Years Of Missing The Point of 'Tropic Thunder's' Thoughts On Mental Disability." *Forbes*, 2018. Accessed July 21, 2021. https://www.forbes.com/sites/kristenlopez/2018/11/02/ten-years-of-missing-the-point-of-tropic-thunders-thoughts-on-mental-disability/?sh=7c93683e34bd.
Lopez, Kristen. "'Forrest Gump' at 25: Disability Representation (For Better and Worse)." *Forbes*, 2019. Accessed July 20, 2021. https://www.forbes.com/sites/kristenlopez/2019/07/05/forrest-gump-at-25-disability-representation-for-better-and-worse/?sh=76e62e38664d.
Murray, Stuart. *Representing Autism: Culture, Narrative, Fascination.* Oxford University Press, 2008.

Rashid, Robia. "Antarctica." Episode. Atypical 1, no. 1. *Netflix*, August 11, 2017.
Rashid, Robia. "That's My Sweatshirt." Episode. Atypical 1, no. 5. Netflix, August 11, 2017.
Rashid, Robia. "The D-Train to Bone Town." Episode. Atypical 1, no. 6. Netflix, August 11, 2017.
Rashid, Robia. "Penguin Cam and Chill." Episode. Atypical 2, no. 2. Netflix, September 7, 2018.
Rashid, Robia. "Little Dude and the Lion." Episode. Atypical 2, no. 3. Netflix, September 7, 2018.
Rashid, Robia. "In the Dragon's Lair." Episode. Atypical 2, no. 6. Netflix, September 7, 2018.
Rashid, Robia. "The Smudging." Episode. Atypical 2, no. 7. Netflix, September 7, 2018.
Rashid, Robia. "Cocaine Pills and Pony Meat." Episode. Atypical 3, no. 3. Netflix, November 1, 2019.
Shore, Stephen, and Linda G. Rastelli. *Understanding Autism for Dummies*. John Wiley & Sons, 2011.
Shakespeare, Tom. "The Social Model of Disability." *The Disability Studies Reader* 2 (2006): 197–204.
Smith, S. E. "Why I Say 'Disabled Person' Instead of 'Person With Disabilities'." *Rewire News Group*, 2016. Accessed August 10, 2021. https://rewirenewsgroup.com/article/2016/09/14/say-disabled-person-instead-person-disabilities/.
Union of the Physically Impaired Against Segregation. n.d. "Policy Statement." Accessed August 14, 2021. https://disability-studies.leeds.ac.uk/wp-content/uploads/sites/40/library/UPIAS-UPIAS.pdf.
Wolff, Sierra M. ""Because He Is Different": Shifts in Discourse and the Increasing Presence of Autism in Fictional Television." PhD diss., The University of Wisconsin-Milwaukee, 2018.
Zemeckis, Robert, dir. 1994. *Forrest Gump*. *Netflix* video. https://www.netflix.com/title/60000724.

Chapter 5

"But can we agree that he's unwell?"

Narrative Resistance in Legion's *Approach to Mental Disability*

Julia E. Kiernan

In October 2015, Marvel and cable network FX announced the development of *Legion*, a television series to be written and produced by *Fargo* showrunner Noah Hawley, and based on a Marvel comics character of the same name. Their early description of the show read:

> Since he was a teenager, David has struggled with mental illness. Diagnosed as schizophrenic, David has been in and out of psychiatric hospitals for years. But after a strange encounter with a fellow patient, he's confronted with the possibility that the voices he hears and the visions he sees might be real. (Slezak)

As the 2017 launch date approached, the show's official Twitter account tweeted out a short teaser video featuring disjointed scenes that mixed violence, drama, interrogation, and treatment. The tweet itself read: "Does David Haller know what he is?" (@LegionFX).

These early glimpses into *Legion* suggested a new take on David Haller—a character whose identity has been defined by mental illness across the print Marvel comics—one in which David's "illness" might be nothing more than mutant powers. The first few episodes reinforce this idea, showing David being rescued from a psychiatric hospital to join a band of young mutants. As reviewers noted at the time, the psychiatric hospital as prison and site of abuse is a familiar narrative trope and (in addition to being played out) presents a damaging model of psychiatric treatment. From there, though, the show took a turn—the first of many.

Over the course of the first season, David and, increasingly, his new allies come to question his sanity as they struggle to find a satisfactory explanation for his erratic behavior, deceptions, and betrayals. Although *Legion* presents an array of possible explanations—David is schizophrenic, David is a powerful mutant, David has been possessed by a psychic enemy, David isn't delusional but everyone else is—all are ultimately undermined. Near the end of the second season, one character asks "But can we agree that he's unwell?" a question that is never quite answered, and which seems less a question than an encapsulation of the *Legion* experience. In these ways, *Legion* represents a new take on the character *and* a new approach to disability, a topic regularly mishandled in popular media and superhero narratives alike.

Until recently, the term "disability" has almost always been associated with physical impairment, seen as a static, often visible condition. Early research in disability studies reflects this approach, focusing primarily on physical handicaps and accessibility rights. However, recent work in the field has turned its attention to "unseen" disabilities; namely, chronic illness, intellectual disability, sensory impairment, and mental illness, the latter of which is the focus of this chapter. Historically, the psychological narratives represented across popular media have embraced tropes of madness and insanity, promoting and vindicating biomedical models of diagnosis and recovery and using them in ways that regularly subvert, alienate, and demonize mentally ill characters. Such models are especially prevalent in superhero narratives where representations of mental, or cognitive, disability are often reserved for villains; when mental disability *is* connected to a superhero, it is often due to external influences—a traumatic event, an emergent power, a psychic attack—which render the hero literally "not himself" until the cause can be explained, eliminated, or otherwise resolved. In drawing attention to this phenomenon, this chapter considers how contemporary trends in comics and superhero narratives have begun to move away from deficit models of mental disability. This chapter positions that such outdated "narrative choices" are "not simply rational or medical choices" but "also ethical choices" (Lewis 2017, 1) that perpetuate deficit-based narratives of disability, which disempower disabled characters through expectations of definitive diagnosis and recovery, serving to obstruct the social, cultural, and philosophical (re)framing of disability in viewers' daily lives.

In order to surface how narratives can more ethically represent mental disability, this chapter offers David Haller (a.k.a. Legion), the central protagonist of *Legion* which aired on the FX network from 2017 to 2019. Although Legion is many things—a powerful mutant, a villain, a hero, the son of X-Men founder Charles Xavier—it is mental disability that most clearly defines him in the print comics. That *Legion* has been adapted into a television show is appropriate, given the greater opportunity for "extended character depth, ongoing plotting, and episodic variation" that television offers over film (Mittell 31). Similarly, that it is a superhero story is appropriate, given the popularity of superhero genres over the last decade. Finally, that *Legion* is not only a narratively complex, serial story, and a superhero story, but also a superhero story that engages seriously with psychological health is appropriate, given the increase in demands for recognition of neurodiversity and greater representations of neurodiversity in popular culture and media. In short, *Legion* feels like a show that could only happen now.

As such, *Legion* serves as a unique point of inquiry because it circulates multiple framing narratives in efforts to explain David's "instability," questioning and testing possible answers without ever committing to a linear narrative. Although an early biomedical explanation for David's condition (schizophrenia) is provided, it gives way to myriad others: mutant powers, possession by the Shadow King[1] group hysteria, manipulation by others (as well as various combinations of these factors)—none of which provide closure or certainty. Using a rhetorical framework, this chapter analyzes the ways that the television series moves away from the source material, offering a particular understanding of the relationship between semiotics and power that resists hegemonic biomedical discourses of mental disability. Accordingly, this chapter interrogates the ways the *Legion* television series undermines deficit discourses of mental illness that dominate superhero narratives and, in doing so, moves away from the compartmentalization and reduction of disability into one-dimensional, socially sanctioned narratives of diagnosis and recovery.

DISABILITY, NARRATIVE, AND THE SUPERHERO

Scholarship and academic attention to disability emerged in response to the disability civil rights movement of the late twentieth century; at that moment disability studies was primarily concerned with physical impairment framed by competing medical and social narratives. As Prendergast (2001, 46) has argued, early work in "disability studies, with its emphasis on the body and not the mind, create[d] fissures through which attention to the mentally disabled easily f[ell]." Such critiques have pushed recent work in the field not only to broaden its scope and include mental and psychological well-being but to also "value disability as a form of cultural difference" (Mullaney) rather than solely a medical difference. This chapter is primarily concerned with the social constraints of disability, where emphasis is placed not explicitly on diagnosis and recovery, but the social contexts that define disability (Squier 2008; Lewis 2017).

A survey of both print comics and recent film and television adaptations further emphasizes the frequency of deficit-based representations of mental health in superhero culture. Prevailing depictions of mental disability in these narratives are usually connected to villains who are regularly described as "mad"—it is their madness that makes them so dangerous, and that simultaneously justifies the actions (and existence) of heroes. For an example, we need look no further than DC Comics' Batman franchise, where the ubiquity of Arkham Asylum,[2] the mental hospital that serves as the periodic residence of famous villains like the Joker, Two-Face, and the Riddler, suggests that mental illness and violence, if not criminal behavior, are certainly linked. Furthermore, while depictions of mental disability in heroes themselves do exist, these are often transient; numerous one-off stories show superheroes becoming temporarily "insane" as a result of injury or illness, a villain's interference, or other external influences.

As mentioned above, narratives most often frame heroes as being accused of insanity, persecuted by doctors who tell them their powers are all in their heads and subject them to inhumane or traumatic "treatments." Marvel's *Iron Fist*, which aired on Netflix at nearly the same time as *Legion*, uses this trope in its first and second episodes, where protagonist Danny Rand is institutionalized after returning from a fifteen-year absence with a fantastic tale about the hidden land of K'un-Lun and his role as the Iron Fist. In these stories, while others question the hero's sanity, the audience is wise to the truth, able to appreciate that while the hero's reality may sound like delusion, the hero is quite sane.

Exceptions to the above scenarios do exist but are often short-lived. As comics writer Suzanne Walker (2016) notes,

> The statistics are pretty clear-cut—whether it's Hawkeye getting his hearing restored or Oracle walking again in the New 52, characters with disabilities have historically been erased or "cured" in comics. And if they haven't, their disability is supplemented by their own superpower. The same radioactive material that caused Daredevil's blindness also gave him the heightened senses that allow him to defend Hell's Kitchen, and Charles Xavier's paralysis is augmented by his telekinesis. There is so very rarely a character who doesn't have some sort of ability ex machina.

This holds true for mental disability as well. There are few examples. Netflix's *Jessica Jones* consistently shows the title character struggling with Post Traumatic Stress Disorder (PTSD) as a result of the violence and loss she's endured. Tom King's 2018 *Heroes in Crisis* story introduces comics fans to Sanctuary, a facility in the Midwest, built with "the will of Batman! The compassion of Wonder Woman! And of course: the honor of Superman!" (King 2019). Sanctuary provides heroes marked by the violence they've seen, endured, and inflicted with a place to process traumatic moments and heal. A number of prominent and obscure DC heroes—Superman, Batman,

Arsenal, Blue Jay, Cyborg, and so on—are depicted in confessional-style scenes where they discuss their struggles with inadequacy, fear, grief, addiction, and depression. While these narratives are in many ways nuanced and sympathetic, they nonetheless frame mental disability as something that can be overcome and present PTSD as the only mental disability heroes are subject to. Whether physical or mental, these examples show that when superheroes' identities are yoked to disability these moments are generally fleeting, suggesting that creators find disability too difficult to write about or are concerned that audiences won't be receptive. Consequently, narratives of diagnosis and recovery dominate these comics rather than narratives of agency and autonomy.

Examples of superheroes for whom mental disability is an enduring part of the character are rarer, and Marvel appears to have a better track record than their competitor DC. In addition to having a physical disability (blindness), Daredevil has struggled with chronic depression; Deadpool has been variously described as having schizophrenia and dissociative identity disorder; Moon Knight, a less prominent hero, also has dissociative identity disorder, in connection with his powers; and within the last few years, fans learned that both Hank Pym (the original Ant-Man) and his daughter Nadia are bipolar. While the scarcity of positive examples of disability in comics speaks to a broader pattern in popular media, the popularity of comics suggests that these stories have the potential to socially influence audiences' understandings of mental health and disability. Accordingly, the genre of comics, and superhero narratives more broadly, can be positioned to "challenge and reinforce societal attitudes towards both emotional and physical disability," where "representations of disability in comic[s] . . . not only provide visual depictions of disability, but they also serve to ignite conversations regarding the complexities and interpretations surrounding the disabilities they present" (Germaine 2016). In this way "Disability Studies theory offers some productive possibilities for exploring the tension between [the] reality and representation" (Jacobs and Dolmage 2012, 75) of superhero narratives.

The field of rhetoric, as a lens through which to explore narrative, provides insight into the construction and power of discourse about disability and the disabled. Catherine Prendergast notes that the *DSM IV* (*The Diagnostic and Statistical Manual of Mental Disorders* published by the American Psychiatric Association) "has been viewed by many as an illness-constructing document of incredible rhetorical power," a master narrative serving as "the psychiatric profession's main vehicle for maintaining dominance over other mental health disciplines, firmly entrenching the biomedical model of mental disorder" (2001, 48). The influence of biomedical narratives like those of the *DSM IV* are problematic due to their suppression of individual experiences of disability as well as biased cultural contributions, both of which serve to influence broader, commonplace constructions of disability in our social lives. Rhetorical scholars James Wilson and Cynthia Lewiecki-Wilson (2001) point to the way that "what it means to be disabled, indeed the very conditions of a disability, are crucially determined by the society in which one lives," as well as by factors such as race, class, and gender, concluding that "disability is not a universal category but a strategic name marking diverse differences" (10). It is not simply this marking of difference that is important to this chapter, but also the ways that superhero narratives can and should shift in efforts to humanize and, therefore, legitimize the experiences of those who embody a spectrum of mental health conditions.

Narrative, then, functions as a means of exerting rhetorical power, allowing a deeper understanding of the ways that disability is experienced by differently situated individuals, and revealing their relationship with broader social narratives that attempt to push definitions of disability onto them. Far from being mere stories, narratives are the primary means through which "human beings make sense of our identities and the social spheres in which we exist," an ongoing process of self-construction that we engage in both "to ourselves and to others" (Jacobs and Dolmage 2012, 72). The stories we tell and those told about us—and about people we recognize as being like us—have significant impact.

Nevertheless, dominant narratives about disability have traditionally been far from positive. G. Thomas Couser (2005) identifies five rhetorics that dominate these narratives: triumph, horror, spiritual compensation, nostalgia, and emancipation; as Jacobs and Dolmage (2012) explain:

> The rhetoric of triumph demands that people with disabilities overcome or compensate for their disability; horror renders disability abject and terrifying; spiritual compensation implies that disability is a punishment for a moral failing; the memoir of nostalgia longs for the time before the author became disabled. Finally, the rhetoric of emancipation, while not leading to the overcoming of disability, instead removes "physical, social and cultural obstacles" for people with disabilities. (76)

The ubiquity of these rhetorics makes it difficult for stories about disability to be told that don't embrace one or more of these frames.

Narratives informed by these rhetorics are common in superhero stories across a variety of media. Walker's (2016) observation about the "ability ex machina" that allows disabled superheroes to compensate for their limitations suggests the way this trope functions in rhetorics of triumph, emancipation, or both, while *Heroes in Crisis* is the rare exception in a history of narratives where heroes triumph over PTSD, depression, anxiety, and other psychological conditions not through treatment, but through sheer willpower.

The rhetoric of horror is plain in the way villains such as the Joker are framed as more frightening, deadly, and grotesque than other villains, not in spite of, but *because* of their mental disabilities. Similarly, rhetorics of spiritual compensation are present not only in these depictions of villains but also in stories about heroes as well. Famously, 1988's *Superman* #22, an issue which ends a fifty-year policy against killing with the Man of Steel killing three people, frames mental illness as punishment. This immoral act damages Superman's psyche so much that he experiences a mental breakdown and develops a form of dissociative identity disorder. Finally, narratives of nostalgia are often built into the origin stories of disabled superheroes, presenting us with idyllic stories of the time before Daredevil became blind, before Cyborg became dependent on his cybernetic body, or, in the case of the Legion in the comics, before traumatic events and his emerging powers fractured his mind.

As a counter, rhetorical scholars call for a rethinking of disability that shifts away from biomedical deficit narratives and limiting options like those described by Couser (2005). James Wilson and Cynthia Lewiecki-Wilson (2001) "argue both for the broadest possible definition of disability and for the right of the disability community to debate, contest, and change their preferred definitions of disability" (10). Similarly, Lewis (2017) argues that "how we decide to engage with our mental difference is shaped by the kinds of worldviews we bring to bear on the question and the kinds of narrative communities we choose to join" (Lewis 2017, 5). He calls for a "deep ethics" approach to disability, one which allows not only for different narratives but also for a multiplicity of narratives, allowing "one narrative of the self for one situation and another narrative for another situation" (Lewis 2017, 5). This approach is socially meaningful in that it neither eliminates nor validates narratives (of triumph, nostalgia, etc.), but presents them as elements of a wider narrative, enabling multiple narratives to be told instead of, or alongside, others.

I AM LEGION

Enter the FX series *Legion* and an examination of the ways that its approaches to disability have served to reimagine not only the character of David Haller but also the relationship between superhero narratives and mental health. Although *Legion* makes use of both biomedical discourse and rhetorical frames such as triumph or nostalgia, these are ultimately undermined in ways that resist their ability to reduce disability to a single type of story, or the disabled person to a single identity. Instead, *Legion* offers multiple, shifting narratives, in something closer to a deep ethics approach.

As in the print comics, FX's David Haller is the son of Charles Xavier and Gabrielle Haller; he is immensely powerful, and often depicted as dangerous, with powers that include telepathy, telekinesis, pyrokinesis, and the power to shape reality. In both, he initially appears at the mercy of powers he cannot fully control, and in both, he is often ambiguously situated—sometimes a hero, sometimes a villain—capable of disastrous mistakes even when his intentions are good. However, while the comics provide a relatively unambiguous narrative—that David is both a powerful mutant and mentally unstable,—diagnosing his mental illness in terms of trauma and paternal abandonment, the FX series refuses this.

Although *Legion* does make use of biomedical discourses of mental illness, these are regularly undermined. The first episode of *Legion* introduces David as a patient at the Clockworks Psychiatric Hospital, where he has been diagnosed as a paranoid schizophrenic, and boasts a history of drug use, violence, and suicidal tendencies (Hawley "Chapter 1," 2017); David seems to accept this diagnosis, not questioning or pushing back, but receiving the diagnosis of mental disability as a normative evaluation. That is until the close of this first episode when David (still unconscious of his powers) is rescued by his girlfriend Syd and her allies, who usher him away to Summerland, a safe house for mutants. At Summerland, David is confronted with the possibility that he is not delusional, but instead a powerful telepath who has not yet learned to harness his powers. Dr. Melanie Bird, the human leader of Summerland who teaches mutants how to control their powers, is adamant in her belief that David is not mentally ill, challenging him by asking "What if I told you every voice, every part of your mental illness was just your power?" and insisting that their work at Summerland will make David "whole" (Hawley "Chapter 2," 2017)—implying that the medical discourses that diagnosed David have somehow divided him from himself, rather than helping him.

This simple shift in setting—out of Clockworks and into Summerland—serves as a plot device that mirrors the replacement of the early narrative, that David is schizophrenic, with Dr. Bird's counternarrative: David isn't mentally ill, but merely a mutant. At the same time that Dr. Bird's explanation resists the biomedical model, her assertions operate according to the same logic, not suggesting that the model is limited or flawed—merely misapplied in this case. Both in this episode and throughout the remainder of the season Dr. Bird repeatedly emphasizes "That's the old narrative, son. The schizophrenic delusions. *You* are not schizophrenic" (Hawley "Chapter 2," 2017). Her emphasis on "you" places David in the same kind of "misdiagnosed" story as in the *Iron Fist* example above.

That David is tempted by the allure of this explanation is clear; in the episodes immediately following his removal to Summerland, David makes protests that echo Dr. Bird's, telling his friend Lenny "I'm not sick. I have powers" (Hawley "Chapter 3," 2017), and responding to his sister's concerns by insisting "I don't have an illness" (Hawley "Chapter 5," 2017). At the same time, David is also unable to accept this explanation as sufficient, saying of the Summerland team, "everybody in here keeps saying that I'm sane. What if they're wrong?" (Hawley "Chapter 3," 2017); warning Syd that "the most dangerous thing about schizophrenia . . . is believing you don't have it . . . your disease convinces you, you don't have it" (Hawley "Chapter 8," 2017). The character of Amahl Farouk further complicates the question of David's mental state: David's actions and impressions of the world could be attributed to mental illness, to his powers, or to his possession by this powerful enemy. This narrative shift encourages the audience to consider the complexities of mental illness as well as the ways that outsiders (and insiders) approach and interpret disability—it is meaningful that opinions about David's mental health constantly waver among his allies and foes, with no definitive diagnosis ever being reached. Moreover, rather than eventually revealing which option is "correct," *Legion* forces its characters, and viewers, to consider that there may be no single, correct answer.

The question of diagnoses is further confused by a series of embedded narratives that occur both alongside and within the larger plot. Season two introduces, jarringly and without explanation, the infusion of mini-mental health "lessons" by an unseen, unnamed narrator, voiced by Jon Hamm. These narratives complicate commonplace understandings of mental health in the ways they uphold *and* undermine hegemonic biomedical models and, as such, serve as a metanarrative that invites the audience to diagnose David themselves.

These narrative interjections, which span the entirety of season 2 are positioned at unpredictable points—sometimes opening an episode; sometimes occurring right in the middle of plot progression—and while each of these vignettes opens with a title (respectively, Part Two: The Madness of Crowds; Chapter Three: Delusions; Chapter Four: Umwelt; Chapter Six: Conspiracy; Part Eight: Moral Panic), even this framing is chaotic and disorderly. In one sense, these narratives function well inside the logic of biomedical discourse. The calm, authoritative voice of the narrator lends these segments the air of lectures, which discuss symptoms and case studies, making use of familiar terminology: disorder, delusion, nocebo effect, infected, and so on. For instance, in "Chapter Three: Delusions," the visual imagery of healthy and unhealthy ideas, juxtaposed as a baby chick and a skittering, sludge-covered monster, suggests that we can easily distinguish between those ideas which are and aren't delusional (Hawley "Chapter 9," 2018). In this way, these embedded narratives argue against a definition of disability that is focused on the personal, challenging the notion of mental disability as an individualized "condition." Instead, these narrative intrusions suggest, to the audience specifically, that there are ways of being "unwell" that are social, even collaborative. At the same time, these segments make clear the socially constructed nature of reality, and, thus, the necessary variations in how it can be interpreted, as well as the unreliable nature of our memories and perceptions. While providing us with language to diagnose the behavior of others, these segments remind us that we are subject to the same socially constructed reality—the same flawed tools of perception—that we have no "outside" position from which we can confidently diagnose others.

It is this refusal to bring any sense of definitive diagnosis to David that shifts *Legion* away from easy and socially commonplace representations of mental disability. Those looking for answers or hoping to plumb the depths of *Legion* are met with an endless procession of new questions and false bottoms. Far from being an empty shell game, however, this chapter argues that *Legion*'s approach to mental illness embodies a model of disability that extends a deep ethics approach.

For example, in season 2, episode 6 one encounters what initially seems to be a "filler" episode where the plot diverges into myriad storylines: David as successful corporate mogul; David as homeless drug addict; David as happy suburban family man; David as over-medicated, lethargic store clerk (Hawley "Chapter 14," 2018). Initially, there seems to be no forward movement of the plot in this episode, that is not until the final scene that closes with the (now familiar) montage of David's life progressing through happy child, troubled teen, suicidal adult, to Clockwords patient. As with much of *Legion*, this montage is backed by music that supplements the plot, in this instance "Superman" (Hawley and Russo 2018) repeats a chorus of: "I am, I am Superman/And I know what's happening/I am, I am Superman/And I can do anything," which serves to confuse the multiple stereotypes of mental disability evoked in this episode (e.g., homeless, medically numbed, deranged), and instead positions David as a character with agency and self-determination. These lyrics, if taken at face value, suggest that David's actions are his own and that the choices he makes are not defined by his mental illness, an idea further enforced in the final moments of this episode when the voice of Amahl Farouk explains these branching possibilities, or alternatives, as reality: "You decide what is real and what is not—*you* will" (Hawley "Chapter 14," 2018). While it is possible to read Farouk's comment in the context of David's powers—his ability to influence others and warp reality—his words also forward a position that identity isn't reducible to disability alone, providing David with a level of autonomy. The insinuation that all of the narratives are equally real suggests that David's story can be any of these, perhaps all of them, at different times in his life. This deep ethics approach to disability, which invites the audience to acknowledge the multiplicity of narratives as an avenue to diversify meaning-making, illustrates how the ways one engages with mental disability are (in actuality) shaped by the worldview of ourselves and those around us, rather than the single lens of biomedical rhetoric.

"BUT CAN WE AGREE THAT HE'S UNWELL?"

Ultimately, what characterizes disability in *Legion* is its refusal to give the audience familiar, easy, or even definitive answers. One of the most telling moments comes near the end of season 2, when David has deserted his friends in pursuit of the Shadow King, despite promising he wouldn't. His girlfriend Syd confides in Clark Debussy (a character who appears first as an antagonist, then an ally, then somewhere between the two) expressing concern that she pushed David away. While the conversation starts out about the nature of romance, about David's ability to commit, it takes a turn in the following exchange:

Syd: He's a good person. You know? He tries so hard.
Clark: But can we agree that he's unwell?
Syd: What does that mean?
Clark: You tell me.
Syd: Maybe he doesn't know . . .
Clark: Go on.
Syd: the difference between things real and not real, right and wrong . . .
Clark: So he's delusional, you're saying.
Syd: No . . . I don't know.
　(Hawley "Chapter 16," 2018)

As Syd invites Clark to agree with her that David is a good person, and Clark invites Syd to agree with him that David is unwell, the result is a stalemate. As mentioned, this moment seems to encapsulate the audience's experience of *Legion*. They, like Syd and Clark, are unable to find satisfactory explanations for David's behavior: to agree on whether or not he is "unwell." Rather than seeing this as an omission on the show's part, this chapter argues that it is an indication that perhaps we don't need to agree that he's unwell, which is a call to engage with David, and *Legion*, on their own terms, rather than seeking to fit them into the biomedical molds.

In short, *Legion*'s avoidance of easy answers offers a sharp contrast to familiar popular culture and media narratives about mental disability; in doing so it resists deficit-based rhetorics that work to compartmentalize and reduce mental illness to a diagnosis or push narratives about disability into these (and other) familiar patterns. In these ways, *Legion* breaks from dominant social representations of mental illness, where too regularly "image and power work in concert to stimulate interpretations of disability such that disabled people may be thought of as incomplete humans whose very identities are altered by their disability" (McIlvenny). Consequently, this analysis of comics broadly, and *Legion* specifically, has worked to address the social constructs that shape disability studies, especially psychological health in popular media, and the ways that representational shifts in superhero narratives can (and cannot) align with cultural values and representations of mental health.

Ultimately, *Legion* offers insight into the ways that biomedical narratives are problematic, not least of all because of the way they suppress individual experiences of disability and cultural contributions to the construction of disability. The multiplicity of narrative choices within this superhero narrative, particularly, functions as a means of exerting rhetorical power, allowing a deeper understanding of the ways that disability is experienced by differently situated individuals, and revealing their relationship with broader social narratives that attempt to push definitions of disability onto them.

NOTES

1. The Shadow King, a.k.a. Amahl Farouk, is an immensely powerful, immoral, telepathic enemy who has been residing in David's mind since he was a child. His character appears in both the print comics and FX adaptation.

2. Although best known by this name, this institution was originally introduced as Arkham Hospital (O'Neil 1974), and was officially named the Elizabeth Arkham Asylum for the Criminally Insane in 1989 (Morrison 1989). In addition to functioning more like a prison for some of the worst villains of the DC Universe, Arkham also plays to stereotypes about psychiatric hospitals, boasting a history of mistreatment of patients and a floorplan that supposedly forms occult runes (Wallace 2012, 117).

WORKS CITED

@LegionFX. "Does David Haller know what he is? #LegionFX arrives February 2017 on FX." *Twitter*, 18 Oct. 2016, 12:30 p.m., https://twitter.com/LegionFX/status/788416879761108992.

Alaniz, José. *Death, Disability, and the Superhero: The Silver Age and Beyond.* University Press of Mississippi, 2014.

Buck, Scott, creator. *Iron Fist.* Netflix, 2017.

Couser, G. Thomas. "Disability, life narrative, and representation." *PMLA/Publications of the Modern Language Association of America* 120, no. 2 (2005): 602–6.

Germaine, Alison Elizabeth. "Disability and depression in Thor comic books." *Disability Studies Quarterly* 36, no. 3 (2016).
Hawley, Noah. "Chapter 1." Episode. *Legion* 1, no. 1. FX Productions, February 8, 2017.
Hawley, Noah. "Chapter 2." Episode. *Legion* 1, no. 2. FX Productions, February 15, 2017.
Hawley, Noah. "Chapter 3." Episode. *Legion* 1, no. 3. FX Productions, February 22, 2017.
Hawley, Noah. "Chapter 5." Episode. *Legion* 1, no. r. FX Productions, March 8, 2017.
Hawley, Noah. "Chapter 8." Episode. *Legion* 1, no. 8. FX Productions, March 29, 2017.
Hawley, Noah. "Chapter 9." Episode. *Legion* 2, no. a. FX Productions, April 3, 2018.
Hawley, Noah. "Chapter 14." Episode. *Legion* 2, no. 6. FX Productions, May 8, 2018.
Hawley, Noah. "Chapter 16." Episode. *Legion* 2, no. 8. FX Productions, May 22, 2018.
Hawley, Noah and Jeff Russo. "Superman." *It's Always Blue: Songs from Legion*, Lakeshore Records, 2018.
Jacobs, Dale, and Jay Dolmage. "Difficult articulations: Comics autobiography, trauma, and disability." *The Future of Text and Image: Collected Essays on Literary and Visual Conjunctures*, edited by Ofra Amihay, Lauren Walsh, WJT Mitchell, and Marianne Hirsch. Cambridge Scholars, 2012, 67–89.
Jacobs, Dale, and Jay Dolmage. "Accessible articulations: Comics and disability rhetorics in Hawkeye# 19." *Inks: The Journal of the Comics Studies Society* 2, no. 3 (2018): 353–68.
King, Tom, writer. *Heroes in Crisis*. Art by Clay Mann, Travis Moore, Lee Weeks, Mitch Gerads, Jorge Fornes. Colors by Tomeu Morey, Arif Prianto, Mitch Gerads. Letters by Clayton Cowles. DC Comics, 2019.
Lewis, Bradley. "A deep ethics for mental difference and disability: The 'case' of Vincent van Gogh." *Medical Humanities* 43, no. 3 (2017): 172–76.
McIlvenny, Paul. "The disabled male body 'writes/draws back:' Graphic fictions of masculinity and the body in the autobiographical comic in 'the spiral cage.'" In *Revealing Male Bodies*, edited by Nancy Tuana. Bloomington: Indiana University Press, 2002. Print.
Morrison, Grant, writer. *Arkham Asylum: A Serious House on Serious Earth*. Art by Dave McKean. Letters by Gaspar Saladino. DC Comics, 1989.
Mullaney, Clare. "Disability Studies: Foundations and Key Concepts." https://daily.jstor.org/reading-list-disability-studies/.
O'Neil, Dennis (w), Irv Novick (p). "Threat of the Two-Headed Coin." *Batman* #258 (Oct. 1974), DC Comics.
Prendergast, Catherine. "On the rhetorics of mental disability." *Embodied Rhetorics: Disability in Language and Culture*, edited by James C Wilson and Cynthia Lewiecki-Wilson. Southern Illinois University Press, 2001, 45–60.
Pryal, Katie Rose Guest. "The creativity mystique and the rhetoric of mood disorders." *Disability Studies Quarterly* 31.3 (2011).

Rashed, Mohammed Abouelleil. "In defense of madness: The problem of disability." *The Journal of Medicine and Philosophy: A Forum for Bioethics and Philosophy of Medicine* 44, no. 2. US: Oxford University Press, 2019.

Siebers, Tobin. 2008. *Disability Theory*. Ann Arbor: University of Michigan Press.

Slezak, Michael. "FX Orders Legion Adaptation From Marvel, Fargo EP Noah Hawley." *TV Line*, 14 Oct. 2015, tvline.com/2015/10/14/legion-marvel-tv-series-pilot-fx/.

Squier, Susan M. "So long as they grow out of it: comics, the discourse of developmental normalcy, and disability." *Journal of Medical Humanities* 29, no. 2 (2008): 71–88.

Walker, Suzanne. "Mooncakes and hearing loss: Taking my own advice." *Women Write About Comics*, 8 Jan 2016, womenwriteaboutcomics.com/2016/01/writing-disability-in-comics/. Accessed 31 July 2020.

Wallace, Daniel. *Batman: The World of the Dark Knight*. New York: DK Publishing, 2012.

Wilson, James C., and Cynthia Lewiecki-Wilson. "Disability, rhetoric, and the body." *Embodied Rhetorics: Disability in Language and Culture*, edited by James C Wilson and Cynthia Lewiecki-Wilson. Southern Illinois University Press, 2001, 1–24.

Chapter 6

Diagnosing Mental and Moral Disability in Post-9/11 Popular American Film Narrative

Carol Donelan

Silver Linings Playbook (David O. Russell, The Weinstein Company, 2012) and *Where'd You Go, Bernadette* (Richard Linklater, Annapurna Pictures, 2019) are narrative feature films adapted from popular novels by Matthew Quick (2008) and Maria Semple (2012), respectively. The films, like the novels, are centered on a white protagonist with a mental disability. In *Silver Linings Playbook*, protagonist Pat Solatano Jr. (Bradley Cooper) is diagnosed with bipolar disorder, and in *Where'd You Go, Bernadette*, protagonist Bernadette Fox (Cate Blanchette), with depression and anxiety. For both protagonists, mental disability is their tragic flaw, marking them as exceptional and therefore worthy of narrative attention in the first place. However, the conflicts in these narratives are not attributed to mental disability, but rather moral disability. The displacement from mental to moral disability corresponds with a displacement in narrative storytelling that is conventional of popular American film: from myth to melodrama, or from the static form of ancient sacred tragic myth to the evolving content of modern secular melodrama. In both films, mental disability is consigned to mythical space outside of time rather than to the melodramatic past and present, aligned with "what is" in nature rather than "what is becoming" in culture. In these films, one cannot change mental disability; it is human nature determined by fate, the origins and purpose of which is unknowable and undialectical in tragic myth. One can only change how one thinks and acts in culture, in relation to others, as moral identity evolving in time dialectically, from unknown to known, in melodrama.

The displacement from mental to moral disability aligns with David T. Mitchell and Sharon L. Snyder's (2014) notion of "narrative prosthesis," how narrative is dependent on physical and mental disability not only as a stock feature of characterization for differentiating characters from the norm but also as an "opportunistic metaphorical device" for lending a material body to textual abstractions, to social commentary (47). Physical and mental disability become symbolic of something else, rather than experienced by a material body in social reality. Mitchell and Snyder are interested in how "the ruse of prosthesis fails to return the incomplete body to the invisible status of a normative essence" in literary narrative (8). This is precisely what happens in the film narratives which are the focus of this chapter. The protagonists in *Silver Linings Playbook* and *Where'd You Go, Bernadette* are ultimately exnominated as symbolic of a normative essence, as morally enlightened, but only by displacing mental disability into moral disability in melodrama. The mentally disabled "incomplete body" is left behind, static and unchanging in tragic myth.

In the displacement from ancient sacred tragic myth to modern secular melodrama that is conventional of popular film narrative, unanswerable enigmas give way to answerable riddles. Protagonists Pat and Bernadette are melodramatic mutes, unable to know or name the unknown of moral identity in the present, their own as well as that of others (Brooks 1995, 56). Therein is their moral disability, premised in not-knowing. And yet, in melodrama, that which is unknown can become known in time. The protagonist's evolution from the moral disability of not-knowing to the moral enlightenment of knowing depends on moral literacy, learning to comprehend and interpret the cues of moral identity, implicitly and explicitly, past and present. Misreading the cues produces the conflicts in the narrative—conflicts in social relations with others in the present. Overcoming moral disability requires the self to nominate or name the moral identity of the underrated other as evolving toward virtue. Doing so facilitates the evolution of the self toward virtue. Nomination, a convention of melodrama, is the dramatic moment when the unknown of moral identity becomes visibly known and named (Brooks 1995, 39; Williams 2001, 352). Moral identity that has been nominated as evolving toward virtue or villainy is visualized as an allegorical emblem (Benjamin 1990, chap. 3; Buck-Morss 1991, 161; Whissel 2014, 6), a visible emblem of melodrama.

In both films, the evolution of moral identity in the content of melodrama culminates with an involution in the narrative structure, to the static form of melodramatic myth. In other words, the narrative structure turns inside out, involving from spatialized time in melodrama to timeless space in melodramatic myth. Ultimately, there are two displacements framing these narratives, both of which are conventional of popular American film narrative. The first displacement is from the static form of ancient sacred tragic myth to the evolving content of melodrama. The second displacement is from the evolving content of melodrama to the static form of modern secular melodramatic myth. Popular American film narrative begins and ends in myth, alternating between stasis and flow, spiraling asymmetrically, starting from the static form of myth in timeless space, displacing into the evolving content of melodrama in spatialized time, and involving back into the static form of myth, but in a different space and time from where it started. The trajectory is from undialectical to dialectical being and thinking, from "what is" to "what is becoming" and "what has become" for now, for this moment. In both films, self and other, having nominated each other as moral identities evolving toward virtue in visible emblems of melodrama, are ex-nominated collectively as a visible symbol of moral enlightenment in melodramatic myth. In contrast with emblems, which evolve in time, symbols are static and timeless. Moral identity is nominated in emblems and ex-nominated in symbols. Ex-nomination refers to "that which does not want to be named" or "for which a name is unnecessary" (Barthes 1989, 138). History is transformed into nature, mobilized content into immobilized form. Historical identities are emptied of historical specificity, mythologized as timeless essences. In popular American film narrative, that which is ex-nominated visibly symbolizes not "what is" ontologically for all time, as in ancient sacred tragic myth, but rather "what has become" morally enlightened for now, for this moment, in modern secular melodramatic myth. Whether mythologized as mentally disabled from the beginning or morally enlightened at the end, white, cisgendered, heterosexual Americans are the alpha and omega of these narratives, ex-nominated as that which goes without saying in relation to all others.

DIAGNOSING MORAL DISABILITY IN MELODRAMA, INDIVIDUALLY AND COLLECTIVELY

Ancient sacred tragic myth is storytelling about ontological being—the ontology of human being, specifically. Who are we? Where did we come from? In ancient sacred tragic myth, human being is timeless and of unknowable origin in nature. Melodrama, a modern secular narrative mode, replaces the static unknowable of ontological being in nature with the evolving unknown of moral identity in culture, which can become known in time, dialectically. The protagonists in *Silver Linings Playbook* and *Where'd You Go, Bernadette* are melodramatic mutes, not-knowing, unable to name the unknown of moral identity in the present, their own as well as that of others (Brooks 1995, 56). Muteness is a symptom of their moral disability. That which is unsaid—unknown and unnamed—is expressed implicitly rather than explicitly, in the elements of film style (Nowell-Smith 1987, 73). The displacement of expression from content to form, from spoken words to visuals and music, is conventional of melodrama as a narrative mode.

In both films, whereas mental disability is ontological being, originating in nature, moral disability originates in culture, in a traumatic event, premised in violence and destruction. The traumatic event is displaced into the past and expressed implicitly in the present, in visuals and music. The morally disabled protagonist is situated in the present as the receiver of a film within the film about the traumatic past, paralleling the viewer, seeing and hearing. In *Silver Linings Playbook*, speaking to a therapist, Pat revisits the trauma of seeing his wife Nikki (Brea Bee) showering with another man, Doug Culpepper (Ted Barba), with whom she is having an affair. Pat's verbal recounting of the traumatic event is displaced into a flashback, a film within the film, the camera adopting his subjective point of view as he confronts the couple. The flashback is accompanied by the faint sounds of an expressionistically modulated Stevie Wonder song, "Ma Cheri Amour," Pat's wedding song, subjectively imagined rather than objectively heard. Pat confesses to his therapist that he snapped and almost beat Doug to death, but the visual and musical depiction of this violence is only partially seen and heard, representing Pat's psychological repression in the present, his melodramatic muteness. In *Where'd You Go, Bernadette*, the traumatic past is likewise expressed retroactively in the present, in visuals and music. During a sleepless night, Bernadette revisits the bulldozing of her award-winning architectural masterpiece, the Twenty Mile House, googling an online video, a film within the film, a narrated retrospective of her career as a renowned architect. The perpetrator of the destruction, her wealthy neighbor, the villainous Nigel Mills-Murray, a television game show host, paves the land for an overflow parking lot. Seeing him hosting his successful game show, hearing his name accompanied by a musical jingle, Bernadette slams shut her laptop, visualizing in a gesture her psychological repression in the present, her melodramatic muteness.

For both protagonists, melodramatic muteness affects who they are becoming, morally. For Pat in *Silver Linings Playbook*, the traumatic event leads to a restraining order and eight months of court-ordered residential treatment in Baltimore. We meet him in the present as he returns to his parents' home in Philadelphia and sets out on a course of self-improvement to win Nikki back. In terms of mood, he's up, determined to move forward, to overcome the "negativity" of the past and evolve toward virtue. For Bernadette in *Where'd You Go, Bernadette*, the traumatic event prompts her to stop creating professionally as an architect in Los Angeles. Instead, she follows her husband Elgie Branch (Billy Crudup) to Seattle as he pursues his career at Microsoft. We meet her in the present as an unhappy homemaker, jealous of her husband's career success. In terms of mood, she's down, unable to move forward, to evolve toward virtue. Whether up or down, east or west, for both protagonists, the evolution from moral disability to moral enlightenment depends on moral literacy, learning to comprehend and interpret the cues of moral identity, implicitly and explicitly, past and present. Misreading the cues produces conflicts in social relations with others in the present. In *Silver Linings Playbook*, the conflicts are explicitly comprehended as "negativity." Not-knowing the traumatic past, misreading the cues, Pat overrates the virtue of his estranged wife Nikki, which leads him to underrate the virtue of his prospective lover Tiffany (Jennifer Lawrence) in the present. In *Where'd You Go, Bernadette*, the conflicts have to do with competitive jealousy. Not-knowing the traumatic past, misreading the cues, Bernadette overrates the virtue of her husband Elgie, which leads her to underrate the virtue of her neighbor Audrey (Kristin Wiig) in the present.

Only by nominating the moral identity of the underrated other as evolving toward virtue can the self evolve toward virtue. In *Silver Linings Playbook*, Pat's therapist, Dr. Cliff Patel (Anupam Kher), encourages Pat, a willing patient, to take responsibility for himself by learning to "read the signs" of his social reality. In time, Pat learns to comprehend and interpret the moral identity of his underrated other, Tiffany, overcoming negativity and nominating Tiffany as a candidate for marriage, a visible emblem of melodrama evolving toward virtue. She, in turn, nominates Pat as a candidate for marriage, a visible emblem of melodrama evolving toward virtue. The implied viewer of *Silver Linings Playbook*, white and male, is likewise invited to read the signs of social reality as a therapist does a patient and to develop an optimistic strategy for his life, for clarifying his own moral identity emblematically, for visibly embodying his evolution toward virtue in relation to others.

As in *Silver Linings Playbook*, in *Where'd You Go, Bernadette*, the self evolves toward virtue only by nominating the moral identity of the underrated other as evolving toward virtue. Bernadette, an unwilling patient, flees the psychiatric intervention initiated by her husband Elgie and facilitated by Dr. Janelle Kurtz (Judy Greer). Hiding out in neighbor Audrey's house, Bernadette learns that she and Audrey have more in common than expected. Each is struggling in her social relations with family members, Audrey with her lethargic son and Bernadette with her workaholic husband. In time, Bernadette learns to comprehend and interpret the moral identity of her underrated other, Audrey, overcoming competitive jealousy and nominating Audrey as a virtuous mother, a visible emblem of melodrama evolving toward virtue. Audrey, in turn, nominates Bernadette as a virtuous wife, a visible emblem of melodrama evolving toward virtue. With Audrey's help, Bernadette sets out on a solo "fishing expedition" to the "white continent" of Antarctica, which involves taking solo responsibility for herself in the present rather than abdicating responsibility for herself and passively following the lead of her husband Elgie, as in the past. The implied viewer of *Where'd You Go, Bernadette*, white and female, is likewise invited to take responsibility for herself, to expand her life beyond home and family, to visibly embody the virtues of self-determination and creativity—virtues historically embodied by white men in the past, in the frontier mythology of the American West—and to fish within herself for implicit meanings proliferating in her mind, which may be affecting her relations with others in social reality.

COMPREHENDING AND INTERPRETING THE CUES OF MENTAL AND MORAL DISABILITY, EXPLICITLY AND IMPLICITLY

Popular American films are allegorical narratives structured by a relation of myth and melodrama. Visualize the structure as two axes, a vertical y-axis representing myth, or static form in timeless space, and a horizontal x-axis representing melodrama, or historical content evolving in spatialized time. In receiving a film, viewers comprehend and interpret the cues in space and time, shifting attention between surface and depth on the spatialized vertical axis of myth as the content evolves in time on the horizontal axis of melodrama. Explicit meaning is constructed by comprehending what the film is about overtly, based on what is seen, known, and named on the surface of the text. Implicit meaning is constructed by interpreting what the film expresses indirectly or implies, based on what is unseen, unknown, and unnamed in the depths of the text (Bordwell 1991, 9). Both films are explicitly about mental disability, implicitly about moral disability, individually and collectively.

Explicit cues in both films prompt viewers to comprehend the protagonists as mentally disabled. In *Silver Linings Playbook*, explicit cues include verbal references to Pat's delusional thinking and the partial visualization of his violent "explosion" upon witnessing Nikki's infidelity. The opening of the film visualizes Pat's release from a psychiatric facility. In a subsequent therapy session, Dr. Patel describes Pat's mental state at the time of his explosion as "undiagnosed bipolar with mood swings and weird thinking brought on by severe stress." In the present, Pat visibly experiences a panic attack every time he hears or imagines his wedding song. In terms of a treatment plan, Dr. Patel insists that Pat stay in therapy, take his medication, and "work on a strategy," which involves developing his moral literacy. Pat cannot change his mental disability, but he can learn to recognize and control the feelings of negativity that trigger his panic attacks, thereby taking responsibility for himself morally.

In *Where'd You Go, Bernadette*, explicit cues prompting viewers to comprehend that Bernadette is mentally disabled include visualizations of her social anxiety and insomnia as well as verbal references to her Xanax prescription. Daughter Bee speculates about the "design flaw" in her mother's brain. Husband Elgie remarks that he has "no idea what's wrong with Bernadette, whether she's depressed, manic, agoraphobic, hooked on pills, or paranoid." Dr. Kurtz thinks Bernadette may be having suicidal thoughts and proposes an intervention leading to residential treatment in a psychiatric facility. The origin of mental disability is a source of concern and uncertainty for the characters, who manifest different ways of knowing. Husband Elgie, a scientist, tacitly agrees with Dr. Kurtz that Bernadette's mental disability originates in nature, upholding the medical model as a mode of knowing. Daughter Bee, the film's narrator, thinking holistically, theorizes that her mother's mental disability has hybrid origins in nature and culture. Bernadette, an artist, does not think of herself as mentally disabled. She resists medical intervention and treatment, insisting that she simply needs to spend more time with her husband and daughter, without the competing pressures of work and school. Implicitly, Bernadette perceives the problems she's experiencing as originating in culture, in social relations with others. In short, she diagnoses her disability as moral rather than mental, in keeping with the conventions of melodrama as a narrative mode.

Whereas explicit cues prompt viewers to comprehend the protagonists as mentally disabled, implicit cues prompt viewers to interpret them as morally disabled. For protagonists and viewers alike, the evolution from moral disability to moral enlightenment depends on moral literacy, learning to comprehend and interpret the cues of moral identity, implicitly and explicitly, past and present. Misreading the cues produces conflicts in social relations in the present. In *Silver Linings Playbook*, the conflicts have to do with negativity. Not-knowing the traumatic past, morally disabled, melodramatically mute, Pat overrates the virtue of his estranged wife Nikki and underrates the virtue of his potential lover Tiffany. In the present, his goal is to evolve beyond the negativity of the past and win Nikki back. His strategy is to improve himself physically and intellectually. He jogs regularly and reads the novels on Nikki's high school English syllabus, developing his literacy, despite disliking the negativity of their endings. Even Tiffany cannot help but be impressed by Pat's description of the positive chemistry he had with Nikki in the past. Meanwhile, Pat underrates Tiffany's virtue, dismissing her as "crazy" and a "slut," proliferating negativity in the present.

A romantic comedy, the explicit conflict in *Silver Linings Playbook* is between the prospective lovers (Grindon 2011, 3), which manifests implicitly as hesitation about moral identity, especially as related to sexuality and violence. Is Tiffany monogamous (virtuous) or promiscuous (villainous)? Is Pat protective (virtuous) or violent (villainous) toward women? On the implicit level of meaning, the symbolic monsters needing to be slain before the prospective lovers can unite as a couple are Tiffany's potential for promiscuity and Pat's potential for violence (Lévi-Strauss 1963). Tiffany had sex with everyone at work after her husband Tommy died, her way of coping with

Tommy's death, but she was faithful to Tommy when he was alive. Nikki, on the other hand, had sex with Doug Culpepper while she was married to Pat. Nikki and Tiffany were both sexually promiscuous in the past but only Tiffany was faithful in marriage. The symbolic monster of Tiffany's promiscuity is therefore slayed by her faithfulness in marriage, rehabilitating her as a viable potential marriage partner for Pat in the present.

The problem of Pat's potential for violence against women runs deeper. Pat, like his father Patrizio (Robert DeNiro), manifests a tendency to explode violently, represented explicitly as mental disability, implicitly as moral disability. Moral disability persists across the generations, individually and collectively. Patrizio was barred from the Eagles football stadium in the past, where he once beat up some fans, exploding violently, for reasons that remain implicit—unseen, unknown, and unnamed. Meanwhile, in the present, Pat gets mixed up in a fight with some racist fans in the stadium parking lot, who taunt and beat up some Indian American fans, for reasons that are explicit—seen, known, and named. Pat joins the fight to protect his older brother Jake (Shea Whigham), who joins the fight to protect the virtuous Indian American fans from the villainous racist fans. Pat's fight against racist male villainy in the present is explicitly justified, morally. By extension, Patrizio's fight against unspecified male villainy in the past is implicitly justified, morally. Inasmuch as moral disability persists across the generations, so does the potential for evolving toward virtue.

In the present, the negativity in Pat's life is not manifested in race but rather gender relations. He misreads the moral identities of women, overrating or underrating their virtue. Late one night, after a confusing interaction with Tiffany wherein she alternately comes on to him, hugs him while crying, and slaps him, Pat tears apart his parents' home in search of his wedding video, needing to restore a vision of unity and happiness from the past in response to moral uncertainty in the present. Is Tiffany promiscuous? Will Pat respond to her with violence? Pat is unable to shake the song stuck in his head, his wedding song, which differs from the nondiegetic song viewers hear, underscoring through sound style the gap that may exist between internal and external realities, individually and collectively, post-9/11. The song triggers in Pat's mind's eye visible images of the traumatic past—Nikki's infidelity, his beating of Doug—and he explodes violently in the present, accidentally knocking his mother Dolores (Jacki Weaver) to the floor and punching his father Patrizio. Pat's behavior evidences a repetition compulsion, a psychological condition wherein the trauma of the past is repeated in the present (Laplanche 1978, 78). Repetition compulsion, manifesting in the content of the film, is also expressed on the level of form, as repetitions in the structure of the plot (Brooks 1984, 124). Awakened by the noise, fearful of the violence, neighbors call the cops. Officer Keogh (Dash Mihok) arrives and threatens to send Pat back to residential treatment. Pat's father Patrizio attempts to defuse the situation by cautioning Pat to shut up about his "crazy theories," which are premised in misreading moral identity. Among Pat's crazy theories is the notion that Nikki is morally virtuous, not responsible for her promiscuity in the past, that the blame lies entirely with Doug.

On a subsequent date with Tiffany, Pat implies that Tiffany is "crazy" and a "slut," underrating her virtue, misreading her moral identity, proliferating negativity in the present. Tiffany, feeling judged, accuses Pat of harassing her, replaying in the present her unknown, unresolved traumatic past, wherein she accused her boss of harassing her after he fired her for sleeping with everyone at work, her way of coping with her husband Tommy's death. In turn, Pat, feeling judged, has a panic attack, replaying in the present his unknown, unresolved traumatic past, wherein he discovered Nikki's promiscuity and exploded violently. Tiffany, reading the signs, recognizes Pat's panic attack as prompted by imagined fears rather than an actual external threat and attempts to calm him down. "It's a song. Don't make it a monster," she counsels. Fearful of Pat's potential for violence, kids nearby call the cops. As in the scene with Pat's family, Officer Keogh arrives and threatens to send Pat back to residential treatment. Tiffany attempts to defuse the situation by blaming Pat's behavior on the kids: "They started it; he didn't do anything." This is yet another crazy theory premised in misreading moral identity. Tiffany's crazy theory, blaming the kids, explicitly absolves Pat of moral responsibility for harassing her in the present: "They started it; he didn't do anything." Tiffany's crazy theory also implicitly slays the symbolic monster of Pat's potential for violence against women, rehabilitating him as a viable potential marriage partner in the present.

The narrative structure of popular American film is self-similar, a time-developing phenomenon wherein the parts maintain the same shape as the whole. Thus, Tiffany's crazy theory not only explicitly absolves Pat of moral responsibility for harassing her but also implicitly absolves the collective American nation for harassing global others in the wake of 9/11: They started it; we didn't do anything. Cultural anthropologist Margaret Mead, writing in 1942 at the start of World War II, identified "who started it" as a central theme in the American national character, involving "a general prohibition of fighting, but an enjoinment to fight if one is picked on, pushed around, or taken advantage of" (Alexander et al. 2004, 272). Jeffrey C. Alexander et al. (2004) update this theme in relation to the events of 9/11, noting the framing of events in terms of a dualistic moral orientation, pitting innocent victims against evil villains, a cultural discourse that absolved the nation of guilt or responsibility for subsequent aggression (276). The narrative counterpart to the cultural discourse described by Alexander et al. is melodrama, the "fundamental mode of popular American 'moving pictures'" (Williams 2001, 13) and the "best example of American culture's (often hypocritical) attempt to construct itself as the locus of innocence and virtue" (17), wherein the suffering of the persecuted innocent gives moral authority to action, justifying aggression and violence.

Like Pat in *Silver Linings Playbook*, Bernadette in *Where'd You Go, Bernadette* can be interpreted as morally disabled, implicitly. Her moral disability, rooted in not-knowing the traumatic past, leads to unspoken jealousy and competition with her husband Elgie over his successful career. Melodramatically mute, morally disabled, not-knowing her own moral identity, Bernadette displaces her competition with Elgie into competition with her neighbor Audrey in the present. An inciting incident in Bernadette's competition with Audrey involves invasive blackberries on Bernadette's hillside, which are encroaching on Audrey's property. Without consulting Bernadette, Audrey enlists Tom to get rid of the invasive blackberries. Later, Bernadette watches passively as Tom removes the blackberries from her hillside with a bulldozer, a symbol of Bernadette's unknown, unresolved traumatic past, when her former neighbor Mills-Murray bulldozed her architectural masterpiece, the Twenty Mile house. An architect, Bernadette knows that the blackberries are the only thing preventing her hillside from sliding down and destroying Audrey's house in the present, but she says nothing. The subsequent destruction of Audrey's house in a mudslide parallels and repeats the destruction of Bernadette's house in the traumatic past. Moral identity in the past is clear. Mills-Murray, Bernadette's former neighbor, was overtly villainous, directly responsible for the destruction of Bernadette's house in the past. Moral identity in the present is unclear. Is Bernadette indirectly responsible for the destruction of her neighbor Audrey's house? In the past, Bernadette built the Twenty Mile house using only local materials gathered within a twenty-mile radius. In the present, Audrey accuses Bernadette of not caring about the local neighborhood where Audrey's grandmother, mother, and Audrey herself grew up, within a four-mile radius. The remedy for moral disability, individually, and collectively, as a nation, is expanding the radius of virtue, nominating neighbors locally and globally as evolving toward virtue.

Bernadette's unspoken jealousy and competition with her husband Elgie is rooted in the personal and cultural valuing of his career as a scientist over hers as an artist. The cultural valuing of (male) science over (female) art is implicitly reinforced by Audrey. Riffing on images of success that the Galer Street school might use to promote itself, Audrey rejects the handprints proposed by an artist mother in favor of a "coat of arms, with something in it, a calculator, or diplomas, a rainbow of diplomas, maybe there's a sketch of a brain, and it has a cap and gown on it, right?" The image of success to which Audrey implicitly refers is Elgie, a scientist father who works for Microsoft, is repeatedly visualized against a backdrop of mathematical symbols (calculator), and is developing a next-generation digital assistant technology that can be applied directly to the forehead (brain). Elgie's next-generation mind-reader is designed to interpret that which is unspoken, but it is still in development. In the meantime, Elgie the scientist comprehends explicit cues but misinterprets implicit cues. This has implications for how he knows Bernadette, which is different from how she knows herself. Elgie comprehends Bernadette as mentally disabled while misinterpreting her moral identity, underrating her virtue as a mother and professional artist. Thus, whereas Bernadette thinks her maternal investment in their daughter Bee is normative, Elgie thinks it is excessive, underrating Bernadette's virtue as a mother caring for a child with a heart defect. Whereas Bernadette thinks her fulminating about Seattle's restrictive city planning rules and regulations is warranted, Elgie thinks it is evidence of an unhealthy mental fixation, underrating Bernadette's virtue as a professional artist who understands building codes and spatial design. And whereas Bernadette insists that she is collecting pills in a mason jar because she is drawn to the combinations of shapes and colors, Elgie thinks she may be intending to commit suicide, underrating Bernadette's virtue as an artist who likes to experiment with shape and color. Increasingly concerned, Elgie joins Dr. Kurtz in comprehending the explicit cues of Bernadette's behavior scientifically, as evidence of a mental disability requiring intervention. And yet, the cues of Bernadette's behavior can also be interpreted otherwise, more in keeping with how she knows herself. By escaping the intervention and embarking on a solo trip to Antarctica, Bernadette is implicitly taking responsibility for herself, her own moral identity, rather than following Elgie's lead, as in the past.

Bernadette's solo trip to Antarctica expands the radius of virtue to encompass self and other as mutually evolving toward virtue. For Bernadette, a female protagonist, the underrated other is not only her neighbor Audrey, another woman, but also herself. Bernadette confesses to a female scientist she meets while kayaking in Antarctica that she never considered herself much of an architect, but rather "a creative problem solver with good taste and a soft spot for logistical nightmares," thus nominating as virtuous the underrated moral identity of wife and mother, thereby confirming her virtue as a female career professional. Meanwhile, Elgie confesses to daughter Bee that he failed Bernadette, that he should never have let her stop creating as an artist, thus nominating as virtuous the underrated moral identity of the artist, thereby confirming his virtue as a scientist. Elgie also tells Bee that he is taking time off from work, that he is now a free agent with time on his hands to be present to her and her mother, nominating himself as a virtuous father and husband. Bernadette then puts in a call to Bee and Elgie, seeking their consent for her to proceed as a free agent to the South Pole, "the most competitive place on earth, where only scientists are allowed to go," to pursue a career opportunity as a professional artist, during which time she will not be present to them as wife and mother. She explains that she will be devoting her time to designing the new South Pole Station and that any structure she builds will be coordinated out of the United States, with every material flown in and nothing wasted, implicitly forgiving Mills-Murray, her former neighbor, for having flown in a million dollars-worth of nonnative plants and ruining the local neighborhood in the past. "Nothing of what has become of me is Seattle's fault," she adds, forgiving the city planners for restrictive building codes that prevented her from remodeling her house in the present, thus ruining the local neighborhood in the present, but joking that she is withholding final judgment until she "starts being more of an artist and less of a menace," cooperative rather than competitive in her social relations with others, morally literate rather than morally disabled.

INTERPRETING THE IMPLICIT CUES OF COLLECTIVE MORAL DISABILITY

Moral disability is cued not only individually in both films, with respect to the protagonist, but also collectively, with respect to the nation. Both films imply that the post-9/11 American nation is melodramatic mute, not-knowing the traumatic past and misreading the cues of moral identity in the present. In *Silver Linings Playbook*, collective moral disability is rooted in negativity, past and present. Negativity in the present is cued explicitly, in economically emasculated husbands and materialistic wives, while negativity in the past is cued implicitly, in dead husbands and estranged wives. Materialism in the present masks the pain of traumatic loss in the past. Returning home after eight months in residential treatment, Pat attends a "hoity-toity" dinner hosted by his underrated Latino friend Ronnie (John Ortiz), a commercial real estate flipper, and Ronnie's overrated haughty white wife Veronica (Julia Stiles)—Ronnie's name, a diminutive of Veronica's, signifying an imbalance in the cultural valuing of their moral identities. Ronnie leads Pat into his recently remodeled family room filled with idealized family portraits and confesses in a hoarse whisper that he feels suffocated by the demands of his materialistic wife, their new baby, and the "dicks" at work. Ronnie visualizes his feelings by placing his hand over his face, a gesture conventional of melodrama, signifying muteness. Ronnie and Pat agree that the economic downturn has affected everyone they know, but the emphasis is on how it has affected men, stifled and emasculated them. Pat's dad and Ronnie's uncle have both lost their pensions. "You can't be happy all the time. You just do your best, you have no choice," Ronnie concludes fatalistically. Pat starts to object to Ronnie's negativity but is interrupted when Ronnie announces that Veronica's sister Tiffany will be joining them for dinner. Tiffany's husband Tommy, a cop, has died "because cops die," Ronnie explains, but Pat is not to bring it up, implicitly referring to the loss of first responders on 9/11 and its repression in the national imagination. "How did who die?" Tiffany blurts as she suddenly enters the room. The "meet cute" of the primary couple, a convention of the romantic comedy (Grindon 2011, 8), is reworked for maximum awkwardness as Pat proceeds to say all the wrong things, misreading the cues.

Inasmuch as negativity in the present is cued explicitly, in economically emasculated husbands and materialistic wives, negativity in the past is cued implicitly, in dead husbands and estranged wives. As the prospective couple stares each other down, materialistic Veronica joins the group and declares that it will be fun to give Pat and Tiffany a tour of her whole house. Veronica is particularly excited to show off recently installed high-tech gadgetry. In the living room, Tiffany interprets a metal frame hanging on the wall not as a fireplace but as "a drawer in a morgue where they pull out dead bodies and shoot them with formaldehyde," invoking her dead husband, a source of negativity originating in the traumatic past. In the bathroom, showcasing an iPod port, Veronica demands that someone hand her an iPod, prompting Pat to say that he does not own an iPod, and neither does he own a cell phone, but if he did, he would call Nikki, invoking his estranged wife, a source of negativity originating in the traumatic past.

The implication in these scenes is that rather than explicitly acknowledging the traumatic losses of the past (dead husbands and estranged wives), Americans in the present are not-knowing, distracting themselves by buying stuff they cannot afford (emasculated husbands and materialistic wives). Materialism is a symptom of the collective moral disability of the nation, post-9/11.

In *Where'd You Go, Bernadette*, the collective moral disability of the nation is manifested in valuing virtual over real social relations—valuing time spent on screens rather than with each other. Socially anxious, Bernadette leaves Audrey and Tom to the implicitly racialized material business of "removing all things blackberry" and retreats into her information-economy house purchased with Microsoft money, where she orders Manjula, a virtual digital assistant based in New Delhi, to work her "Hindu magic" on a huge project, implicitly the film itself, booking tickets to the "white continent" of Antarctica for a family trip, a middle-school graduation present for daughter Bee. Bernadette confesses to Manjula that she does not want to go on the trip to the white continent, mainly because she will be "surrounded by people," casting her gaze directly at white viewers, acknowledging her awareness of their presence in the virtual social reality of the film. During her confession, which evolves into a competitive rant, Bernadette cuts a hole in her carpet in the shape of a cross, allowing an invasive blackberry taking root underneath to enter her home. Her confession is interrupted by the whimpering of the family dog, Ice Cream ("I scream, you scream"), who has somehow gotten himself locked in a closet called the confessional, inspired by the cross on the door. Despite the expressiveness of Bernadette's ranting and Ice Cream's "screaming," both are melodramatic mutes, unable or unwilling to confess directly, in so many words, the known of moral identity, their own as well as that of others. Bernadette orders a fishing vest from Manjula, ostensibly to wear on the trip to the white continent, but which also implies that she is—and viewers are—on a fishing expedition of sorts, fishing for implicit meanings which are unknown and unnamed but nevertheless expressed visually (crosses, closet, invasive blackberries, fishing vest) and aurally (ranting, whimpering, screaming), conventional of melodrama as a narrative mode.

Since moving to Seattle to pursue Elgie's career, Bernadette and Elgie have both become more invested in their virtual digital assistants than each other. Whereas Bernadette's digital assistant Manjula can type spoken words, Elgie's digital assistant Samantha can type unspoken thoughts. The relation of spoken words and unspoken thoughts points to the relation of explicit and implicit meaning structuring the film. In their lives together, Bernadette says too much, Elgie does not say enough, and his next-generation mind-reader, Samantha 2, is still in development. It is up to viewers to mind-read the implicit thoughts of this film, having to do with collective moral disability. Ultimately, Manjula turns out to be a front for a Russian identity theft ring and Samantha 2 gets canceled and folded into games, implying that viewer-citizens of the post-9/11 American nation are distracted and vulnerable to scamming due to their valuing of virtual over real social relations.

THE INVOLUTION OF MELODRAMA INTO MELODRAMATIC MYTH

In both films, the evolution of moral identity in the content of melodrama culminates with an involution in the narrative structure, to the static form of melodramatic myth. The narrative structure turns inside out, involving from spatialized time in melodrama to timeless space in melodramatic myth. In *Silver Linings Playbook*, Pat is finally able to accept his own "crazy" by accepting Tiffany's "crazy." He forgives Tiffany for giving him a letter supposedly authored by Nikki that Tiffany wrote herself, therein slaying the monster of judgment and nominating Tiffany as a candidate for marriage, a visible emblem of melodrama evolving toward virtue. Tiffany, in turn, nominates Pat as a candidate for marriage, a visible emblem of melodrama evolving toward virtue, declaring him O.K. As the couple kiss, the camera circles around them, ex-nominating them collectively as a visible symbol of moral enlightenment in melodramatic myth.

Where'd You Go, Bernadette also culminates with an involution in the narrative structure, to the static form of melodramatic myth. The conclusion of the film performs a miracle of dialectical reconciliation on behalf of viewers that parallels the "Hindu magic" performed by digital assistant Manjula on behalf of Bernadette. In a final vision attributed to Saint Bernadette, a Christian visionary, scientist husband Elgie and artist wife Bernadette embrace, reconciling the contradictions they embody in an emblem of melodrama, mutually nominating each other as evolving toward virtue. Husband and Wife, Science and Art, two halves of a whole, are coupled and birth a divine child, their daughter Bee, a hybrid identity named after the Hindu god Balakrishna, creator and destroyer, the film's narrator. Father, mother, and child embrace, producing a secular vision of the holy family, ex-nominated collectively as a visible symbol of the morally enlightened Christian-Hindu nation in melodramatic myth.

A coda concludes each film, cuing viewers to perceive the film itself, the narrative structure that produced the visible symbol of secular moral enlightenment, a vision of timelessness within time. In *Silver Linings Playbook*, the camera withdraws from the ex-nominated couple, tracking backward on the cobblestone street decorated with Christmas lights—backward in the narrative, to ancient sacred tragic myth, and forward into Tiffany's dance studio, where the couple learned to read the cues of moral identity and stop judging each other negatively in time—forward in the narrative, to modern secular melodrama. The camera then tracks forward into Pat's home for the hybridity of the happy ending, with his entire family together for now, for this moment, on Sunday (ancient sacred tragic myth), game day (modern secular melodrama), to watch the Eagles (nation) play. In the coda of *Where'd You Go, Bernadette*, narrator Bee, speculating on whether penguins in nature mate for life, implies that the reason her parents are staying together in the present is not located in nature but rather culture, not a matter of fate in ancient sacred tragic myth but rather moral choice in modern secular melodrama.

THE INVOLUTION OF HISTORY INTO MYTH

Popular American film narrative involves emblems of melodrama in spatialized time into symbols of melodramatic myth in timeless space, thereby producing visions of mythical timelessness within historical time. These visions of mythical timelessness are not for all time, as in ancient sacred tragic myth, but for now, for this moment in history, in modern secular melodramatic myth. Involving historical content into timeless mythical form is how film narrative functions ritually in culture (Altman 1999, 218). The involution in narrative structure enacts a ritual involution in the experience of viewers. For viewers, evolving in time can be associated with negativity or jealous competition in social relations with others, at home, school, and work, with family members, neighbors, and friends. Feeling negative, jealous, and competitive toward others—these are emotions. Film narrative functions ritually to convert the inner, individualized emotional experience of viewers in social reality into outer, collectively experienced affect in film narrative (Jameson 2017, 31; 2019, 325). In other words, film narrative functions ritually to ex-nominate and mythologize not only protagonists but also viewers, giving viewers a collective experience of themselves, outside of themselves—an affective, euphoric experience of timelessness in film narrative.

The involution from historical content to timeless mythical form not only serves a ritual but also an ideological function in culture (Altman 1999, 218), given that the identities of viewers are far more diverse, in terms of race, gender, sexuality, and ability, than the identities onscreen. In popular American film narrative, the ex-nominated mythical self tends to be a white, cisgendered, heterosexual, able-bodied American. The protagonists in *Silver Linings Playbook* and *Where'd You Go Bernadette* pose a challenge to this norm, at least on one level, in that they are mentally disabled. This difference is the impetus to narrate a story in the first place. However, the story becomes about something else, something other than a material body's experience of mental disability in social reality, something more abstracted, textually: moral disability. In both films, mental disability is a pretext, an opportunistic metaphorical device for lending a material body to textual abstraction, for exploring the moral identity of white, cisgendered, heterosexual Americans, individually and collectively, in history and myth. As the morally disabled self evolves in time, in melodrama, and involves to moral enlightenment in melodramatic myth, the mentally disabled material body is left behind, left to fate, static and unchanging in tragic myth. Ultimately, popular film storytelling essentializes mental disability, upholding the intuitive belief that human beings are what they are, immutably—a belief cognitive science reveals as biased, irrational, and at odds with science (Berent).

WORKS CITED

Alexander, Jeffrey C., Ron Eyerman, Bernard Glesen, Neil J. Smelser, and Piotr Sztompka. *Cultural Trauma and Collective Identity*. Berkeley: University of California Press, 2004.

Altman, Rick. *Film/Genre*. London: BFI, 1999.

Barthes, Roland. *Mythologies*. Trans. Annette Lavers. New York: Noonday Press, 1989.
Benjamin, Walter. *The Origin of German Tragic Drama*. Trans. John Osborne. New York: Verso, 1990.
Berent, Iris, and Melanie Platt. "Essentialist Biases Toward Psychiatric Disorders: Brain Disorders are Presumed Innate." *Cognitive Science: A Multidisciplinary Journal* 45, no. 4 (19 April 2021): 1–21.
Bordwell, David. *Making Meaning: Inference and Rhetoric in the Interpretation of Cinema*. New Haven: Harvard University Press, 1991.
Brooks, Peter. *The Melodramatic Imagination: Balzac, Henry James, Melodrama, and the Mode of Excess*. New Haven: Yale University Press, 1995.
Brooks, Peter. *Reading for the Plot: Design and Intention in Narrative*. Cambridge: Harvard University Press, 1984.
Buck-Morss, Susan. *The Dialectics of Seeing: Walter Benjamin and the Arcades Project*. Cambridge: MIT Press, 1991.
Grindon, Leger. *The Hollywood Romantic Comedy: Conventions, History, Controversies*. New York: Wiley-Blackwell, 2011.
Jameson, Fredric. *Allegory and Ideology*. London: Verso, 2019.
Jameson, Fredric. *The Ancients and the Postmoderns: On the Historicity of Forms*. London: Verso, 2017.
Laplanche, J. and J.-B. Pontalis. *The Language of Psychoanalysis*. Trans. Donald Nicholson-Smith. New York: W. W. Norton, 1973.
Lévi-Strauss, Claude. "The Structural Analysis of Myth." In Claude Lévi-Strauss, *Structural Anthropology*, 206–31. New York: Basic Books, 1963.
Linklater, Richard, dir. 2019. *Where'd You Go, Bernadette*. Burbank, CA: 20th Century Fox. 2020. DVD.
Mitchell, David T. and Sharon L. Snyder. *Narrative Prosthesis: Disabilities and the Dependencies of Discourse*. Ann Arbor: University of Michigan Press, 2014.
Nowell-Smith, Geoffrey. "Minnelli and Melodrama." In Christine Gledhill (ed.), *Home is Where the Heart Is: Studies in Melodrama and the Woman's Film*, 70–74. London: British Film Institute, 1987.
Quick, Matthew. *Silver Linings Playbook: A Novel*. New York: Farrar, Straus and Giroux, 2008.
Russell, David O., dir. 2012. *Silver Linings Playbook*. New York: The Weinstein Company, 2013. DVD.
Semple, Maria. *Where'd You Go, Bernadette: A Novel*. New York: Little, Brown and Company, 2012.
Whissel, Kristen. *Spectacular Digital Effects: CGI and Contemporary Cinema*. Durham: Duke University Press, 2014.
Williams, Linda. *Playing the Race Card: Melodramas of Black & White from Uncle Tom's Cabin to O.J. Simpson*. Princeton: Princeton University Press, 2001.

Part II

RENEGOTIATING AND RESISTING NARRATIVES OF DISABILITY

Chapter 7

"A document in madness?"
Disability Erasure in Contemporary Rewrites of Ophelia
Lindsay Adams Kennedy

I remember my first-time teaching *Hamlet* to a college class of all nonmajors—students who had signed up for a Literature and Film class, expecting to watch movies in class, only to discover four Shakespeare plays on the required textbook list. When we started reading *Hamlet*, even I was surprised by how vehemently my students defended Ophelia in the text—criticizing Hamlet for not listening to her and forcing himself into her rooms, and Polonius for his paternalistic attempts to control her. There's *something* about Ophelia—it's undeniable. My experience teaching *Hamlet* confirms Ophelia's continued appeal and fascination, especially for young women; they are passionate, confused, and furious about her treatment in the play, both by the playwright and the other characters. My students were further angered at how she just disappears from the text—their frustration returning me to my first reading of the play when I was a teenager—a frustration that always brings me back to this character. It is Ophelia's very inscrutability that makes her rife with potential interpretations, making her both identifiable and relatable.

It is easy to think we no longer need to engage with Ophelia in our current day when we do have nuanced and empathic depictions of women with mental disability in popular culture—one such example being the character of Rebecca Bunch in *Crazy Ex-Girlfriend*; however, those depictions are the exception, not the norm. As the character of Ophelia continues to be adapted, and the play of *Hamlet* performed, this text continues to be not only a part of the narrative of mental health but one of the most influential. As Duncan Salkeld points out, "our concepts of madness are rooted in social and historical contexts which have influenced the way in which madness down the years has been (mis)understood" (Salkeld 1994, 10). Ophelia speaks to a mass audience, both in Shakespeare's time and in our own. She has become deeply associated with suicidal teenagerhood due to psychology books like Mary Pipher's *Reviving Ophelia: Saving the Selves of Adolescent Girls*. This, and the use of the play as a teaching text at the high school and collegiate level, has solidified Ophelia as both a trope and point of identification for young adult women, especially those with invisible disabilities. The three more popular, recent adaptations of *Hamlet* that this chapter will focus on center around Ophelia and attempt to bring to light her narrative, or her other possible narratives: *Elsinore*, a point-and-click video game, and *Ophelia*, both the 2006 young adult novel written by Lisa Klein and the 2018 film based on Klein's novel.

In this chapter, I will explore the ways that these three adaptations attempt, but fail, to re-claim the character of Ophelia; I attribute this failure to their inability to engage with her identity as a disabled woman. Their adaptive choices, while seemingly progressive and responsive to issues of representation, continue to reiterate the same sad tropes of mental disability that make canonical works like *Hamlet* so fraught from a disability studies perspective. These adaptations' attempts to approach Ophelia from a feminist perspective do not lead to a more nuanced depiction of mental disability but renders it invisible. In erasing Ophelia's disabled identity, they keep the problematic rhetoric and representation of mental disability of the source text. Ultimately though, these works are indicative of a much larger sociocultural issue: the ways female agency is framed as being dependent on ability. Culture and media affect each other—the stories we tell about disability shape the day-to-day experiences and interactions that people with disabilities face. It is time to change outdated narratives—something that all three of these adaptations attempt to do—but we can only do this by identifying the misunderstandings and assumptions around mental health that permeate *Hamlet* as well as the deeper ableist social structures that underpin and are influenced by the play even today.

ADAPTING *HAMLET* AND THE FEMINISM PROBLEM

The women of *Hamlet* (Ophelia and Gertrude) are famously underwritten and play into many problematic tropes—from their passivity in the larger plot to the constant whore/virgin dichotomy of Hamlet's language and his conflating of all women as the same. These issues are something that productions and adaptations often work to fix. This is clearly a primary goal of the three adaptations that I am analyzing in this chapter. In the video game *Elsinore* (2019) Ophelia is the player-character whose decisions define the entire narrative; *Elsinore* deconstructs the source play through its time-loop game mechanic that allows Ophelia (and by extension the player) to make a variety of discursive choices that disrupt the original story and unlock thirteen possible endings. The young adult novel Ophelia (2006), and the following film adaptation of Klein's novel (2018) do this through cleverly rewriting the plot of Hamlet, particularly in changing the context to shift how the audience understands the play's famous scenes. These adaptations are unapologetically feminist in their concerns, looking at the events of *Hamlet* through Ophelia's eyes and interrogating the limitations placed on the female characters of the original work because of their gender. While they all attempt to reclaim Ophelia and they do a lot of work with their feminist frame, they fall short in representing her disability. I believe the erasure of her disability in these adaptations is a side-effect of their feminist concerns. The feminist imperative is to make Ophelia empowered; however, this empowerment assumes, and often requires, ability. In this section, I will explore the adaptational choices that, in an attempt to bring a feminist lens to Shakespeare's play, end up failing to show Ophelia's intersectional identity.

The insertion of new female characters in *Elsinore* and the novel and film of *Ophelia* (as well as the additional identities and backstories given to those featured in *Hamlet*) creates more nuanced conversations about the multiplicity of the female experience and differing challenges women face based on a variety of factors including social status and identities. Klein's novel introduces a broader cast of female characters that include Mechtild, a healer woman who teaches Ophelia the uses of different herbs, as well as a host of nuns she meets after "getting herself" to a French convent, as Hamlet suggests. In *Ophelia*, not only does Lisa Klein dig into the titular character, but we also see a more complex Gertrude and are meant to sympathize with the impossible situations in which she finds herself. She takes Ophelia in as a lady-in-waiting despite her low birth and treats her with an almost maternal love. The film adaptation of *Ophelia* gives female characters even more of an active role in the narrative—in the film version Gertrude is the one who stabs Claudius through the chest. The film also adds a subplot about Mechthild, who is adapted as Queen Gertrude's sister and King Claudius's ex-lover. Her backstory creates a conversation around the defining of women's epistemologies as "witchery," and the double standard around men and women when it comes to sexual promiscuousness. In Klein's novel as well, Ophelia sees the hypocrisy of gender expectations and sexual expression in the court. She wonders, "Why should men be allowed freedoms that were deemed sinful for women to take?" (Klein 2006, 106). Later in the novel she bemoans "the insecure state of women, who must always abide by the earthly authority of men" (253). Unlike in *Hamlet*, Ophelia is allowed to voice her frustrations with the status quo.

Elsinore engages even more deeply than *Ophelia* (2006 & 2018) with the complexities of female experience and some intersectional identities, by engaging with race and sexual identity. In *Elsinore*, Ophelia is a biracial woman who grapples with prejudice due to her interlocking identities, and the game also gender-swaps and adapts Rosencrantz and Guildenstern as women of color. The video game also features some entirely new characters like Lady Brit, some that were referenced but not seen in *Hamlet* (the pirate captain is revealed to be the historical pirate Grace O'Malley), and others pulled from other Shakespeare plays. *Elsinore* leverages characters with diverse identities into an opportunity to have conversations about power dynamics that are constructed around gender and racial identities. As *Elsinore*'s Guildenstern points out to Hamlet, with whom she had an affair, "At Wittenberg, women who looked like Ophelia and me were *afraid* to refuse you. You're a Prince" (*Elsinore* 2019). This interaction allows us to see Hamlet realize his level of power and privilege for the first time, recognizing that despite his own feelings of powerlessness, there are others with far less authority and agency than him.

The importance of support and allyship between women is another theme running through all these adaptations, which recognize how female community protects women from patriarchal systems that would render them marginalized. *Ophelia* presents the bullying lady-in-waiting Cristiana with nuance—allowing her to grow from harassing Ophelia due to socially constructed notions around unhealthy female competition to showing female solidarity and warning Ophelia when she fears that her life could be at risk (Klein 2006, 157). There is a similar antagonistic relationship between Lady Brit and Ophelia in *Elsinore*, one that plays out the ways that women are often pitted against each other, while offering (depending on the player choice) a brighter possibility where they can recognize the other as not the real enemy. As Gertrude says in *Elsinore*: "This can never be a world worth living in if women don't protect one another" (2019). This is a necessity in a patriarchal society where, "Men will sell us, breed us, hit us, dishonor us, and kill us. They rend us apart the moment they're born from us" (2019). Adding more female characters, giving them agency, and engaging with some intersectional identities are strong adaptive choices. Through these choices, *Elsinore* and *Ophelia* (the book and film) highlight the challenges women faced (and face) as well as offering them the opportunity for solidarity (and extended dialogue) with each other—something the source material sorely lacks.

Yet, these feminist rewrites of Ophelia repeatedly fail in their engagement with her disability by framing her madness as either make believe or a misunderstanding. Not only that, but the adaptations also use questionable rhetoric in referring to her madness—language that perpetuates rather than frees Ophelia from stereotypes. In Klein's novel and its film adaptation,

Ophelia fakes madness to protect herself and only pretends to commit suicide to escape Elsinore and assassination. *Elsinore* makes it explicit that Ophelia is only *believed to be mad* by other characters, either because she talks to the wrong people about time repeating or tells the truth about Claudius' guilt. In all three works, Ophelia is made a protagonist with agency over her own choices, but her madness becomes a performance or a false patriarchal assumption. The adaptations seem to find it impossible for Ophelia to be both empowered and disabled, as if the two are mutually exclusive.

This is in line with a great deal of feminist scholarship looking at madness and gender in relation to Ophelia, much of which also relies on a kind of erasure of her intersectional identity as a disabled woman.[1] As Tobin Siebers notes in his groundbreaking work *Disability Theory*, "ability appears unmarked because it is the norm, while disability, as an affront to ability, feels the full and persistent force of an ideological impulse to erase from view any exception to ability" (2008, 102). One example of this in the source text, *Hamlet*, is Gertrude's reticence and (at first) outright refusal to see or engage with Ophelia once she bears the markers of "madness," once her mental disability is visible. Abled people (of which I am one) rarely think of themselves as such, because they rarely think about disability; the only time this identity becomes manifest is when in the presence of a person with a disability. Because of this, as Rosemarie Garland-Thomson points out, abled people try to "domesticate" the alarming challenge to the status quo those with disabilities represent to the abled and "reassert the equilibrium of familiarity" (2009, 19). Often, this takes the form of attempting to "fix" the disabled person through medical means. To make Ophelia "sane" is to render her normal and to thus "fix" her "mental defect" and tragic ending.

Thus, disability is made *a problem to be solved* in media depictions—an impulse that comes from our instinctive wish to other the disability and normalize the person experiencing it. It is also an ongoing problem with the character of Ophelia. The "ideological impulse" that Siebers describes is evident in the refusal to engage with Ophelia's madness, with readers, critics, and adapters choosing to erase her identity as a person living with a mental disability. As Elaine Showalter points out, certain feminine characteristics are often coded in terms of madness or hysteria, this is especially evident in relation to Ophelia's performance history and interpretations (1992, 281–93). The instinct of feminist readings and reimaginings of *Hamlet*, then, is to turn Ophelia's madness into a metaphor for the relationship between female subjects and patriarchal control. This chapter argues that the lived experience of mental disability deserves better than to be made into a metaphor for something else—this becomes a bizarre appropriation of a marginalized identity. As Siebers writes, "disability is not a physical or mental defect but a cultural and minority identity" (Siebers 2008, 4). However, to those that view mental disability as a defect, removing Ophelia's madness by making it merely a performance or misunderstanding is the natural move to strengthen her character and give her an uplifting ending. This ideation leads inevitably to the flawed conclusion that Ophelia can only achieve happiness and avoid suicide by *not being mad in the first place*. The refusal to engage with her "madness" as an integral part of her intersectional identity in these adaptations, not only erases her disability but also ends up perpetuating disability stereotypes.

Due to the feminist empowerment offered to audiences in these adaptations, this form of erasure is easy to miss. It seems likely that the mostly female authors and creatives produced these works with only the best of intentions. The team lead and writer of *Elsinore*, Katie Chironis, describes her first experience with Hamlet very similarly to those of my students:

> So, I read Hamlet for the first time in high school, and I was very drawn to Ophelia as a character, even then. I remember thinking that I didn't really feel like she got a fair shot in the original play. (Lachenal 2015)

Chironis and the game designer Connor Fallon are clearly invested in creating a diverse cast of characters. In another interview about *Elsinore*, Fallon explains,

> Diversity was something we as a team cared about. Everyone deserves to be able to find heroes that look like them. We live in a diverse world, and while many performances of the original play don't reflect that, there is no reason our own take on it can't. (Ingram 2015)

The video game adaptation features diverse heroes—heroes that are women, heroes that are people of color, heroes that are queer, heroes of a variety of shapes, experiences, and identities. Yet, there are no heroes that are disabled in *Elsinore*; for young people with disabilities, there is nobody that "looks like them." Similarly, Klein's acknowledgments in the novel thank the people that helped her make sure that "Ophelia now has her due" ("Acknowledgements" 2006). Their intentions, however, do not fully exculpate them or change the fact that creators have an ethical responsibility when handling narratives of disability, along with other identities. This is further heightened when adapting for mass consumption one of the few canonical characters that have an invisible disability. Writers and casting directors in the film industry are being widely criticized for things like white-washing characters and redface,[2] as should have been happening long before now—it is time for the same awareness and advocacy to occur in relation to disability.

THE REPRESENTATION AND RHETORIC OF MADNESS IN *ELSINORE* AND *OPHELIA*

The narrative erasure of mental disability in these three adaptations is a microcosm of an issue that is widespread in contemporary media. While attempting to empower the character (and the mostly female audience the works are speaking to), decisions made by the creators of these works to remove disability are ultimately damaging. While positioning Ophelia as a feminist (and in *Elsinore* a queer) icon, they ignore the part of her character that is perhaps her strongest point of identification for many audience members—her mental disability, which they render invisible. Ophelia is one of a handful of canonical characters that give representation to those living with mental disabilities and is especially important for young women. The potential value of these adaptations showing another, rewritten ending for Ophelia that does not involve suicide but instead embraces her disabled identity is exponential. Unfortunately, this potential is not realized. The adaptive choices of these works depict Ophelia as an abled woman, erasing the lived truth of her mental disability—her madness is merely a misunderstanding or tactical self-preservation.

All three adaptations make explicit the fact that the madness presented by Ophelia, or assumed by other characters, is pretense only. In Klein's novel, both Hamlet and Ophelia feign madness at different times for different purposes. Hamlet pretends that he is made mad by his love for Ophelia: "I will appear mad with love for you—or with a general madness—but I put on this disposition to divert and test them all" (Klein 2006, 131). By getting the court to doubt his sanity due to his melancholy over thwarted love he will keep his marriage to Ophelia secret. Ophelia follows his example once Hamlet is sent away to England and her father is dead. Her singing and flower sharing are part of a performance to protect her from the King's wrath and suspicion. As Ophelia says, "I wear this madness for a purpose. I may put it on and take it off at will" (185). Mental disability is a mask that she wears as needed, like the Janus necklace given to her by Hamlet that depicts a comic and tragic face. Positioning Ophelia as abled but pretending to be disabled, turns her mad scenes into mockery of mental disability, utilizing as a survival strategy a disability that in reality can make it a daily struggle to survive. She is coopting the disabled experience, which in itself is problematic, even more so, when one considers the ways that disability is often doubted. In the Early Modern era, the physically disabled, such as the blind, were often cast as fakers and con artists; however, it is not so different today for those with invisible disabilities. The validity of mental disabilities is often questioned—challenged by some as not being a "real" disability, but instead a character flaw. Disclosure of mental disability can come with intense societal stigma; it is unsurprising that many living with these disabilities stay silent from a fear of being disbelieved or being othered.

What makes Ophelia's mad performance even more dangerous is that she imitates madness without ever having watched it closely. As she herself admits, "I had never observed such a creature, for whether from shame or fear I had ignored the madmen and the poor who lived among us" (179). She is expressing the discomfort, the "affront to ability," viewing those with disabilities can create for abled people (Siebers 2008, 102). Part of why Ophelia is successful in her disguise, despite her complete lack of knowledge about the mentally disabled, is because those around her turn away and ignore her. This is just another example of the "ideological impulse" of the abled to ignore and erase disability. If the abled are unwilling to look closely at disability, they will never learn more about this identity and experience. Ophelia does not have to be particularly successful in her performance of madness, as her peers wouldn't be able to tell the difference. Here Klein is clearly and empathetically articulating the marginalization and invisibility of the mad in Elsinore. What is profoundly difficult about this articulation is that the text of *Ophelia* is doing the exact same thing as these villagers—choosing to ignore rather than interact with Ophelia's madness.

Similarly, in *Elsinore* only one of the game's many final endings for Ophelia addresses her madness in the source material, but even this is only perceived madness. This ending, as well as several different scenes and outcomes, is unlocked if Ophelia talks to the wrong people about her visions of death or being in a time loop. In one of these possible dialogue scenes, Claudius and Polonius conspire together to have her sent off to an asylum. While he is clearly reluctant, Polonius sees no other choice but to have her institutionalized. Claudius strengthens his resolve, saying: "As we discussed earlier, her mind's not well. She needs help" (*Elsinore* 2019). In the other possible scene, Ophelia is poisoned as an act of "mercy" to save her from her supposed insanity. This leads to a *Game Over* that restarts the clock with Ophelia saying: "I tried. I tried to tell them. But they wouldn't believe me." What Ophelia has been saying is assumed to be proof of her madness, when it is in fact proof of her "sanity." Ophelia being declared crazy and institutionalized by her father unlocks one of the final endings—the one that is tagged as "Sacrifice REALITY for JOY." This ending involves her in an asylum, but living out the world she wishes she could have created in her head. In *Elsinore*, then, madness and mental disability are framed as un-reality. They are states that are not real—both in the sense not only that no one in this game is living with mental disability but also that they are consistently declared only as delusion and dissociation. Ophelia rejects Polonius's claims that she is mad by saying, "I'm not delusional, Father." When the player discovers the ending, Ophelia has a last line of dialogue: "I could use the Book of Fates to embrace madness, if I wanted to." Thus, madness and mental disability is made a choice, not an inherent part of the character's identity.

While these adaptations reframe Ophelia's "madness" in different ways, the choices they make in relation to her disability all amount to erasure, just with differing methods. It doesn't matter if Klein obliquely references the othering of those who are poor or "mad" if she turns the mental illness that Ophelia has in the source material into a charade. Those with mental disabilities do not need our pity, they need representation. They need to be truly seen. The film adaptation of *Ophelia* keeps this madness-as-performance and has no mention at all of other characters or people with disabilities. While *Elsinore* does not have its protagonist pretend to be mad, like in *Ophelia*, her sanity is explicitly stated and unquestionable. People calling her mad is a misunderstanding stemming from patriarchal stereotypes of female instability or an excuse to silence her. In *Elsinore*, Ophelia being mad may not be a tactic, but it is something tragic to be avoided. Making Ophelia, a character that is canonically a woman with a mental disability, into an abled person is not different than adapting a character of color as white. Removing her disability is erasing her identity, and ultimately erases a potentially important representation of the disabled community.

Even worse than the erasure of Ophelia's disability are the ways in which the adaptations utilize ableist frameworks from Hamlet and deploy dangerous Early Modern disability tropes; this indicates the purchase and power that these stereotypes still have in our present day. While departing in many ways from the source material, in certain ways these adaptations hew very close to Shakespeare's play—specifically in relation to the language used around mental and cognitive disability. Writing about a frenzied man regaining sanity, St. Thomas More wrote that he "gathered hys remembraunce to hym and beganne to come agayne to hym selfe" (1979, 118). To be distracted was to have forgotten oneself, to have lost the person that you "truly are." In Klein's novel, madness is similarly framed. Ophelia describes having "lost my wits through grief" (2006, 178). Thus, madness becomes a "loss" of the self, not another facet of a personal identity. Ophelia's very identity has been obliterated by the madness. *Elsinore* plays into this trope through its game mechanics as well. If the player, as Ophelia, tells the wrong information to characters it will "shatter" them. They are marked—after the character's name there is "shattered" in parenthesis—and Ophelia cannot interact with them further or share more information. This is based on the language of the source play itself: Ophelia says of Hamlet that "he raised a sigh so piteous and profound/

as it did seem to shatter all his bulk/And end his being" (Shakespeare 2016, 2.1.91–93). Melancholy, or any other Early Modern coded term for mental imbalance, is a "shattering" of the person, a separation between that person and themselves. Thus, madness comes to be all the person is, according to the language used in these works. This mental imbalance separates the person from the world, rendering them unable to communicate or be engaged with. These adaptational choices end up formalizing implicit (and dangerous) claims from the source text.

It may seem like these Early Modern notions should have little impact on conversations about contemporary media and mental health representation. Yet, as Carol Thomas Neely writes: "Although Renaissance conceptions, representations, and treatments of madness seem at first impossibly distant and alien, our own debates about the condition often recapitulate or grow out of those early ones" (1). There are ramifications for reiterating certain kinds of structures from this play. *Hamlet* has and will continue to influence how we understand mental disability, and the potential impact is broadened through uncritical dissemination of the play's problematic "conceptions, representations, and treatments of madness" in contemporary adaptations. As a text that is still very much part of our educational system, and one of the primary canonical representations of mental disability, our conversations around Hamlet have the power to change misconceptions—but we have to start reading it differently. Ophelia has become a prototype in popular culture, as perhaps the single most influential, and broadly known representation of mental illness, especially in relation to the female experience. The failure to engage ethically with mental health issues and suicidal ideation is still very present in contemporary works. The media idealization (accidental or not) of the dead Ophelia has continued past the pre-Raphaelite paintings glorifying her suicide—one need look no further than the outcry at the adaptational decisions made in the Netflix Original Series *13 Reasons Why* as well as criticisms of the source material. There is deep risk involved in this conversation, because of the many mistakes that can be made in engaging with it as authors, artists, and critics—but we risk more by refusing to address it. This is a conversation that one must be willing to have when you choose to adapt the character of Ophelia. But instead, these adaptations attempt to entirely distance themselves, and her character, from real discussions of mental illness.

The way madness is described in *Elsinore* and *Ophelia* (2006 & 2018) is as something that happens to a person, not as an embodied part of their identity—something that they live with daily. The separation between the two is what still today leads to the marginalization and medicalization of disabled persons. When mental disability is made separate from the disabled person, it becomes something to be stamped out or destroyed. The goal becomes to return them to "normality," at which point they become not just their ideal self, but the able person they were *meant to be*. This pathologizing language frames mental disability as something outside of the person, or something that happens to them, is problematic, but common. In the Early Modern period, madness and distraction (while having the self-obliterating/agency-removing qualities previously discussed) were understood as a "temporary derailing" of the mind (Neely 2004, 2). Rather than a permanent state, the distracted were grouped in with the sick, suffering from that which are "temporary curable disruptions of health" (Neely 2004, 4). Madness was and still is viewed as a treatable, solvable medical illness. This ideation is carried through in what is often called the medical model of disability, which is the framework used by these adaptations of *Hamlet*. This medical model is heavily criticized for its focus on diagnosing and curing the disability. Many literary critics also attempt to diagnose Ophelia; but, as Richard A. Ingram, one of the leading theorists of Mad Studies and coiner of the term, points out, "trying to pin down madness as one thing is, I think, to miss the point: It is a million things" (2006, 15). As long as these depictions of Ophelia continue to use this language, people will continue to "miss the point."

One could argue that the issues I have raised with the disability frameworks and language are merely these works representing bias against and misunderstandings of mental disability, not perpetuating them. However, unlike all the other marginalized identities that are explored, there is no counternarrative presented to this notion of disability—in part because people with mental disabilities do not get to voice them. In *Elsinore*, they simply do not seem to exist. In Klein's *Ophelia*, they are not given much voice at all, and our experience of them is mediated through Ophelia's, who in this work is a fully abled woman that admits she never looked very closely at the mentally disabled in her community. All three of these adaptations make it explicit that Ophelia is not in fact living with mental disability. All we get in *Ophelia* is her mad performance but no one who genuinely lives with mental illness to compare it to. In *Elsinore*, there is no mad representation outside of other characters misreading the explicitly sane Ophelia, or worse this character choosing insanity as if it is a piece of clothing to be taken on or off at will. Part of what makes these works so disappointing is that they create conversations around Ophelia's other identities by giving her a multiplicity of characters who have lived experience with them to engage with—all, that is, except for her disabled identity.

Due to the fact that this is an industry-wide and society-wide issue, I think it is necessary to acknowledge that *Elsinore* writer Katie Chironis, *Ophelia* novelist Lisa Klein, and the adapting screenwriter Semi Chellas should not be held single-handedly accountable.

I also do not want to suggest that Chironis failed at her attempt to go down some kind of checklist, making sure to hit every marginalized or narratively-often-neglected identity. To suggest that would be to sell *Elsinore* short—the way that these characters are fleshed out with their own wants, needs, and history make it clear that that is not the case. There are nuanced, three-dimensional characters, not tokens used for performative posturing or virtue signaling. My point is that this is a much larger and systematic problem surrounding disability as a marginalized identity. Disability, especially mental disability, is still often erased or ignored in contemporary media, even in excellent works created by well-intentioned writers who are clearly invested in character diversity. It is long past time, as Catherine J. Kudlick puts it, that we "think about disability not as an isolated, individual medical pathology but instead as a key defining social category on a par with race, class, and gender" (2003, 764).

AGENCY, CHOICE, AND DISABILITY ERASURE

These works were created with good intentions, and yet all of them fail in relation to Ophelia's mental disability in surprisingly similar ways. Why does this keep happening? It feels almost like we are caught in a time-loop like the Ophelia of Kudlick. This erasure comes down to contemporary notions around agency, as well as the consistent tension between societal views on self-determinacy and disability. It makes sense that the reason these adaptations struggle with disability representation is because of the vital question at the heart of *Hamlet*—action or inaction? The play and its protagonist are obsessed with choice and these concerns are carried into these adaptations. The thirteen different endings of *Elsinore* all tellingly begin with the line: "This is the fate I choose" (2019). The importance of choice is also made manifest in the mechanics—the plot and events of the game are based on the decisions the player makes.[3] Using Boolean logic, characters are coded with specific wants and beliefs that change their direction and narrative. The game is all about interrogating choices and agency, whether it be addressing the lack of choices that many of the women, especially women of color, have in *Elsinore*, as well as questioning whether the choices made by Ophelia, and by extension the player, are meaningful. The novel and film of *Ophelia* engage with this by exploring the agency of controlling the telling of the narrative. In the opening voiceover to the film, Ophelia warns the audience that while they may think themselves familiar with her tale, "it is high time I should tell you my story . . . myself" (Chellas 2018, 01:13–02:03). The film ends with a voiceover that returns to the same themes, as Ophelia watches her daughter playing: "I found my way to hope . . . that one day I would tell my own story. As one day you, my love . . . you will tell yours" (01:38:40–01:39:34). This framing makes the film (even more than the novel) explicitly about the importance of what stories get told, who tells them, and supports the next generation of women in having agency over their narrative. These are the very concerns I have with the adaptive choices made in these works. They reject the stories told in *Hamlet*, the woefully underwritten female characters, the misogyny of male characters, but with that comes the problematic rejection of the disabled identity.

A large part of these three adaptations deciding to ignore mental disability is due to our uncertainty around what to "do" with madness in contemporary discourse as well as the ways that cognitive and mental disability break down abled, simplistic notions about choice. All of the works are focused on giving Ophelia choices and control over her own destiny—opportunities that the canonical source work do not give her. This is part of the feminist lens that Klein, Chironis, and Chellas are bringing to their adaptations. Choice is predicated on agency and self-determinacy, which in large part is located in our *ability* to take action or make any decision we want. When we talk about decision-making, we discuss whether someone has the *ability* to make a choice—the binary of abled or disabled is coded into the language we use. Madness, and I would argue disability in general, breaks down binaries like this. Sandra J. Levi writes about limiting the self-determinacy of people with disabilities as being one of the hallmarks of ableism and how it manifests in society. While agency is often a value that is held in high regard, "disabled persons often are not able to exercise their rights to self-determination" (2006, 3). Part of this stems from another foundational tenet of ableism, which is the paternalistic attitude toward those with disabilities, one that assumes their incapacity to "achieve." This is often based on abled notions and frameworks of both what success is and looks like, as well as the false assumption that "low achievement in one performance domain automatically transfers to low achievement in other performance domains" (Levi 2006, 2). There are various laws in place that are constructed to remove these abled structures and systems; however, as Levi points out, it is impossible to "protect persons from unspoken judgments of inadequacy." Exacerbating this problem and tension is the fact that capitalist, Western society in general, is "predicated on able-bodied ideals of independence, strength, control, self-mastery, and struggle" (Kudlick 2003, 766). There is a narrative in Western culture that privileges and prioritizes individual achievement and agency, but then removes the possibility of that narrative for specific groups.

When feminist agency is inherently tied to self-determinacy, from which disabled women are societally and systematically disallowed, what we get is a form of exclusionary pop-feminism. Ophelia's sanity is necessary to keep our understanding of choice as something stable that is "clearly" and "rationally" made. Madness is made inherently limiting in *Elsinore*; the player must make specific choices to make sure people do not think Ophelia is mad, as otherwise it becomes a hindrance to the player unlocking all the possible endings. While her being viewed as mad is necessary to achieving one ending, it pre-empts and shuts down the opportunity for the player to find the others. Once the player has unlocked this ending, her being considered mad is only a deterrent that will lead to her death and a restart of the game. At a certain point, Ophelia bearing any "markers" of disability means the player cannot complete the game. Ophelia being abled is required to continue assumptions around agency being inherently tied to ability. In Ingram's article outlining the goals for Mad Studies, he references *Hamlet* not once but twice, which I think speaks to the ways that this play (and its narrative that continues to be replicated and remixed in various forms) has become a kind of definitive, influential text in conversations around madness. Ingram says,

> To make sense or not to make sense, maybe that's the question! Or maybe it is a matter of both making sense and not making sense, so that there can be a making sense at times and not making sense at other times. (2006, 14–15)

Some critics, Ingram included, have described disability as having a "queering" effect, especially in relation to constructs of time. I am cautious about certain theoretical and critical tendencies in my field to broaden that term too far so as to make it mean everything, and yet nothing. Yet, it is fascinating that in a work like *Elsinore*, especially that is all about warping and changing our notions of time, disability is still erased. This decision is even more frustrating in that work due to the fact that it is in many ways trying to break down binary notions, and instead welcome the player into a multiplicity of endings and universes.

CONCLUSION

With her novel *Ophelia*, Lisa Klein has the opportunity to allow young women living with a mental disability to see themselves represented, while changing Ophelia's tragic ending. Instead, what we get is a simplistic feminism that refuses to engage with the character's intersectional identity. In *Elsinore*, the choice to ignore Ophelia's disability is even more perplexing, due to its engagement with intersectionality and the complexities of choice and control. Instead of grappling with the ways that choice-based games often assume ability, *Elsinore* erases Ophelia's experience living with a mental disability. The narratives we tell about disability matter; as Siebers writes, disability is an "elastic social category both subject to social control and capable of effecting social change" (2008, 4). Its elasticity stems from the breadth of this identity category, including wildly different experiences of disability, including mental, cognitive, developmental, and physical. Most importantly, disability has a reciprocal relationship with culture and society, which is why engaging with Ophelia's disability is vital.

We cannot continue to be the villagers in *Ophelia* who look away when faced with "extraordinary bodies," to use Rosemarie Garland-Thomson's term (2017, xii). We cannot continue to erase disabilities. As Garland-Thomson points out in her work *Staring:* increased disability presence and visibility in society changes how the abled view those with disability and it broadens our notions of what it is to be human. Disability representation in media has the same potentiality. If staring can be made into an occasion of learning, it "becomes a starer's quest to know and a staree's opportunity to be known" (Garland-Thomson 2009, 15). This beneficial and transformative staring force is what she calls "beholding," and it allows for a "mutual recognition" (Garland-Thomson 2009, 185). We need to truly behold the character of Ophelia, and welcome and acknowledge her many complexities and identities. Erasing Ophelia's disability suggests that the only way to be empowered or have agency over one's life is to be able-bodied. The implicit assumption in these adaptations is that the only way for Ophelia's story to end up happily is for her not to have a mental disability. She can survive as a biracial woman in Elsinore's court, but if she is "crazy" it would seem that ending up in a river drowned is her only possible conclusion. We need a new narrative of Ophelia, one that isn't ableist in its assumptions and concerns. We need the narrative where Ophelia is both living with her invisible disability and surviving with it.

NOTES

1. A few examples include Showalter, Elaine. 1992. "Representing Ophelia: Women, Madness and the Responsibilities of Feminist Criticism." In *Shakespearean Tragedy (Longman Critical Readers*, edited by John Drakakis, 280–295. London: Longman Publishing, as well as Neely, Carol Thomas. 2004. *Distracted Subjects: Madness and Gender in Shakespeare and Early Modern Culture*. Ithaca: Cornell University Press.

2. Just a few recent examples include the casting of Tilda Swinton as The Ancient One in *Dr. Strange*, even though in the comics the character is of Tibetan descent, as well as the casting of Johnny Depp (another white actor) as Tonto (a character who is explicitly Native American) in *The Lone Ranger*.

3. *Elsinore* doesn't follow the traditional narrative of most choice-based games or have the usual branching mechanics where a choice is given to the player who has to make a decision that is clearly marked in how it will affect the outcomes.

There is a lot more trial and error required. There is risk at play in the choices the player makes; Ophelia can be murdered or locked away based on sharing the wrong information with the wrong person at the wrong time. There are some moments in In Elsinore (only a few) where a window comes up to give a "Yes" or "No" choice to the player. Usually, this is a consent-based situation, such as Ophelia deciding whether to rekindle her romance with Hamlet or kissing one of her alternate love interests like Othello, Guildenstern, Grace, or Claudius. Although, I must note different games use branching mechanics in wildly different ways when it comes to the level of certainty a player can have going into their decision on how their choice manifests. The point and click choice games (like *The Walking Dead* and *Game of Thrones*) made by Telltale Games (now defunct) would have a script appear at the bottom of the screen that tells you that the character you are speaking to will remember your choice. Other games like *Mass Effect* build in a level of surprise or uncertainty. Sometimes the dialogue choices lead to actions that a player couldn't have anticipated and may quickly perhaps regret. Just one example being that a player choosing the answer "They know better" in response to a reporter asking if the Citadel has requested Shepard prioritize their agenda over Earth leads to Shepard punching the reporter in the face (*Mass Effect*, 2007).

WORKS CITED

Chellas, Semi. *Ophelia*, directed by Claire McCarthy. Covert Media, 2018.
Elsinore. Created by Katie Chironis and Connor Fallon. Golden Glitch Studios, 2019.
Game of Thrones: A Telltale Games Series. Directed by Martin Montgomery et al., designed by Ryan Kaufman and Matt Allmer. Telltale Games, 2014–2015.
Garland-Thomson, Rosemarie. *Extraordinary Bodies: Figuring Physical Disability in American Culture and Literature*. Vol. Twentieth anniversary edition. New York: Columbia University Press, 2017.
Garland-Thomson, Rosemarie. *Staring: How We Look*. Oxford: Oxford University Press, 2009.
Ingram, Jackson. 2015. "Interview: Elsinore Developer Gives us New Insights into Ophelia's Heroic Comeback." *Game Skinny*, June 24, 2015. https://www.game-skinny.com/akzwd/interview-elsinore-developer-gives-us-new-insights-into-ophelias-heroic-comeback.
Ingram, Richard A. "Doing Mad Studies: Making (Non) Sense Together." *Intersectionalities: A Global Journal of Social Work Analysis, Research, Polity, and Practice* 5, no. 3 (2016): 11–17.
Klein, Lisa. "Acknowledgements." In *Ophelia*. London: Bloomsbury Press, 2006.
Klein, Lisa. *Ophelia*. London: Bloomsbury Press, 2006.
Kudlick, Catherine J. "Disability History: Why We Need Another 'Other.'" *The American Historical Review* 108, no. 3 (2003): 763–93.
Lachenal, Jessica. "The Mary Sue Interview: Katie Chironis and Connor Fallon on Elsinore." *The Mary Sue*, May 1, 2015. https://www.themarysue.com/tms-elsinore-interview/.

Levi, Sandra J. "Ableism." In *Encyclopedia of Disability*, edited by Gary L. Albrecht, vol. 1 (2006): 1–4. SAGE Reference. Gale eBooks.

Mass Effect. Created by Casey Hudson, Preston Watamaniuk, and Drew Karpyshyn. BioWare, 2007.

More, Thomas. *The Complete Works of St. Thomas More*, vol. 9, edited by J. B. Trapp. New Haven: Yale University Press, 1979.

Neely, Carol Thomas. *Broken Nuptials in Shakespeare's Plays*. Champaign: University of Illinois Press, 1993.

Neely, Carol Thomas. *Distracted Subjects: Madness and Gender in Shakespeare and Early Modern Culture*. Ithaca: Cornell University Press, 2004.

Pipher, Mary. *Reviving Ophelia: Saving the Selves of Adolescent Girls*. New York: Riverhead Books, 2005.

Salkeld, Duncan. *Madness and Drama in the Age of Shakespeare*. Manchester: Manchester University Press, 1994.

Shakespeare, William. "Hamlet." In *The Norton Shakespeare: Tragedies 3rd Ed.*, edited by Stephen Greenblatt. New York: W. W. Norton, 2016.

Showalter, Elaine. "Representing Ophelia: Women, Madness and the Responsibilities of Feminist Criticism." In *Shakespearean Tragedy (Longman Critical Readers)*, edited by John Drakakis, 280–95. London: Longman Publishing, 1992.

Siebers, Tobin. *Disability Theory*. Ann Arbor: University of Michigan Press, 2008.

The Walking Dead: The Game. Directed and designed by Sean Vanaman et al. Telltale Games, 2012.

Chapter 8

"You're All about 'Crazy'"

Rendering the Visibility of Trauma in Alias and Jessica Jones

Whitney Hardin

The arrival of Netflix series *Jessica Jones* in 2015 came as something of a surprise. In an otherwise masculine landscape of superhero films and television shows (broken only by supporting female characters, the inclusion of Black Widow on the otherwise male Avengers team, and exceptions such as the DC/CW show *Supergirl*, which premiered a month before *Jessica Jones*), a superhero story with a strong female lead was refreshing. The character of Jessica Jones is a relatively recent one, introduced in the comic book series *Alias*, a twenty-eight-issue series published by Marvel Comics, running from 2001 to 2003 and fronted by writer Brian Michael Bendis and artist Michael Gaydos. The opening season of Netflix's *Jessica Jones*, which draws on *Alias*, differs from the comic in several ways, not the least of which is a definitively female production team, led by creator Melissa Rosenburg and supported by a number of female staff writers and story editors.

The existence of *Jessica Jones* speaks to the current "age of the superhero"; the last two decades have brought numerous adaptations of superhero narratives to screens big and small (Hardin and Kiernan, forthcoming). This insurgence of comic narratives within various popular culture milieus is noteworthy for multiple reasons; however, this chapter is concerned primarily with Germaine's (2016) observation that heroes and heroines who "symbolize strength, courage, and invincibility" are also often "battling disability, depression, and disease." Characters who bring together these two elements are important in terms of audience consumption and awareness because—when told thoughtfully and critically—narratives of disability, particularly mental disability, can potentially ignite moments of genuine change. To date, however, attention to disability in superheroes has been predominantly seated in androcentric, physical disability; this chapter extends work in this field to consider mental disability through the lens of disability studies with a focus on Jessica Jones, a female character diagnosed with PTSD. This chapter looks at both *Alias* and the first season of *Jessica Jones*—the latter of which derives from the source text in ways that later seasons do not. The protagonist of both series is Jessica Jones, a hardboiled detective with a shadowy past; the primary similarities across the two narratives are framed by Jessica's character development, which is impacted by trauma, including PTSD. As audiences move through either text, a combination of visual and textual narrative choices, including flashback, art style, and character interactions, work to articulate Jessica's experiences of trauma.

From a disability lens, the narrative choices of rendering trauma visible across both texts are noteworthy because, in a literal sense, the visual media allow both *Alias* and *Jessica Jones* to represent trauma in new ways; in a less literal sense, both source text and adaptation make visible some of the burdens of trauma, especially for women, who may be required to prove to others that their trauma exists, particularly when a male abuser is involved. Both texts offer examples of the ways that "comics represent a rich but fraught medium for mapping the ways that bodies are shaped by disability and trauma—and also how they might re-shape these experiences" (Jacobs and Dolmage 2012, 70). Attention to these moves emphasize shifting approaches to how audiences consume narratives of trauma; in illustrating these choices this chapter examines the positioning of PTSD in terms of the social model of disability and the normalization and acceptance of trauma in popular media. Superhero stories, especially, have rarely confronted mental disability and trauma outside of leveraging them as hero or villain motivation or as plot devices; Jessica Jones is an important point of analysis because hers is one of the few stories that engages directly and realistically with trauma, specifically PTSD. Moreover, rather than depicting trauma as an affliction of men, particularly men of war—the traumatized (male) veteran is a common trope in pop culture, so much so that another Netflix superhero show, *The Punisher*, features a protagonist who is traumatized first by his experiences as a military sniper, and then by the violent deaths of his family—*Alias* and *Jessica Jones* depict trauma as something more common, harder to recognize, and more likely to be experienced by women. Jessica's trauma is not the result of impersonal yet spectacular acts of violence by faceless enemies, but a violence that is intimate, subtle, and often hidden by the trappings of romantic/sexual love.

Accordingly, this chapter summarizes some of the ways that representations of trauma, particularly PTSD, have been addressed both in the field of disability studies and in comics and superhero narratives more broadly. Following this, Jessica Jones, as a character in both *Alias* and *Jessica Jones* is analyzed, with attention to how these two texts render visible Jessica's experience of trauma and its ongoing impact in her life. Finally, in how other characters in the texts respond to Jessica, both the comic and Netflix series pay heed to rendering visible some of the burdens of trauma, specifically for women who may be asked to justify, prove, and perform their trauma for disbelieving audiences.

REPRESENTATIONS OF TRAUMA: A SURVEY OF DISABILITY STUDIES AND COMICS NARRATIVES

Dominant representations of trauma, including PTSD, in popular media are androcentric and focused primarily on male narratives of war (Powell 2014; Wilson 2020; Rothe 2011; etc.); however, as discussed below, these reductive depictions of trauma are problematic given their dismissal of the many commonplace sexual aggressions and microaggressions experienced daily by women. This section, in unpacking this neglect of female trauma across popular media, opens with an examination of what PTSD is, moves to consider how the field of disability has discussed PTSD to date, and closes with attention to the ways that trauma has been addressed in superhero narratives.

The American Psychological Association defines trauma as "an emotional response to a terrible event" ("Trauma and Shock" 2021). The experience of trauma can be tied to a single event (such as a near-death experience), or as something ongoing (the experience of a long-term abusive relationship, or long-term insecurity about food or shelter)—it is also possible to experience multiple sources of trauma at the same time. It is important to note that this definition locates trauma not inside the event itself, but in the person responding. Carter (2021) argues that while anyone can experience a catastrophic event or hardship, trauma "is marked by an affective embodiment that disrupts the ability to perform the hegemonic standards of personhood" and is thus tied "not to the horrendousness of the event or events, but rather to the debilitating sociopolitical responses and the overlapping attributes of instability that often accompany it."

Although the two terms are often used interchangeably, PTSD can be distinguished from trauma and is usually regarded as an ongoing, disruptive response to trauma. In other words, while an emotional response to catastrophe or hardship is regarded as normal, a person who continues to experience an intense emotional response long after the event is over is said to be suffering from PTSD. As Snipes et al. (2017) note, common signs of PTSD include intrusive symptoms such as flashbacks to the traumatic event(s), avoidance of people or situations that trigger memories of the traumatic events(s), negative affect, and hyperarousal (2454). Moreover, as explained by the American Psychiatric Association (2021),

PTSD has been known by many names in the past, such as "shell shock" during the years of World War I and "combat fatigue" after World War II, but PTSD does not just happen to combat veterans. PTSD can occur in all people, of any ethnicity, nationality or culture, and at any age.

Of note within this definition is the lack of attention to gender—a common reality within medical landscapes, which tend to favor the heteronomative male experience—and while this definition goes on to note that "women are twice as likely as men to have PTSD," the details of this remain vague and underdeveloped (APA 2021). This negligence has been noted by Judith Herman (2015) who explains that "not until the women's liberation movement of the 1970s was it recognized that the most common post-traumatic disorders are those not of men of war but of women in civilian life" (28); moreover, "women are at an increased risk of developing PTSD in general" (Snipes et al. 2017, 2456). Yet, narratives of PTSD in popular media remain androcentric.

While scholarly intersections in trauma and disability studies would appear to best engage academic understandings of PTSD, for the most part the field of trauma studies has largely proceeded independently of the field of disability studies. This may be the result of the often-psychological nature of trauma; early work in disability studies is concerned primarily with physical, or visible, arguments of bodily oppression, where "disability studies, with its emphasis on the body and not the mind, [has] create[d] fissures through which attention to the mentally disabled easily falls" (Prendergast 2001, 46). While current scholarship in disability studies strives to encompass both physical and mental disability, disability studies overall has been "remarkably silent on matters of the traumatic origins of many disabilities, and on the ongoing relationship between shocking events, their abrupt and chronic impacts, and experiences of disability" (Morrison and Casper 2012). This silence is perhaps especially surprising, given disability studies' increased attention to mental disability and the fact that "much psychiatric disability is closely linked to trauma" (Nicki 2001, 80). Noting this, and the greater likelihood that those living with mental disability will also be exposed to trauma, there is little reason to exclude trauma, and representations of trauma, from the realm of disability studies. To fully understand "the many ways that the disabled body is constructed is [therefore also] a means of recognizing the social (and rhetorical) construction of all bodies" (Jacobs and Dolmage 2012, 75). To refuse to recognize trauma as part of this social/rhetorical construction can only provide an incomplete understanding of the disabled body.

As referenced above, superhero and comics narratives offer one inroad to recognize the social construction(s) of trauma as represented across popular media. Comics and adaptations of these narratives are important sites of scholarly attention because of their tendency to both erase and cement disability. Representations of physical disability are rare in the world of superheroes, and representations of mental and cognitive disability are especially limited, which is only exacerbated by the "unseen" nature of these disabilities. When invisible disabilities do appear in superhero stories, they are often tied to villains rather than heroes or are temporary states that the hero is able to throw off through an effort of will or a timely rescue by allies.

Trauma, on the other hand, is more pronounced in superhero stories. It is extremely common for heroes (again, largely male heroes) to be motivated by trauma. Popular heroes such as Batman, Robin/Nightwing, Spider-Man, Daredevil, and The Punisher are motivated to fight crime after experiencing the violent deaths of their loved ones. In these instances, the ongoing effects of trauma are seldom explored in realistic ways—not only does trauma fail to keep these heroes from functioning, it is presented as the driving force that allows them to function at greater-than-human levels. More recent depictions have made more of an attempt to grapple realistically with trauma. The Marvel Cinematic Universe's 2013 *Iron Man 3* shows its protagonist suffering from debilitating panic attacks, the result of traumatic events in a previous film. Moreover, when writer Gail Simone was tapped to write a rebooted Batgirl series, she reached out to real-life clinician Dr. Andrea Letamendi for advice on realistically depicting Batgirl's response to trauma at the hands of the Joker; Dr. Letamendi was eventually incorporated into the comic as Batgirl's psychologist (Hayasaki 2015). A few years later, writer Tom King and artist Clay Mann created *Heroes in Crisis*, a limited series running from September 2018 to May 2019, which was devoted explicitly to answering the question of how a wide variety of heroes in the DC universe experience and attempt to navigate PTSD. In spite of these developments PTSD is still often depicted as the province of men, treated as something motivating (for heroes) or the source of their evil deeds (for villains); as something that can be overcome by an effort of will. *Alias*' and *Jessica Jones*' embodiments of PTSD offer rare exceptions and are important points of analysis because Jessica's narrative renders trauma visible and, in turn, offers a glimpse into the ways that comics are attempting to shape social representations of mental health and disability across popular media.

What *Alias* and *Jessica Jones* allow for is—in the very least—recognition and acknowledgement of representations of trauma that are heterogeneous and discordant, a viewing reality that is largely missing across both popular and transmedia narratives of PTSD.

The following sections discuss how the two texts allow for divergent narrative choices when storying trauma, including PTSD.

A CRITICAL ANALYSIS OF PTSD IN
ALIAS AND *JESSICA JONES*

Both *Alias* and *Jessica Jones* focus on Jessica Jones, a no-nonsense private investigator haunted by her past and who often turns to alcohol and sex in order to escape. This past is marked by multiple instances of trauma, including the deaths of Jessica's family members in a car accident; the discovery that she has superpowers; an ill-fated career as an active superhero; and her eventual kidnapping, exploitation, and violation by the Purple Man—a supervillain with mind-control powers. Both the source comic and its Netflix adaptation introduce us to Jessica after these events have happened to her, revealing her past over a series of issues and episodes (respectively).

Despite these similarities, there are also notable differences between the two versions of Jessica's story. *Alias* provides Jessica with a superhero name (Jewel) and costume, and a short-lived career that brings her into contact with more famous heroes such as the Avengers; one of Jessica's only friends is Carol Danvers (Captain Marvel), and Scott Lang (Ant-Man) features as a love interest. *Jessica Jones*, however, downplays Jessica's status as a superhero and presents her as an anonymous vigilante; Trish Walker (not yet in her Hellcat persona) takes the place of Carol as Jessica's closest female friend, and although Jessica still associates with Luke Cage (also not yet in his superhero persona), she doesn't otherwise engage with the wider universe of superheroes. Moreover, the primary villain of *Alias*—the Purple Man—is stripped of his supervillain name in *Jessica Jones* and altered from a public figure with purple skin and a history of conflict with other superheroes (notably Daredevil) to an average-looking private citizen whose predatory behavior has largely gone unnoticed. Even his surname is slightly altered in the show, from Killgrave to Kilgrave. In *Alias* we don't encounter this villain until the last four issues of the comic's twenty-eight-issue run—although Jessica's past with him is hinted at earlier in her interactions with other characters. In *Jessica Jones*, however, her past with the Purple Man is the focus of the entire first season.

What both adaptations share, however, is a blunt look at how Jessica has been shaped by trauma. Specifically, in both the comic and Netflix series trauma is about violence, coercion, and sex. Killgrave/Kilgrave causes Jessica to experience physical, sexual, and psychological violence, and forces her to engage in physical and sexual acts against her will. In the television series, while we never see Kilgrave having sex with Jessica, we learn about this sexual trauma through conversations (Rosenberg "AKA WWJD?," 2015). In the first of these Kilgrave says to Jessica "I promise I won't touch you until I get your genuine consent," hinting at a past of nonconsensual sex; in a later exchange in this same episode it is made explicit that, for Kilgrave, there was neither consent nor any admission of culpability in their shared past:

Kilgrave: We used to do a lot more than just touch hands.
Jones: Yeah—It's called rape.
Kilgrave: What? Which part of staying in five-star hotels, eating in all the best places, doing whatever the hell you wanted, is rape?
Jones: The part where I didn't want to do any of it!

In the comic, although Jessica says that she didn't have sex with Killgrave and rejects the label of rape when asked about it (Bendis and Gaydos "Issue #18," 2015), she makes it clear that their relationship was nonetheless sexualized. For instance, Jessica experiences flashbacks in which Killgrave has forced her into various states of undress, and describes instances where he had her bathe him and lay at his feet, made her watch him have sex with others, and beg him to have sex with her. While Bendis has indicated that *Alias*'s reluctance to call Killgrave's behavior rape was an attempt to avoid an admittedly over-used narrative device (Hurley 2016), it also contributes to a harmful discourse about what "counts" as sexual assault. As a result, this chapter contends that while it is important to respect Jessica's understanding of what happened to her, *Alias*'s wholesale rejection of the term doesn't have to mean we, as viewers, also have to reject it. In both adaptations, the trauma Jessica experiences at the hands of the Purple Man is clearly sexual.

Making Trauma Visible

In rendering Jessica's trauma visible, it is both texts' reliance on the narrativization of intrusive symptoms, most commonly portrayed via the subjective mode of flashback, that is most prevalent to this analysis. Flashbacks, particularly when used across the mediums of comics and television, are noteworthy points of inquiry due to their ability to combine verbiage and gesture to convey distress and "mental impairment" (Squier 2008). Comics, in their capacity to portray "embodiment through gesture, posture, and design choice; through choice of panel, frame and character; and through the conventions of character creation," are well situated to represent "how disability feels and what an impairment means socially for the disabled person" (Squier 2008). Moreover, in regard to both versions of Jessica, specific moments of said embodiment are rendered visible through the use of flashbacks. Flashbacks also point to shared circumstances of both medicine and popular media. The flashback, noted in medical terminology as "distressing, sensory-based involuntary memories of trauma . . . [which are also] the hallmark symptom of PTSD" (Borne et al. 2012, 1521), is a staple of popular media depictions of PTSD as well (De Bruyn 2014). As such, it is important to recognize the visual and gestural nature afforded to the trauma-induced flashback; it is not just simply a symptom but also a standard design choice in both comics and television, evidenced across both *Alias* and *Jessica Jones*.

Alias is especially focused on portraying elements such as gesture and posture during flashbacks. For instance, in spite of having something of a reputation for mouthing off, Jessica is often silent for long stretches of time, the audience getting her reaction through nonverbal means. During flashbacks to her past, we see that Jessica responds to moments of stress (e.g., being told by a social worker that someone wants to adopt her, being bullied at her high school, becoming free of Killgrave's mind control) without words, but with expressions of uncertainty, distress, or anger—close up shots of her face in these panels show her with brow furrowed, lips compressed, or eyes closed. Similar expressions of distress, and defensive body language, accompany her attempts to discuss the traumatic events of these flashbacks in the present. By including these "pre-verbal components," the medium of the comic adds a dimension to Jessica's narrative, allowing us to see not only what happened to her but also how she is physically impacted by reliving and communicating these events (Squier 2008).

In *Jessica Jones* flashbacks are used in the episodes leading up to the introduction of Kilgrave; in the first four episodes, Kilgrave is only present in the form of flashbacks, most of which are sensory-based and involuntary. These flashbacks are triggered as Jessica, in the role of PI, carries out an investigation that leads her to familiar Kilgrave haunts—many of which cue emotions of a traumatic, mind-controlled past. Visiting these places, Jessica suffers a string of flashbacks tied to place: streets, restaurants, and hotels. These flashbacks trigger (what come to be familiar) verbal and gestural responses, wherein the audience sees Jessica shift into fetal-like bodily contortions, accompanied by camera shots that are blurry and distorted as well as aural bass rhythms that are panicked and rapid, serving to both match and further dramatize Jessica's escalating pulse and erratic breathing. These flashbacks almost always end with an image of Jessica, body limp, reciting the names of the streets from her childhood neighborhood—an action that the audience later learns is a coping mechanism suggested by a medical professional to circumvent panic attacks. By including these verbal, gestural, and aural components, the medium of television adds a dimension to Jessica's narrative that allows the audience not just simply to learn about Jessica's past but also to experience the ways that trauma continues to physically impact her present.

Recognizing the ways that flashbacks are able to represent and embody trauma is important because, as Jacobs and Dolmage (2012) note, "Disability Studies theorists argue that attitudes towards disability are constructed powerfully through visual means" (80). These attitudes include not just simply the generation of sympathy for the character but also the opportunity to move closer to empathy—to experience what the disabled and traumatized person experiences. While verbal and nonverbal elements play a role here, so too does style, given that "different styles of illustration can also express . . . the disability experience" (Squier 2008). In *Alias*, during Jessica's long confession to Cage, readers experience several flashbacks, which are drawn in different artistic styles (these flashback sequences even include different creative teams). The flashback where Jessica reveals how her family died has a style reminiscent of the Silver Age of comics—in part, this choice makes continuity sense, as the flashback discloses that Jessica Jones and Peter Parker were classmates, and the character of Spider-Man emerged during the Silver Age, but it also suggests that Jessica's memories of that time are, like the style, simpler and less shadowed. By contrast, her flashbacks to being the superhero Jewel and coming under the thrall of the Purple Man are drawn in yet another style, this one closer to the style used in the bulk of the comic, but nonetheless distinct. The lines are more exaggerated, at times reminiscent of a cartoon, and Jessica is drawn with absurdly long legs and a tiny waist, with larger eyes and a wide smile. While this too might be paying homage to the dominant artistic style of an earlier decade, it also suggests that Jessica's memories of this time are disconnected from her present life—these events seem to have taken place in different worlds than those of the present.

In the Netflix series, flashbacks are not styled to indicate shifts in time, but like with *Alias* style in the show serves to represent distress. This distress, while often accompanied by muffled and cacophonic sound, is primarily visual. During the spatially triggered flashbacks images become warped and fold in upon themselves, images are also sped up and/or slowed down; these choices mimic Jessica's trauma-induced sensory overload, illustrating her consciousness moving from lucid and coherent to distorted and confused. And, while the *Jessica Jones* flashbacks do not necessarily offer the same depth of narrativizing Jessica's trauma as do the drawing styles in *Alias*, what both do attempt is to offer a story wherein the viewing audience witnesses the debilitating and demobilizing impact of trauma.

In these ways, both series can be positioned within a critical disability studies lens because both narrativize trauma as something "to be understood from the perspective of the person who experiences it" (Reaume 2014, 1248). These choices illustrate how *Alias* and *Jessica Jones* (and, thus, comics and comics adaptations more broadly) "can serve as incubators of understanding, which can promote positive societal attitudes regarding disability and depression" (Germaine 2016); in regard to representations of PTSD, it is important for audiences to not only hear about the trauma from the survivor but also witness the ways that trauma is physically debilitating. In *Alias*, this is achieved via artistic choices that serve to represent Jessica's pained silences and disconnections from the past; in *Jessica Jones*, this is achieved via distorted camera shots accompanied by sound discordance. These visual and aural choices are important sites of inquiry in regard to trauma and disability studies because they work to

> create a unique conversational dimension and can encourage disability, depression, and disease to be viewed and discussed in terms of visual representation and subsequent understanding . . . which offers a rich and diverse environment for such representation: superheroes may be depicted as disabled, depressed, or diseased, but the true benefit of this depiction is the resulting interpretation and exposure of their conditions. (Germaine 2016)

Accordingly, these representations serve to shape social models of disability—the ways that audiences understand, normalize, and accept trauma narratives—and, in turn, shape society's understanding of what it is to live with and experience mental disability seated in trauma.

The Visibility of Trauma's Social Expectations

As introduced above, in portraying trauma, both *Alias* and *Jessica Jones* attempt to make visible some of the unseen burdens of trauma, and the difficulties of narrativizing trauma. As Carter (2021) argues, those who have experienced trauma are pushed to tell their stories, and when they choose silence—even a productive silence—their audiences are likely to fill that silence with narratives that they find easier to accept. For women, in particular, it is not unusual for audiences to attempt to ignore or dismiss their experiences, denying that trauma occurred or discrediting its severity. In both the source text and adaptation, we see attempts by other characters to push Jessica's story onto one or another of these paths. As a result, in addition to living with the effects of what Killgrave/Kilgrave has done to her, Jessica is frequently forced to live with additional burdens. First, she is often required to prove to others that her trauma exists/that her abuse did happen. Second, even when her trauma is accepted, Jessica is pushed to narrate or perform her trauma in ways that satisfy the needs of the people around her.

Narratives of dismissiveness attempt to minimize or delegitimize trauma by insisting that what happened shouldn't be considered traumatic, that the person is misremembering, wrongly interpreting, and so on. In *Jessica Jones*, the decision to downplay Kilgrave's role as a supervillain shows one avenue for others to dismiss trauma. Unlike *Alias*, where his purple skin, over-the-top tantrums, and ludicrous commands make his mind control easier for others to detect and believe, in *Jessica Jones* Kilgrave's manipulation often takes the form of coercive control, rendering it invisible to others and enabling their disbelief that Jessica was abused at all.

Coercive control, which is most often used against women, is a means whereby victims "lose personal autonomy and safety" through micromanagement, erosion of support networks, and enforcement of stereotypical roles (Green 2019, 176). However, cultural assumptions about the passivity of women make coercive control harder to detect, and

> the notion that behaviours, such as persistent male attention, authoritative decision-making and jealousy, may be predatory and abusive can seem unthinkable to outsiders, partly because these are part of the formalized rituals of masculine courtship that are still culturally privileged as desirable. (Green 2019, 176)

Accordingly, Killgrave/Kilgrave takes the women he controls on dates, buys them gifts, or asks them to smile for him—all seemingly normal courtship behaviors.

The Netflix series draws particular attention to Kilgrave's fixation with smiling. Unlike *Alias*, where Jessica is usually drawn as wide-eyed and slightly slack-mouthed when under the Purple Man's thrall, the Kilgrave of *Jessica Jones* is much more concerned with keeping up appearances and with receiving this visual marker of pleasure from the women around him. As Hill (2015) notes, if the series "was the type of show to have a catchphrase line for each character, 'Smile,' would be Kilgrave's." Just thirty-two minutes into the first episode, a flashback shows us Kilgrave and Jessica together for the first time, a dinner scene in which he instructs her to smile (Rosenberg "AKA Ladies Night," 2017). Recurring references to Jessica not smiling across *Jessica Jones* serve to push back against both normative expectations of female passiveness and harmful narratives of dismissiveness. These culminate in the titling of the first season finale, "AKA Smile," where Jessica finally gets her revenge against Kilgrave.

> *Kilgrave:* My God, it's finally over. You're mine now. No more fighting. No more of these ugly displays. You'll be with me now. Look, after a while . . . however long it takes . . . I know . . . I know you will feel what I feel. *Let's start with a smile.* Tell me you love me (emphasis mine). (Rosenberg 2017)

In response, Jessica, smiling widely, looks past Kilgrave to Trish Walker, says "I love you," and then seconds later instructs Kilgrave to "Smile" before murdering him. This moment works to turn dismissiveness on its head, acknowledging Jessica's trauma and Kilgrave's coercive behavior in their final exchange. Despite this scene, however, the fact that Kilgrave is able to literally control his victims complicates matters throughout the season, his power functions as a metaphor for the helplessness coercive control can instill. Nevertheless, it is meaningful that in the first season finale of *Jessica Jones* we see the narrative turn its back on dismissiveness and legitimize Jessica's trauma.

That said, it takes thirteen episodes for those around Jessica to fully realize the actuality of her trauma. Part of the dismissal she experiences is tied to the fact that when not actively using his mind-control powers, Kilgrave's control of others, particularly Jessica, is difficult for others to detect. This is especially true in *Jessica Jones*, where Kilgrave appears at least somewhat invested in winning Jessica over without the use of his mind control. Moreover, by threatening to harm others if she doesn't comply, Kilgrave is able to coerce Jessica into playing house with him in her childhood home and to send him a photograph of herself every day. Because these "gestures of romance—avowals of affection, gifts, celebratory meals, regulated dominance—follow a desirable pattern of courtship and avowal," Jessica's trauma at Kilgrave's hands is often invisible to others (Green 2019, 176). The more his behavior resembles a normal relationship, and the more he is able to force her complicity in participating in the facade, the easier her trauma is for others to dismiss.

By and large, in both source text and adaptation Jessica is forced to spend significant time and energy trying to *convince* people, and the primary narrative embraced by those around her remains one of dismissal. Others regularly mistake her behavior not as tied to trauma, but as the result of simply being someone who is unreliable, a user, a screw-up, a drunk, a bitch, etc. In *Jessica Jones* this dismissal is also situated within the now defunct medical diagnosis of female hysteria, which was framed as a way to control and dismiss women's emotions. In the episode titled: "AKA 99 Friends" characters dismiss Jessica's concerns about Kilgrave and his surveillance of her, with one stating: "You need to pull yourself together, you are coming across as distinctly paranoid" (Rosenberg 2017). While *Alias* never frames Jessica's reactions explicitly in terms of female hysteria, it's certainly hinted at in the reactions of her friends. One on occasion, having pushed Jessica to talk about her past until she flees his apartment, Scott Lang is indignant and confrontational in their next conversation, saying, "That night—all I was trying to do was *listen* to you and *be* there for you. But you screamed and stormed out," and later accusing her of being "all about 'crazy'" (Bendis and Gaydos "Issue #21," 2015). In another exchange, Jessica asks Scott to leave her alone, attempting more than once to tell him what she needs, only to be repeatedly cut off. In the face of her refusal to conform to his expectations or to accept his reading of the situation, Scott accuses her of being unreasonable: "So, see? See how you're being all paranoid and no one has done *anything* even *remotely* bad to you?" When he once again cuts her off, she chooses (again) to flee, getting out of the cab and yelling "I'll call you later. Respect my fucking boundaries!" (Bendis and Gaydos "Issue #24," 2015). Although this is the only time that Jessica explicitly frames this request in terms of boundaries, it is a request she makes implicitly multiple times over the course of *Alias*. Just as others find it inconceivable to allow Jessica to be silent or to tell her story on her own terms and in her own time, they seem similarly incapable of acknowledging or respecting her boundaries. Consequently, the narrative of dismissiveness often forces Jessica to carry a double (or even triple) burden—first, of living with trauma, but also the necessity of convincing others that this trauma is real, and of doing so in ways that her audience is prepared to take seriously. Similarly, in *Jessica Jones*, we see Jessica struggling against the character Will Simpson, a secondary antagonist who vehemently refuses to believe Jessica until he himself falls under the spell of Kilgrave, and who even then consistently overrides Jessica's plans or advice with his own. As Simpson repeatedly doubts Jessica's claims about Kilgrave, and dismisses her warnings that he isn't equipped to deal with him, we see the consequences as Jessica misses opportunities to stop Kilgrave or sees others being put in harm's way. While Simpson no doubt believes he's aiding Jessica, by dismissing her experience, he compounds her state of mental distress.

This dismissal is further evidenced in *Alias* when Jessica first begins to tell Luke Cage about her history with Killgrave, who responds by asking "The Purple fucker? Guy looks at you and makes you do whatever he says?" and later comments "Guy's a little fuck with an attitude" (Bendis and Gaydos "Issue #25," 2015). Although Cage quickly begins taking her seriously, his initial reaction is to dismiss the Purple Man, and thus, anything Jessica might have suffered at his hands. Later, when Jessica confronts Killgrave, he hints at special knowledge that the two of them shared—a real intimacy that she isn't acknowledging or sharing when she tells her story—again casting doubt on her account (Bendis and Gaydos "Issue #27," 2015). The result of this burden in *Alias* is that at times even Jessica appears to doubt herself. She tells Luke Cage:

> In my *mind*, I can't tell the difference between what he *made* me do or say and what I do or say on my own. The only reason I know I wasn't in *love* with him is that I say to myself: How *could* I be? I *hate* him. That's it. That's what my sanity is holding on to. "How *could* I be?" But that's where it ends. Other than *that* it feels like I *was* in love with him. (Bendis and Gaydos "Issue #25," 2015) Emphasis in original.

This excerpt is especially telling because, unlike *Jessica Jones* where Jessica is certain of her assault, in *Alias* we see Jessica both questioning and, in turn, almost dismissing the trauma forced upon her by Killgrave. In all these instances, Jessica is forced into impossible situations, dealing with the daily burden of trauma, as well as the expectations and demands placed on her by her friends and allies.

While the two versions of Jessica's story narrativize, and even recognize, her trauma differently, what both attempt to do is provide audiences with an experience that validates the impacts of trauma-induced mental disability. Through visually representing intrusive symptoms, like the flashback, as well as the ways that the source comic and the Netflix adaptation thwart what have come to be recognized as normative narratives of female trauma, both texts strive to provide a story that moves away from hegemonic and androcentric representations of PTSD. In these ways, the source comic and the Netflix adaptation make an attempt to provide realistic depictions of female trauma and in doing so work to provide their viewing audiences with renderings of sexual violence that broaden their understanding of how PTSD can manifest in women who have experienced sexual trauma.

WORKS CITED

American Psychiatric Association. "What is PTSD?" 2021. https://www.psychiatry.org/patients-families/ptsd/what-is-ptsd.

Bendis, Brian Michael and Michael Gaydos. *Jessica Jones: Alias*. Vols. 1–4. Marvel, 2015.

Bourne, Corin, C. E. Mackay, and Emily A. Holmes. "The neural basis of flashback formation: The impact of viewing trauma." *Psychological Medicine* 43, no. 7 (2013): 1521–32.

Carter, Angela. "When silence said everything: Reconceptualizing trauma through critical disability studies." *Lateral* 10, no. 1 (2021).

De Bruyn, Dirk Cornelis. *The Performance of Trauma in Moving Image Art*. Cambridge Scholars Publishing, 2014.

Germaine, Alison Elizabeth. "Disability and depression in Thor comic books." *Disability Studies Quarterly* 36, no. 3 (2016).

Green, Stephanie. "Fantasy, gender, and power in *Jessica Jones*." *Continuum* 33, no. 2 (Jan. 2019): 173–84.

Hardin, Whitney and Julia Kiernan. (Forthcoming). "The multiverse paradigm and the reinvention of *Legion*." In L. Piatti-Farnell (Ed.), *Parallel Universes: Remaking Superheroes in Film and Popular Media*. Lanham: Lexington Books/Rowman & Littlefield.

Hayasaki, Erika. "How a psychologist who loves cosplay became a comic book character." *The Atlantic*. Atlantic Media Company, January 27, 2015. https://www.theatlantic.com/health/archive/2015/01/batgirls-psychologist/384661/.

Herman, Judith Lewis. *Trauma and Recovery: The Aftermath of Violence–from Domestic Abuse to Political Terror*. Hachette UK, 2015.

Hill, Libby. "'Smile!' How a Villain's Phrase in 'Jessica Jones' Exposes Modern-Day Sexism." *Los Angeles Times*. Los Angeles Times, November 24, 2015. https://

www.latimes.com/entertainment/herocomplex/la-et-hc-jessica-jones-smile-sexism-20151123-story.html.

Hurley, Laura. "How Jessica Jones' creator feels about the show's biggest change from the comics." *Cinemablend*. June 30, 2016. http://www.cinemablend.com/television/1529159/how-jessica-jones-creator-feels-about-the-shows-biggest-change-from-the-comics.

Nicki, Andrea. "The abused mind: Feminist theory, psychiatric disability, and trauma." *Hypatia* 16, no. 4 (2001): 80–104.

Nicki, Andrea. "Feminist philosophy of disability, care ethics and mental illness." *Nursing Philosophy* 3, no. 3 (2002): 270–72.

Powell, Laura. "Glorification of the military in popular culture and the media." *Good Intentions* 4 (2014): 167.

Prendergast, Catherine. "On the rhetorics of mental disability." *Embodied Rhetorics: Disability in Language and Culture* (2001): 45–60.

Rakes, H. "Crip feminist trauma studies in Jessica Jones and beyond." *Journal of Literary & Cultural Disability Studies* 13, no. 1 (2019): 75–91.

Reaume, Geoffrey. "Understanding critical disability studies." *CMAJ* 186, no. 16 (2014): 1248–49.

Rosenberg, Melissa. "AKA ladies night." Episode. *Jessica Jones* 1, no. 1. Netflix, November 20, 2015.

Rosenberg, Melissa. "AKA 99 friends." Episode. *Jessica Jones* 1, no. 4. Netflix, November 20, 2015.

Rosenberg, Melissa. "AKA WWJD?" Episode. *Jessica Jones* 1, no. 8. Netflix, November 20, 2015.

Rosenberg, Melissa. "AKA smile." Episode. *Jessica Jones* 1, no. 13. Netflix, November 20, 2015.

Rothe, Anne. *Popular Trauma Culture: Selling the Pain of Others in the Mass Media*. Rutgers University Press, 2011.

Snipes, Daniel J., Jenna M. Calton, Brooke A. Green, Paul B. Perrin, and Eric G. Benotsch. "Rape and Posttraumatic Stress Disorder (PTSD): Examining the mediating role of explicit sex–power beliefs for men versus women." *Journal of Interpersonal Violence* 32, no. 16 (2017): 2453–70.

Squier, Susan M. "So long as they grow out of it: Comics, the discourse of developmental normalcy, and disability." *Journal of Medical Humanities* 29, no. 2 (2008): 71–88.

"Trauma and Shock." American Psychological Association. American Psychological Association. Accessed August 30, 2021. https://www.apa.org/topics/trauma.

Wilson, Graeme John. "'When the Gunfire Ends': Deconstructing PTSD Among Military Veterans in Marvel's The Punisher." *Popular Culture Studies Journal* 8, no. 1 (2020): 101.

Chapter 9

Subspaces Run through Your Head

Scott Pilgrim, *Intertextuality,* and *Visualizing the Traumatized Mind*

Guy Spriggs

Near the end of *Scott Pilgrim's Precious Little Life* (2004), the first volume in Bryan Lee O'Malley's *Scott Pilgrim* graphic novel series (2004–2010), the title character's band Sex Bob-omb takes the stage for a set when their opening song is interrupted by a new character who crashes through the venue's ceiling, flying toward the band and looking for a fight. Unfazed, Scott sets down his bass guitar and heroically steps in front of his bandmates before blocking the attack and reversing it with a devastating punch of his own. The attacker is revealed to have "mystical powers," which include the ability to shoot fireballs and summon "demon hipster chicks" (O'Malley 2004), but surprisingly doesn't seem much of a challenge for the heretofore listless Scott. After Scott himself flies to deliver the final punch, his opponent—shocked at being overwhelmed so easily—vanishes with a "poom" and leaves behind coins as a reward. Scott then leaves the failed concert with mysterious new girlfriend Ramona Flowers, who explains the story's plot to him and the reader. The flying, fireball-throwing attacker was the first of Ramona's "evil exes," and for Scott to continue to date her—the literal girl of his dreams—he'll have to fight and defeat six more: a professional skateboarder turned actor, a rock star with psychic powers enabled by veganism, a teleporting lesbian "half-ninja," a pair of twin experts in robotics, and the vengeful record producer who organized these evil exes to sabotage Ramona's future suitors.

Of course, we recognize the fantastical turn at the end of *Scott Pilgrim's Precious Little Life* (2004) as something other than normal. But Scott's bandmates and friends in the audience don't respond with shock or amazement at what they see but instead comment on the battle as it unfolds, questioning the strategy of Scott's opponent—"Doesn't he know Scott's the best fighter in the province?"—and counting his consecutive landed punches as he goes for a video game-style "air juggle" (O'Malley 2004). That's because these sorts of things are actually ordinary for the storyworld of *Scott Pilgrim*, which until this point followed aimless twenty-something Scott through his lonely dreams and awkward romantic pursuits. One of the hallmarks of O'Malley's graphic novel series is its incorporation of stylized violence that seems unbelievable even by superhero comic book standards into a story built around traditional, familiar story dynamics that curiously reasserts its grounding in a real place (Toronto). This kind of scene—which becomes commonplace over the next five volumes of the *Scott Pilgrim* series—reflects the intertextuality and hyperactive tone that can encourage reductive readings of the content as simply a goofy or kooky riff on coming-of-age and/or boy-meets-girl archetypes. More importantly, however, the storyworld elements introduced at the end of *Scott Pilgrim's Precious Little Life* (2004) help establish a broad, complex system of representing mental illness that reframes the series as a novel portrait of loss, failure, trauma, and potential growth.

O'Malley's *Scott Pilgrim* series and its 2010 film adaptation are more than intertextual works, they are worlds constructed around and seen through the eyes of an intertextual character: Scott is a protagonist and narrator whose perspective is dependent almost entirely on his understanding of pre-existing texts and conventions. The style of the *Scott Pilgrim* graphic novel series in particular is more than simple allusion, it reflects Julia Kristeva's description of the text as a "permutation" of preexisting creations (1980, 36), a "mosaic" connecting texts and containing intersections of culture and ideology (1980, 60). What makes the *Scott Pilgrim* series an interesting case study for understanding the confluence of trauma, mental illness, and adaptation is that Scott's mental illness seems to be hyper-referentiality or intertextuality itself. Scott is a traumatized subject, constantly reliving a breakup that leaves him lost, his resulting limited cognition manifests itself through the graphic novels' highly referential style. Scott is not just a character involved in a romance or stuck in a state of perpetual adolescence, but he also seems incapable of understanding the world around him except through mediated frames and references, mainly (but not limited to) video games. Scott is also incapable of developing a sense of narrative, understanding how events cohere as part of a larger whole or fit into even a personal idea of the past, present, and future. These aspects of Scott's cognition are reflected in his relationship to the setting of the graphic novel series: just as Scott fails to realize other people have lives themselves or that things happen when he's not around, the representations of his environment, memory, and state of mind are direct manifestations of his limited ability to process the world. Stylized insertions—from pop-up bubbles detailing local history to special items and tokens to progress bars for ordinary functions like working and going to the bathroom and much,

much more—serve as constant reminders of Scott's central place within the text and the traumatized state of mind he not only lives with but also must communicate through.

Perhaps unsurprisingly, Edgar Wright's 2010 film adaptation complicates the graphic novels' portrait of trauma and mental illness, but not through simple infidelity to the source material. Despite Wright's profound interest in visual storytelling as a director, his cinematic adaptation minimizes a more nuanced portrayal of damaged states of mind to expand the graphic novels' hyper-referentiality. Wright's film offers important insights into the complexity of adaptation, revealing how works being translated to a new medium compete with other influences and conventions. These complexities result in a cleaner, simpler storyworld, where trauma and depression are essentially surface-level concerns, able to be resolved through nonpsychological, nonemotional means. If faithful adaptation assumes the "creator's aim to reproduce" the source text, as Linda Hutcheon argues (2006, 4), then Wright's approach to fidelity seems separate from much of the graphic novels' thematic investments. By embracing the visual while abandoning its connection to the interiority of the self as seen in the graphic novels, *Scott Pilgrim vs. the World* (2010) demonstrates the tremendous capacity of adaptation and the cinematic medium while sacrificing explorations that might lead to better understanding of the ways different traumas assert themselves in lived experience.

Approaches to the *Scott Pilgrim* graphic novel series and its film adaptation tend to engage in some type of formal analysis, trying to account for and understand its kinetic, hyper-referential style. For commentary on *Scott Pilgrim vs. the World* (2010) in particular, examining the film's steady barrage of influences seems to take precedent over understanding it in relation to its source text(s). Interestingly, questions of fidelity to source material—the frustratingly prevalent metric and ideal most responsible for the rise of adaptation studies in recent decades—have gone largely unasked. Jason Rothery and Benjamin Woo offer an explanation for this in "Mutatis Mutandis: Constructing Fidelity in the Comic Book Film Adaptation," suggesting the comic creator serves as "guarantor" of an adaptation's faithfulness (2017, 133). Bryan Lee O'Malley's assurance that Wright's film adaptation captures "the *feeling* of his work"—despite profound changes—encourages closer examination of the relationship between form, theme, and content across these works rather than rigorous side-by-side plot or visual comparison (Rothery and Woo 2017, 133, emphasis in original). Regardless, the tendency to overlook or minimize the story's actual content and its relationship to form creates new demand for critical engagement with the adaptation process relating these texts. While the visual and narrative styles of both iterations of *Scott Pilgrim* may deserve the attention they've received, the minimal engagement with their content undermines the potential for understanding how its systems of reference and intertextuality might actually be used in service of story, character, meaning, and representation. Ultimately, these perspectives on the *Scott Pilgrim* graphic novel series and its film adaptation affirm the value of approaching these works with an eye toward representations of mental illness. Understanding Scott's traumatic experiences, the mental illness they cause, and Ramona's own fantastical suffering offers new substance for what could otherwise be ungrounded observation and meaningful connection for unnecessarily singular critical approaches.

Even positive film reviews for *Scott Pilgrim vs. the World* (2010) separate its form from content, engaging its story only for its application of established character and narrative archetypes. Writing in *The New York Times*, critic A.O. Scott mentions the film's "kinetic visual wit"—which he considers a trademark of Wright's style—but is otherwise more focused on how *Scott Pilgrim vs. the World* (2010) acknowledges the struggles of youth (2010). Fellow critic Ty Burr is less convinced of the film's capacity for real meaning and feeling, resulting from its "stutter-stop speed" and video game inserts (such as "extra lives"), which he offers as a sort of ideal for how young adults want to experience life (2010). In his popular video review series "Escape to the Movies with Movie Bob," Bob Chapman contends the film directs its conflicts and emotions through pop culture frames "because that's how a guy of Scott's age and temperament might contextualize his world" (2010). The minimizing of the cognitive limitations informing Scott's behavior and perspective reflected in these reviews demonstrates the drive to read the film in terms of its engagement with classic narrative framing, obscuring its lingering engagement with mental illness and trauma. In particular, Burr's casual contention that Scott's reliance on pop culture is somehow enviable seems a bizarre way to describe a character whose ability to relate to people and surroundings is so noticeably limited. The subtitle of A. O. Scott's review, "This Girl Has a Lot of Baggage, and He Must Shoulder the Load," is, in spite of pointing out the emotional stakes of the story, reflective of the film's minimized portrayal of trauma as well as the broader critical perspective on its content.

Importantly, both A. O. Scott and Ty Burr describe *Scott Pilgrim vs. the World* (2010) in transmedial terms, suggesting it may be "the best video game movie ever" (Scott 2010) and offering that "for all intents and purposes, 'Scott Pilgrim' *is* a video game" (Burr 2010, emphasis in original). This idea is pushed to its logical conclusion by scholar Jeff Thoss, whose contribution to *Storyworlds across Media* argues the graphic novel and film adaptation exist more so in opposition than in relation to one another, competing in simulating video game storytelling. In other words, for Thoss, the graphic novel and film appear to be in a contest to see which can be the better, more complete video game and not much else. This formulation expands and complicates key concepts in adaptation studies, namely the presumed inferiority of adapted works noted in Linda Hutcheon's scholarship. But such a complete reduction to form—proposing *all* elements of story and character as performative simulations done to impersonate different medial systems—reduces the content of both *Scott Pilgrim vs. the World* (2010) and its source text(s) to meaningless fodder. In fact, Thoss insists somewhat dismissively that no one watches *Scott Pilgrim vs. the World* (2010) for its characters or events, but only for "the resulting discursive spectacle" of seeing a film style itself as a video game (2014, 226). Thoss's criticism here isn't limited to the film, and when he asks if *Scott Pilgrim* is "the tale of someone who has played too many games and as a result experiences life as a game, hence prompting this unusual manner of presentation," he critically overlooks or dismisses the central facets of Scott's identity and mental state (2014, 220). The answer to Thoss's question is actually yes, but not in terms of presenting the arrested perspective of a gamer: Scott is best understood as a character if the story's style is recognized as an extension of its protagonist's suffering mental state. Simply put, the *Scott Pilgrim* graphic novels and film adaptation look the way they do and are structured the way they are because of their content, not in spite of it.

John Bodner's scholarship also focuses on the transmedial exchange between the *Scott Pilgrim* graphic novel series and its film adaptation, but importantly concludes that both texts offer "internal perspective[s] of how Scott understands himself and the world" (Bodner 2017, 248). While Bodner doesn't explicitly mention concepts like trauma and mental illness in examining the interplay of content and form, he invaluably acknowledges the centrality of Scott to the perspective of both the graphic novels and film. This is an important contrast to Burr and Chapman: instead of describing Scott's mental state as a more contained cultural or generational phenomenon, Bodner reaffirms how the worlds of both *Scott Pilgrim* texts are projections of the title character's cognition and, by extension, act as lenses into his state of mind. Dru Jeffries echoes this claim in *Comic Book Film Style*, observing that both the graphic novel and film versions of *Scott Pilgrim* are driven by how texts shape interaction with the surrounding environment, further suggesting the need to recognize Scott's cognition in understanding style and narration across these works (2017, 168). These formulations help clarify how the intertextuality and referentiality of *Scott Pilgrim* texts are actually the center of a complicated approach to demonstrating the transcendent power of trauma that might otherwise be ignored or simply written off as "emotional baggage." Scott is a character with almost no interiority: he struggles to understand many basic human and social interactions, demonstrates limited emotional and psychological development, mythologizes himself as a virtuous warrior through distorted recollections of the past, and seems incapable of making new memories. Or, more simply, Scott is a character who should be understood as more than just a bad boyfriend or an ineffectual young adult.

Given that the source material of O'Malley's series steers heavily into all the absurd elements of its story and characters, its adaptation from graphic novel to film seems an unlikely case study for understanding trauma and mental illness. As a mechanism for exploring identity, memory, and language, trauma studies is broadly concerned with the effects of what Nasrullah Mambrol refers to as "severely disruptive experience," that which "profoundly impacts the self's emotional organization and perception of the external world" (2018). Therefore, trauma studies is often used as a tool for examining accounts of the horrors of human history, such as the bombings of Hiroshima and Nagasaki, American slavery, and the Holocaust. But as canonical works such as Cathy Caruth's *Unclaimed Experience* and Felman and Laub's *Testimony* demonstrate, such examinations result (in part) in the identification of traits and qualities that help describe the traumatic subject. Caruth's explorations reflect the incomprehensibility she associates with trauma: it is at once a hidden wound to the mind, a voice that cries out with an unknown truth, and a repeated, "belated" experience that renders "endless impact" on the survivor (1996, 7). The crisis of trauma "simultaneously defies and demands our witness" (Caruth 1996, 4) paradoxically insisting on recognition of its essential unknowability and asking what it means for "consciousness to survive" in the aftermath of such upheaval (Caruth 1996, 61). This sense of absence and fragmentation is echoed by Felman and Laub, who describe testimony as bearing witness to a crisis or trauma but affirming the fragmentation caused by the event and its fallout (1992, 5). They contend the writing and telling of stories is inherently connected to the act of bearing witness, which inscribes "what we do not yet know of our lived historical relation to the events of our times" (Felman and Laub 1992, xx).

In these contexts, the *Scott Pilgrim* graphic novels can—and I argue, should—be understood as a sort of testimony, albeit one dealing with what we might understand as small(er) trauma, personal trauma, or individual trauma. Underneath the allegories for the struggles of personal relationships and surrounding the superheroic battles is an environment built on a complex portrait of what it means to live with loss and personal failing—and, importantly, the difficulty in communicating that experience. In their *Critical Survey of Graphic Novels*, Bart H. Beaty and Stephen Weiner contend that the major conflict of the comics is actually "Scott versus his own issues that prevent him from being a 'grown-up' and a decent boyfriend to Ramona" (2012, 710). Indeed, the graphic novels have far more to say about confronting problems with the self and the obstacles preventing actualization than simply achieving a romantic relationship. But this leaves the question of what issues prevent Scott's ability to grow, and in the graphic novels in particular, both Scott and Ramona suffer through fantastical assaults on their emotional and psychological well-beings—and, accordingly, carry deep wounds that perpetuate their traumatic experiences. Just as importantly, the graphic novels and film adaptation show that Scott's traumatic pain and resulting inability to develop and engage directly with his surroundings cannot be extricated from the story's hyper-referential, hyper-mediated style. Scott's place in the world relies completely on the structure provided by his consumption and deployment of preexisting narratives: there would be no story and no way of understanding Scott without the clearly delineated missions that guide him, archetypal figures that mentor and support him, and his self-conscious, self-styling as the centerpiece of an epic story.

It is less important to compile an exhaustive list of the referential, intertextual, and metatextual elements scaffolding both O'Malley's and Wright's work than it is to recognize the trends or patterns that characterize their use. For O'Malley this seems to be a way to expose the sources shaping the overall approach to story and character of the *Scott Pilgrim* graphic novel series, which can be seen in the author's own notes accompanying the text of certain volumes. Scott similarly uses references to understand and communicate the events of his story, but more importantly, he processes and presents events with an awareness of storytelling, drawing attention to his place within the narrative and communicating to the reader as a means of controlling the telling of his story. Throughout the graphic novel series, Scott tells other characters to read earlier volumes to familiarize themselves with recent history, bemoans how much of an individual book has been occupied by a specific scene when he feels things are drawn out or boring, and requests a "last minute, poorly-set up deus ex machina!" when trapped in a fight he cannot win (O'Malley 2006). In these moments, Scott demonstrates a curious awareness of the way information is shared structurally, and his reliance on presenting the world in this way draws attention to how and why Scott understands his own experiences. These narrative engagements can also act as a sort of internal voice for Scott as audience to his own story, seen mostly clearly when he first kisses Ramona and their embrace is superimposed by an image of him playing the bass guitar underneath the text, "Nice one, Scott! Now turn the page" (O'Malley 2004). Moments like these reveal Scott's reliance on framing every element of his lived experiences using recognizable narrative and cultural patterns, and his interior monologue acts as self-congratulations while encouraging the reader to recognize his own understanding of and central position within the unfolding story.

The *Scott Pilgrim* graphic novel series demonstrates deep investment in how emotions, secrets, depression, and trauma can be depicted in visual media—a pursuit most valuably reflected in the concepts of "the glow" and "subspace highways." In the comics, the interior mind is spatialized: not only does human consciousness exist in a geographic sense, characters' minds are interconnected and even accessible by others. The existence of "subspace highways" means that characters can move through space in a supernatural way while also affording them access to the darkest corners of one's memory and the most essential elements of their identity. Likewise, characters can be left with a sort of indelible psychic scar—one deliberately and purposefully left by a traumatizing agent—manifesting itself as a halo-like "glow," often without the afflicted even being aware of it. The far-reaching implications of the *Scott Pilgrim* graphic novel series storyworld—where no part of you is untouched by suffering, no secret can be completely hidden, and no aspect of the self is safe from outside forces—are inextricable from its visual style. O'Malley's comics depict human consciousness as part of an accessible physical space, offering little defense against catastrophic events or more everyday, seemingly universal pains, visualizing the far-reaching, often unknowable resonance of trauma. So while they aren't survivors of a horrific event of historical magnitude, mechanisms of the *Scott Pilgrim* series reveal the damage Scott and Ramona carry as obscured, recurring, and inescapable in terms similar to the traumatic subject described by Cathy Caruth.

Recurring elements like the "glow" and "subspace highways" are essentially omitted from Edgar Wright's *Scott Pilgrim vs. the World* (2010), obscuring the main devices that connect the graphic novels' intertextuality and metatextuality to an understanding of the traumatized mind. The glow is introduced at the end of *Scott Pilgrim's Precious Little Life* (2004) in the calm following the first evil ex-fight and Ramona's explanation of Scott's quest. Scott asks if Gideon—who was earlier mentioned in passing but is later revealed to be the mastermind of the plot against Ramona—is one of the evil exes he must fight, and the question causes a constellation of lines to form in a circle around Ramona's head. Her eyes are reduced to pinpoints, and instead of answering she simply looks off into the distance. Scott points out that something seems wrong with her head and asks if she's okay, but Ramona smiles flatly and replies with "Yeah. I'm fine" (O'Malley 2004). The first volume ends with Scott staring at his panicked reflection in the subway window, clearly struggling to understand what this unknown glow could mean. This is the first concrete portrayal of trauma in the *Scott Pilgrim* graphic novel series, as the sudden return of Ramona's emotional wound is coupled with her seeming unawareness of its presence, reflecting the looming, returning, unknowing nature of trauma. Ramona is "infected" with the glow throughout the comics, usually as a response to being reminded of Gideon or when events make it seem like her relationship with Scott is unsettled. Ramona's unawareness of the glow becomes a minor plot point, as characters point out when it appears. At first the glow seems to be a natural function of her unexplained past suffering, recurring as past wounds are reopened and affecting her in ways she can't recognize or understand. This is complicated in the series' fifth volume—*Scott Pilgrim vs. the Universe* (2009)—when Ramona is confronted with a photo of the glow but answers cryptically when asked about its meaning, first saying "No idea," and then "Okay . . . I can't tell you."

The significance of the glow is finally revealed through the ultimate confrontation with Gideon in *Scott Pilgrim's Finest Hour* (2010). Gideon explains the glow as a form of emotional warfare, a tool that "Seals you inside your head. Just you and your *issues*. And once you're hit, that's it. No cure. It's chronic" (emphasis in original). Importantly, it is also revealed that Ramona found a way to use the glow to enter her own mind, trying to withdraw from her suffering in the real world and retreat to a place where she ideally has more control. Her trauma is not so easily escapable, though, as we see that Gideon occupies a central place in her mind as well, a function of his powers of manipulation more so than Ramona's own desire. Nevertheless, these moments reveal that while Ramona was aware of the existence and significance of the glow, she was not always aware of being subjected to it, meaning she would suffer unknowingly. These details reflect Caruth's description of trauma, which is "not available to the survivor until it imposes itself again" (1996, 4) and re-subjects the sufferer to "violence [that] has not yet been fully known" (1996, 6). Ramona's vague understanding of her pain also demonstrates Petar Ramadanovic's configuration of trauma, which depends on the awareness of an absence or "tear," forcing a dislocation that "separates feeling from fact" (2001, 2). The glow, then, has the important visual function of pointing out the recurring presence of trauma, but is also a renewed wound the victim is actively subjected to; here the traumatized know they have been hurt and even know the hurt is still with them, but don't know when that wound will reassert itself or how. Gideon says the glow doesn't affect him—melodramatically stating, "I've been trapped in my own head since the day I was born"—but no character in the graphic novels simply obtains the glow as a result of some wound or suffering (O'Malley 2010). Rather, they are *given* the glow by Gideon, touched by his supervillainy in a deliberate way that leaves them irreparably broken. In O'Malley's *Scott Pilgrim* series, trauma is configured as something that is done to you rather than something that simply happens, configuring this recurring suffering as something other than a force of nature and affirming the poisoning role of the offender.

This crucial element of understanding trauma in the *Scott Pilgrim* graphic novel series is virtually eliminated from the film adaptation despite its ability to be visually represented. In the film, Ramona rubs her neck a handful of times but this gesture—perhaps intended to replace the visual effect of the glow—is never really acknowledged. And while the final battle of *Scott*

Pilgrim's Finest Hour (2010) revolves around Scott and Ramona fighting against Gideon in the real world and in their own heads to resist his overwhelming control, in the film Ramona reveals what is presumably a mind control device on the back of her neck and says Gideon "literally has a way of getting into my head" (Wright 2010). In the source text, Gideon's use of the glow means he is able to see what his victims see, secretly tinker with their innermost desires, and even change their memories. It is fundamentally a tool of trauma, removing the victim's agency and forcibly disconnecting them from their identities and personal pasts. The film version of Gideon simply wants to have Ramona "under his thumb"—as the accompanying use of The Rolling Stones' "Under My Thumb" suggests—rendering him a simpler, more generic villain and minimizing the priority placed on Ramona's own profound suffering in the graphic novels. This moment illustrates the film's tendency to use further referentiality (in this case, the soundtrack) instead of modeling the source comics' visual scheme for representing trauma. It is also a notable example of the way Ramona's experiences are minimized in *Scott Pilgrim vs. the World* (2010) and the limitations this absence has on its engagements with style and mental illness. The final showdown in *Scott Pilgrim's Finest Hour* (2010) is arguably more about her struggle with Gideon than Scott's, but in the film adaptation it is Knives Chau—Scott's former girlfriend who he doesn't quite break up with before becoming involved with Ramona—who joins Scott in defeating the "final boss." Ramona's suffering clarifies the graphic novels' portrait of trauma, demonstrating how such a recurring wound can create new pain in others. As Kyle Eveleth insightfully notes, "In each additional volume, Scott's worth as a protagonist is more profoundly questioned until it becomes clear that his story is one of many" (2013, 10). Eveleth's observation encourages us to not only question Scott's self-image and narrative control but also recognize the way his perspective may limit our understanding of the story's events and characters. If the *Scott Pilgrim* graphic novel series (2004–2010) is a sort of testimony, then it "does not offer [. . .] a completed statement, a totalizable account" (Felman and Laub 1992, 5), meaning that we need more than just Scott's perspective—and not just because of his limited cognition. These elements are reduced to the point of total omission in the world of *Scott Pilgrim vs. the World* (2010), and their absence makes Ramona's experiences secondary, blunts the film's portrayal of her relationship with Scott, and further obscures any visual scheme for representing trauma.

    The graphic novel series also uses the glow to demonstrate how trauma can spread to and vary in others, as Scott too becomes subjected to its fragmenting, unsettling powers in *Scott Pilgrim Gets It Together* (2007). The day after an argument that resulted in Ramona suffering with the glow, Scott accidentally enters her mind before noticing one of the evil exes waking up in her house.

This experience is an echo of Scott's primary trauma: he begins the events of *Scott Pilgrim* trying to overcome the emptiness at having been dumped by former girlfriend Envy Adams. Scott has struggled to get over this loss—he is practically crippled by receiving a phone call from Envy in the series' second volume—and his friends generally acknowledge his post-breakup phase as a sort of mourning period. But his feelings of suffering and anxiety are easily triggered, and his attachment to them represent Scott's only accurate memories in the entire *Scott Pilgrim* graphic novel series. The moment of Scott's first glow also reintroduces a representation of trauma specific to Scott and indicative of his further-wounded mind: the Nega Scott. Inspired by the Dark Link figure from The Legend of Zelda video game series, this shadowy figure asserts itself throughout the graphic novel series when Scott is at his most vulnerable. Scott is unsure of what the figure wants or represents, and resists it until bandmate and friend Kim Pine points out that his simple, self-mythologizing memories have no connection to the actual past. During the final confrontation with the Nega Scott, Kim encourages Scott in ways that double as indicators of his traumatized mind, shouting "But if you keep forgetting your mistakes, you'll just keep making them again!" and "Everything you've done wrong is just gonna keep following you around, Scott!" (O'Malley 2010). The failures noted by Kim expose the troubling repetition inherent in trauma, which Caruth describes as "more fundamentally and enigmatically, the very attempt to *claim one's survival*" (1996, 64, emphasis in original). And being afflicted with the glow only further traumatizes Scott, amplifying the ways his emptiness and cognitive limitations have prevented him from engaging with the people and places around him.

In *Scott Pilgrim's Finest Hour* (2010), the confrontation with the Nega Scott ends with the dark figure being absorbed into Scott after he first tries to kill it—in hopes that doing so will allow him to forget—and then experiencing a flashback reflecting how central Ramona is to his understanding of himself. This moment reconnects Scott to his memories in a way he hasn't experienced before: he covers his face in apparent shock and shame, saying he now remembers everything and recognizing his artificial self-image has been hiding all the harm he has caused to others. This reconciliation of the self is side-stepped in the film adaptation, where the confrontation between Scott and Nega Scott ends with the two walking away together without fighting and chatting about brunch, with Scott curiously describing his seeming opposite as "just a really nice guy [. . .] we actually have a lot in common" (Wright 2010). This lack of resolution is particularly limiting to a critical understanding of Scott, as Beaty and Weiner frame these developments with Nega Scott as central to the graphic novels, challenging Scott's unreliable understanding of himself as "awesome," "a paragon of virtue," and "a fantastic boyfriend," ignoring past indiscretions and becoming "the only way he remembers himself" (2012, 711). Previously, his memory had been represented in two ways, either as distortions corrected by his friends (such as saying he doesn't drink alcohol or that previous breakups were completely amicable) or through the use of his "memory cam," which visually recreates moments from the past with a misleading emphasis on his uprightness, heroism, and desirability. Scott's connection to his own past is further obscured by the glow, however, as Gideon later reveals he has been in Scott's head, noting it was "mostly empty" except for memories he "spiced up" (O'Malley 2010). This means Scott is doubly removed from his own identity: even though he has reconnected with his past by joining with the Nega Scott, there's no way to know how many of his recovered memories are unaltered, complete, or true. There is also no way for us to know if Scott has consciously cultivated the self-importance reflected in his memories and is therefore responsible for his dismissiveness toward the pain he has caused for others. His separation reflects the traumatic forgetting described by Ramadanovic, which is not an omission but instead the "opposite of remembering," a failure of integration that "disperses what has happened" (2001, 3).

Gideon's access to Scott's mind in the comics is enabled by "subspace highways," a concept first introduced as a way for Ramona to travel quickly by taking shortcuts through his mind. Scott refers to his interest in Ramona as an obsession after she literally appears in his dreams, which helps explain his interest in her and insistence on their relationship despite knowing nothing about her. The "rules" of subspace are unexplained and cloudy at best: Ramona not only seems to access these highways by entering doors marked with a single star throughout Toronto but also carries a similarly marked purse that also appears to access the seeming infinity of subspace, with a graphic insert noting that its capacity is "unknown." The purse is used primarily for visual gags in the film adaptation, and subspace doesn't figure into its story outside of being a vehicle for bringing Ramona and Scott together in the first act. The absence of subspace highways in the film adaptation illustrates exactly how little we see of Scott's self and state of mind: the graphic novel is filled with his dreams and fantasies—and impositions by outside parties—but the film offers no glimpses into Scott's interiority aside from the first dream of loneliness that introduces Ramona and the interrupted high school dream that leads to their second meeting. The film's emphasis on further intertextuality means employing even more references to make Scott's perspective understandable and relatable, but simultaneously leaves an empty center with less to actually relate to. But subspace highways are integral to the portrait of trauma in the *Scott Pilgrim* graphic novel series, as they reveal both the fragile, accessible nature of our minds and create visual representations of the suffering of Scott and Ramona for readers and in-world characters alike.

These differences are coalesced in the final battles with Gideon in comic *Scott Pilgrim's Finest Hour* (2010) and film *Scott Pilgrim vs. the World* (2010). These conclusions make interesting points of comparison, as John Bodner argues the film's fidelity may be "undermined by co-creation" since Wright's film was written before the completion of O'Malley's final volume, meaning it couldn't use the comic as a source in the same way (2017, 253). The contrasting endings do more, then, to reveal the trajectory of their separate narrative and thematic investments than to act as a test of faithfulness as an inherently positive value. In both texts, Scott initially fights Gideon using a sword called The Power of Love, which emerges from Scott's chest when he tells Ramona he loves her. But Scott loses his primary weapon and is killed by Gideon in each version of the battle, returning to face the final evil ex a second time after utilizing an "extra life" he received for his victory in a previous fight. The unfolding action of Scott's second attempt at closure, however, reveals the diverging investments in the themes of trauma, shared suffering, and the potential for self-actualization. In *Scott Pilgrim vs. the World* (2010), Scott announces he isn't there to fight Gideon for Ramona but for himself, and this declaration earns him a new weapon: The Power of Self-Respect. This weapon isn't enough to best Gideon either, but Scott is able to defeat him with the help of Knives Chau as Ramona mostly watches. Again the film's prioritizing of Scott is clear, as Ramona's potential resolution is sidelined in favor of Scott achieving some sort of self-knowledge on his own, without anyone's encouragement or true newfound understanding. Importantly, he does try to acknowledge his shortcomings to his friends, but the visual tools used to depict Scott's awareness of his flaws and need to resolve them are noticeably absent. Understanding is at the center of *Scott Pilgrim's Finest Hour* (2010): the sword he earns and uses to defeat Gideon—dealing the final blow with Ramona—is called The Power of Understanding. He earns this new weapon after saying he understands Gideon's villainous desires and, as a result, knows he has to be destroyed. Scott says Gideon has to be punished for messing with their heads, foregrounding the graphic novels' acts of emotional warfare and their ensuing trauma and mental illness as the "final boss," the true obstacle that must be overcome. Ramona and Scott both have come to terms with their pasts and used Love and Understanding as tools to push Gideon out of their minds, making it possible for them to move forward with a better understanding of who they are, how they've been harmed, and even their own capacity to harm others.

The stories' endings have significant visual similarity: with all the evil exes defeated, Scott and Ramona say they will try again and hold hands as they walk through a subspace highway door one final time, seeming to accept their uncertain future together. This visual fidelity is key to Wright's adaptive vision: *Scott Pilgrim vs. the World* (2010) pays homage to the comics' visual and narrative style but obscures its underlying meaning in doing so, rendering the source texts as just another group of reference points in its intertextual landscape. The end result is another sort of empty center, exposing the strained connection between the film's kinetic style and the ways it can reflect a traumatized state of mind. Even though the film's conclusion revolves around Scott and Ramona walking away together, their togetherness still has to be encouraged by outside forces. Ramona walks away at the end because she says the past is always catching up with her and hurting other people, and Scott shrugs and says, "Bye and stuff . . ." before letting her go (Wright 2010). Scott only pursues Ramona one final time because Knives Chau tells him he's been "fighting for her all along," prodding him toward a reunion and reinforcing the film's journey as a squarely romantic one (Wright 2010). Solutions in *Scott Pilgrim vs. the World* (2010) can only really be achieved by fighting and for the sake of relationships: Ramona offers some desire to resolve her lingering pain and guilt, but the resolution sidesteps these concerns to deliver Scott the girlfriend he has fought for. The story and conclusion pretty clearly belong to Scott, but only to tell a story about getting the girl, not as a means of representing the trauma and mental illness that still linger through the text's connection to its source.

Scott Pilgrim's Finest Hour (2010), however, brings its tale of absurd, fantastical violence to a close with the couple *talking*, coming to terms with their losses, fears, and potential growth. After they defeat Gideon, Scott asks if things can be the same, and Ramona tells him, "Things never *were* the same. Change is . . . it's what we get" (O'Malley 2010, emphasis in original). They don't talk about leaving things behind but rather about not being stuck, resolving that they can overcome their fear(s) of abandoning and hurting others if they are willing to learn to hold on to each other. Importantly, the final images of the comic draw visual reference from the series itself, with Ramona waiting for Scott at the top of an outdoor staircase before the two walk through a star-marked door—the same sequence of events from their first date in *Scott Pilgrim's Precious Little Life* (2004). This imagery truly suggests the couple will *try again*: not simply that they will give their relationship another chance as implied in the film, but that—just as Scott used his "extra life" to succeed where he initially failed in fighting Gideon—they will continue their lives and try to do better based on what they've experienced and learned. O'Malley's *Scott Pilgrim* graphic novel series, then, uses intertextuality as a tool to reveal the depth of its main characters' suffering and the ways it reasserts itself in Scott's lived experience and storytelling. Scott and Ramona's trauma has been present throughout the six volumes telling their story, and it's also present in their future together. The couple can continue to heal and grow as a unit, not as a means to end the melodramatic loneliness that frames the beginning of Scott's story in the comics—and the entirety of his arc in the film—but to repair the fragmented experiences that come from their individual and shared suffering. The act of trying again is still essentially one of repetition; Scott and Ramona are still traumatized, but now believe it is possible to live with their pain and past(s) rather than hoping in vain to make them disappear. These final images show Scott's capacity for growth: he still suffers but has some awareness of the how and why, and is able to conclude the story he shares with Ramona by revisiting their shared experiences rather than relying on preexisting narratives to supplement his own emptiness. Even though *Scott Pilgrim vs. the World* (2010) builds its style around pushing referentiality and situating Scott within that frame to the very end—complicating the adaptation of its source text in the process—*Scott Pilgrim's Finest Hour* (2010) shows Scott is capable of overcoming the intertextuality that has plagued him and that the graphic novel series' style can be used in the service of telling Scott's own story.

WORKS CITED

Beaty, Bart H. and Stephen Weiner. *Critical Survey of Graphic Novels: Independents and Underground Classics.* Ipswich, Massachusetts: Salem Press, 2012.

Berninger, Mark. "'Scott Pilgrim Gets It Together': The Cultural Crossovers of Bryan Lee O'Malley." In *Transnational Perspectives on Graphic Narratives; Comics at the Crossroads,* edited by Shane Denson, Christina Meyer, and Daniel Stein, 243–55. London: Bloomsbury Academics, 2013.

Bodner, John. "Scott Pilgrim's Precious Little Texts: Adaptation, Form, and Transmedia Co-creation." In *Comics and Pop Culture: Adaptation from Panel to Frame,* edited by Barry Keith Grand and Scott Henderson, 246–64. Austin: University of Texas Press, 2017.

Burr, Ty. "Movie Review: Scott Pilgrim vs. the World." archive.boston.com. Boston Globe, published August 13, 2010. http://archive.boston.com/ae/movies/articles/2010/08/13/ scott_pilgrim_vs_the_world/.

Caruth, Cathy. *Unclaimed Experience: Trauma, Narrative, and History.* Baltimore: Johns Hopkins University Press, 1996.

Chapman, Bob. "Escape to the Movies—Scott Pilgrim vs. the World." escapistmagazine.com. The Escapist, Published August 13, 2010. https://v1.escapistmagazine.com/videos/view/ escape-to-the-movies/1918-Scott-Pilgrim-vs-The-World.

Eveleth, Kyle. "Crucial Convergence: *Scott Pilgrim* as Transmedial Test Case." *Textual Overtures* 1, no. 1 (2013): 1–14.

Felman, Shoshana and Dori Laub. *Testimony: Crises of Witnessing in Literature, Psychoanalysis, and History.* New York: Routledge, 1992.

Hutcheon, Linda with Siobhan O'Flynn. *A Theory of Adaptation.* New York: Routledge, 2006, 2013.

Jeffries, Dru. *Comic Book Film Style: Cinema at 24 Panels per Second.* Austin: University of Texas Press, 2017.

Kristeva, Julia. *Desire in Language: A Semiotic Approach to Literature and Art.* New York: Columbia University Press, 1980.
Mambrol, Nasrullah. "Trauma Studies." Literariness.org. Literariness.org, published December 19, 2018. https://literariness.org/2018/12/19/trauma-studies/.
O'Malley, Bryan Lee. *Scott Pilgrim and the Infinite Sadness.* Portland: Oni Press, 2006.
O'Malley, Bryan Lee. *Scott Pilgrim's Finest Hour.* Portland: Oni Press, 2010.
O'Malley, Bryan Lee. *Scott Pilgrim Gets It Together.* Portland: Oni Press, 2007.
O'Malley, Bryan Lee. *Scott Pilgrim's Precious Little Life.* Portland: Oni Press, 2004.
O'Malley, Bryan Lee. *Scott Pilgrim vs. the World.* Portland: Oni Press, 2005.
"Pop Culture Happy Hour < Does 'Scott Pilgrim Vs. The World' Hold Up, Ten Years Later?." December 7, 2020. 22:02. https://www.npr.org/transcripts/941558942.
Ramadanovic, Petar. *Forgetting Futures: On Memory, Trauma, and Identity.* Lanham, Maryland: Lexington Books, 2001.
Rothery, Jason and Benjamin Woo. "Mutatis Mutandis: Constructing Fidelity in the Comic Book Film Adaptation." In *Comics and Pop Culture: Adaptation from Panel to Frame,* edited by Barry Keith Grant and Scott Henderson, 126–37. Austin: University of Texas Press, 2017.
Scott, AO review. "Movie Review | 'Scott Pilgrim vs. The World." NYTimes.com. The New York Times, published August 12, 2010. https://www.nytimes.com/2010/08/13/movies/ 13scott.html.
Thoss, Jeff. "Tell It Like a Game: *Scott Pilgrim* and Performative Media Rivalry." In *Storyworlds across Media,* edited by Marie-Laure Ryan and Jan-Noël Thon, 211–29. Lincoln, Nebraska: University of Nebraska Press, 2014.
Wright, Edgar, dir. *Scott Pilgrim vs. the World.* 2010: Universal Pictures Home Entertainment, 2010. DVD.

Chapter 10

Minding the Gap

Adaptation of and Mental Disability in Quiet Life *(1990, 1995)*

Rea Amit

Mental disability has played a major role in Japanese novelist Kenzaburō Ōe's prolific oeuvre, but only a marginalized one in his director brother-in-law Jūzō Itami's films. Despite some interest in film as a topic within his novels, only a handful of Ōe's works have been adapted, and arguably the most famous exception is that of the novel *Shizuka na seikatsu* (*Quiet Life*, 1990),[1] which was adapted by Itami into film in 1995. However, the film remains the most understudied among Itami's works, and seemingly the least critically acclaimed. For example, Shigehiko Hasumi, one of Japan's leading theorists who celebrated both Ōe's novels and Itami's films until this adaptation disparaged it (Yomota 2001).

The following pages challenge this tendency and throw new light on both the novel and the adaptation by focusing on gaps between the two, especially as these pertain to and foster nuanced articulations of mental disability. Being cognizant of the gaps between what does and does not exist in the two versions of *Quiet Life* is a deceivingly simple (albeit tedious) endeavor. It brings to the fore omissions and augmentations of elements, sources of influence, as well as accounts of fluctuating mental states. Seen as separate entities, the two versions put forth an aporia; they exist in one medium, but not in another that is conceived as its replica. The works represent an ontological potency, on the one hand, and flickering ephemerality, on the other. Together, as a single phenomenon that is comprised of not only the original and its adaptation but also the multiple sources that are interwoven with it, *Quiet Life* represents the otherwise unrepresentable apparatus of compromised epistemological states of being.

I argue that thinking in tandem with *Quiet Life*'s literary and cinematic versions, as well as the works they refer to as converging cognates (reading/ viewing), reproduces an unstable state of cognitive dissonance that is the rippling effect of the recapitulating procedure. While the works themselves seem to showcase a straightforward representation of a mentally disabled character that stems from real-life (coding), this chapter focuses more on the state of decoding that derives from the reader/viewer. This is not a linear process of identifying differences and similarities, but a circular one that thinks through the film and novel, their sources of influences, and reverts to the reader/viewer as an active, yet compromised, decoder. Thus, by recognizing a precarious middle ground between production and reception in the hermeneutic act itself, the chapter proposes a way to articulate an inherently unarticulated process of cognition.

This examination first introduces the background in which *Quiet Life* has emerged, the novel's author, the cinematic adaptation's director, and the links between them. Next, the chapter contextualizes Foucault's term apparatus following Shelley L. Tremain's recent work and Derrida's aporia with Harold Bloom's famous "anxiety of influence" to articulate mental disability as it emanates from the experience of reading and watching the novel and its cinematic adaptation. Doing so, this chapter aims to rethink these concepts together to consider *Quiet Life* in light of their sources of influence, as a diverging and converging metanarrative. As a guide into the apparatus, and between the discussion of the concepts mentioned above, the chapter pays special attention to Andrei Tarkovsky's 1979 film *Stalker*, which is discussed in the novel but not in its cinematic adaptation. Although seemingly unrelated to the discourse on mental disability, I argue that *Stalker* provides a key to identify gaps between the two versions of *Quiet Life* along lines of a third medium: poetry. The chapter concludes by restating the argument that the act of reading/viewing the works in tandem affectively creates an imaginative, yet forceful, articulation\visualization of mental disability.

(NOT SO) QUIET LIVES

Japan has long been slow to create progressive policies for people with mental disability (Gottlieb 2001). While this is arguably a global phenomenon that has only recently begun to change, representations of disability in general, and particularly of mental disability across Japanese media are still scarce. A striking exception in this regard is Kenzaburō Ōe's oeuvre, including *Quiet Life*. A Nobel Prize laureate, Ōe is widely considered among the most influential writers in modern Japan. Many of his works are known for their depiction of the author's personal life, his family, and especially of

Hikari, his developmentally disabled son. Hikari was born with an encephalocele, and its surgical removal, during the first months of his life, left him with hydrocephalus and neurological deficits.

As mentioned in the outset, Ōe's works have seldom been adapted into films. This is despite the fact that the author's brother-in-law and lifelong close friend, Jūzō Itami (1933-1997), was one of the most celebrated Japanese filmmakers in postwar Japan. The first and only collaboration between the film director and Ōe is the cinematic adaptation of the novel *Quiet Life*, a deeply personal depiction of the writer's family life, and his disabled grown child, and a rather eventless novel. The primary link between *Quiet Life*'s versions, as well as between fiction and real life, is the character modeled after Ōe's son, Hikari. Although the character modeled after Hikari is not the central active agent in either text, he is nonetheless the main subject of both works. In real life, Hikari, despite his disability, has become a composer, a fact that both the novel and the film treat extensively. Yet, unlike the novel, which is a work of a single creator, Hikari the real person was actively involved in the film production by contributing his music to the soundtrack.

Quiet Life is a far cry from the author's more sensational works and, true to its title, depicts mostly dull, everyday life. The narrative portrays a slice of Hikari and his two younger yet more capable siblings' lives in Tokyo while their parents are away. Like many other of Ōe's works, Hikari, or as he is often referred to in his father's fiction, Eeyore, after the donkey in Winnie-the-Pooh books (Ōe 1977, 177), is a pivotal figure in the narrative. Yet unlike probably all other works in the novelist's extensive output, the narrator in *Quiet Life* is the author's daughter, referred to as Mā-chan, a nickname, she explains in the novel, that was given to her due to her round-shaped head, a feature strikingly different than her older brain-damaged brother when he was born. In the opening of the novel, the father is invited to serve as a writer-in-residence at a Californian university, and his wife, the children's mother, decides to accompany him. Mā-chan, the college student, is left to take care of her two siblings, the older handicapped brother, and her younger brother, Ō-chan, who is about to take college entrance exams. The novel is, in a way, a diary that Mā-chan keeps as a promise to her mother, a written record that she acknowledges as uninteresting.

The film adaptation of *Quiet Life* injects another layer of complexity to the already intricate "based-on-a-true-story" conundrum in adaptation studies. Whereas scholars such as Sara Brinch who, following Christine Geraghty, advocate for a method of contextualized reading of a given adaptation considering the reception of the real-life events it depicts (2013, 225), my approach here is different. This is not due to a methodological disagreement, but rather it is because my aim here is less to highlight the gap between the "origin" and the adaptation as a matter in and of itself and to instead accentuate the epistemological states of being mentally disabled across the two works. Rather than pointing to the film's deviations from the novel as indicative of infidelity to an "original" source (an already dubious notion given that the novel itself fictionalizes real-life), this chapter embraces instead truthfulness to what Fredric Jameson dubs a "well-nigh Derridean vigilance to the multiple forms difference takes in the object" of an adapted work (2011, 215). This chapter analyzes the differences that both objects project in respect to one another in addition to the works they refer to, as well as the individuals they represent, and manifests a dissonance akin to the unarticulated state of being mentally compromised. In other words, it is the difference itself—the incongruity that arises from the incapability to differentiate the adapted object from the perceiving subject—that gives birth to an imaginative brainchild in the space that opens between life and fiction.

MENTAL DISABILITY AS AN APPARATUS

Given Michel Foucault's famous work on madness, narrating mental disability along the lines of the Foucauldian notion of the apparatus (or *Dispositif* in French) may seem obvious. Although Foucault himself never properly defined the term, philosopher Giorgio Agamben succinctly characterizes it as a network between discourses, a function located in power-relation, and as relations of knowledge (2009, 2–3). In this sense, the apparatus is concerned with mental or cognitive disparity between the characters in *Quiet Life*, as well as between the novel and its film adaptation.

Implementation of the apparatus in the context of mental disability has been taken into serious consideration only recently by Shelley L. Tremain, who positions it as a "historically contingent network of force relations in which everyone is implicated and entangled and in a relation to which everyone occupies a position"; thus, being disabled in this conception merely means "to occupy a certain subject position within the productive constraints of the apparatus of disability" (2017, 22). Articulating disability in this way does not identify a single disabled source, but only relative states of power or mental abilities in relation to other subjects.

Aware of Foucault's objections to relativism, Tremain nonetheless argues for a position in which one is identified as disabled on an imaginary scale measured against other subjects—based on internal as well as external power dynamics in various fields. Disability, in this conception, is not a quality one possesses, but rather "outcomes of contextually specific and performative relations of power" within the apparatus (Ibid., 23). Applying the concept to *Quiet Life* means to move away from singling out Hikai as the sole representation of disability, and to instead uncover a network of performative relations between not only fictional characters but also sources of influence, as well as those seemingly in position of full mental command. That is, rather than one stable disability state, the works as an apparatus expose a range of mental conditions that are contingent upon interactions, perspectives, and intermediating agents. Moreover, the apparatus in the Foucauldian sense is especially relevant to the depiction of mental disability in *Quiet Life* in its correspondence with the private lives of the author's extended family. Indeed, mental disability remains the author's main driving source, even if the autobiographic authenticity that can be traced back to works such as the 1969 novella "Teach Us How to Outgrow Our Madness" is questionable (Mulvey 2012). In this notable early work, one of the author's earliest depictions of Hikari's disability as a central subject matter, Ōe himself is the object of mental perilous state as he struggles to "normalize" Eeyore. As the end of the story—where the seemingly mentally abled protagonist realizes his own compromised position—shows, being mentally impaired is not an ontological quality, but a state conditioned by different variables across altering states, or indeed, an apparatus. The real-life author's own unstable mental capacity is also a feature that Itami highlights in the film adaptation of *Quiet Life*, where the father's departure to Australia (instead of California as in the novel) is motivated by the novelist's chronic depression. Although Itami frames this in a humorous fashion, he also illustrates the severity of the problem in depicting the author's past suicide attempts (and perhaps even hints by this at his own mental state). Thus, mental disability in both the novel and the film are not presented as a stable predicament, but rather as a relative state contingent upon temporal situations and perspective.

Beyond Foucault, the term "apparatus" in film and media studies is chiefly associated with what has become known as the "apparatus theory." Most notable in this context are thinkers such as Jean-Louis Baudry who identifies the forces at play in film viewing in relation to psychoanalytical and ideological models. While both might be applicable to *Quiet Life*, the former can more readily shed light on the expanded narrative that sprawls from Ōe's novel, Itami's film, and the range of influences between them. In this sense, although psychological identification is not a position this chapter assumes, the specifically disabled cinematic subject can be recognized, following Baudry's closing lines of one of his famous essays, as a "psychic apparatus of substitution, corresponding to the model defined by the dominant ideology" (1974–1975, 46). The model he singles out is a system of repression designed to prevent deviation, and in a mental disability context, it illustrates a model of sanity, mentally capable, and productive subjects. Under both definitions, the apparatus in the context of the novel and its film adaptation lays out networks of probable epistemologically compromised states.

Taking both approaches into account, the apparatus this chapter proposes considers *Quiet Life* as a life work of multiple subjects, including the author and his family (e.g., Hikari and Itami). The apparatus is the network within which they interact with one another, with an array of influential sources, and on a different level, with audiences. The power dynamics between all players in this web is fluid, as it is manifested only in relation to other subjects, and thus it enables even seemingly capable minds to assume, even if only temporarily, an imaginative mentally compromised position.

THE GUIDE TO THE APPARATUS

To access the apparatus that forms *Quiet Life*, as well as to begin articulating the mental disability experience it produces, it is helpful to have a guide, a mediator between the novel and its adaptation. One such guide is found in a section of the book that does not appear in the film, in which the siblings discuss their experience of watching Andrei Tarkovsky's 1979 film *Stalker*.

The youngest brother, Ō-chan, records the film from a late-night television broadcast, and although he is busy studying for university entrance exams, and despite the film's length and high level of abstraction, the three siblings, including Eeyore, watch it. Throughout most of the chapter, Mā-chan contemplates the film's meanings and discusses it with her younger brother. The discussion of Tarkovsky's film fits in the novel due to the novel's episodic, undramatic, and overall eventless narrative, qualities that make it difficult to adapt into a commercial film. The removal of this section of the book from the film is therefore understandable, as Keiichiro Ihara points out, "the reason is clear ... it is simply because it cannot be filmed" (*tanjun ni eiga ni naranai kara da*) (2014, 72). At the same time, the fact that the most palpable gap between the novel and the film is cinematic in essence is emblematic of the web of influences that characterizes a state of flux in depicting mental disability as an apparatus.

Stalker therefore serves as a guide into the mental disability spectrum portrayed between *Quiet Life*'s two media versions. Although the Japanese commercial film adaptation and the Soviet meditative, metaphysical, science fiction film seem worlds apart, some lines of thought connect them. First among these is of course the fact that the book upon which the Japanese film is based directly refers to and discusses *Stalker*. In addition, despite showcasing altogether different cinematic qualities, their narratives converge (albeit unevenly) on alluding to personal matters, disability, and poetry.

It might appear as a deviation to interject another film into a discussion of *Quiet Life*, but as an apparatus, the novel and its adaptation subsume a space (or even a zone) that inhibits sources of influence as organic extensions of themselves. Moreover, in this discussion *Stalker* fulfills two main functions: it introduces a key to unpacking the depiction of mental disability as a relative mode of being, and it provides a link to poetry, a language with which mental disability can be articulated.

Stalker projects a near yet unspecified future where a certain mysterious Zone is discovered and kept out of reach by the army. It is rumored that visiting the Zone might grant individuals their innermost wishes. The film's main character is a stalker, a guide who sneaks visitors into the forbidden area. Most of the film portrays one such dangerous mission. However, in spite of their formal differences, *Stalker* is notably similar to *Quiet Life* in its portrayal of a father who is absent from home during most of the film, and most noticeably, in its presentation of a disabled child, who like Eeyore is named after an animal, Monkey. Moreover, like Eeyore, who is a musical prodigy, Monkey, despite her disability, boasts a remarkable ability of telekinesis. Both characters represent a fluid state that at times also evinces extraordinary capabilities.

Stalker puts forth a discussion on the human psyche, and the Zone it depicts, according to several scholars, that represents the mind (e.g., Martin 2011). While no such Zone exists in either version of *Quiet Life*, it is precisely the synchronization of the two that is at work in analogous ways; ushering in an intricate experience of the apparatus—bodily, intellectually, and psychologically. It is the act of adaptation itself that serves as a "Zone," into which *Stalker* guides what Linda Hutcheon calls the "knowing audience." The knowledge such audiences possess, according to Hutcheon, is simply the awareness of the act of adaptation, which consequently allows for a process of gap-filling through the discursive expansion from the original work to the adapted one (2013, 120–21). In the case of *Quiet Life*, this knowledge is not necessarily the novel itself, but rather the fact that it is based on the real life of one of Japan's most famous authors, and his mentally disabled grown child whose 1992 and 1994 albums won the Japan Gold Disc Award in the classical music category.

Although to a lesser degree, some "knowing audiences" could point out that like *Quiet Life*, *Stalker*, too, is a personal matter for its director, who as Robert Bird mentions, entered the film world after withdrawing his initial intentions to establish a career in classical music due to his lack of perfect pitch (2008, 7), a capability the disabled Eeyore does possess. Tarkovsky injects himself into the film even though *Stalker*, like *Quiet Life*, is an adaptation. Indeed, Tarkovsky is less faithful to his original source of influence, Arkady and Boris Strugatsky's novel *Roadside Picnic* (*Piknik na obochine*, 1972). For example, while the novel suggests that Monkey's disability is visible, in the film she is an ambivalent character who might suffer some physical difficulties, but she does not appear deformed. In the novel, unlike the film, as Vida T. Johnson and Graham Petrie point out, Monkey becomes increasingly "nonhuman both physically and intellectually" (1994, 141). This was expected in the novel, where Guta, stalker's partner, debates having an abortion after her mother warns her: "It's a stalker's child, why breed freaks?" (2012, 54). Although she is not the main character in Tarkovsky's adaptation, Monkey does become, as Nariman Skakov claims, the "ultimate riddle of the film" (2012, 164). As such, from the perspective of more informed "knowing audiences," Monkey and Eeyore are aligned within an apparatus that transcends generic, temporal, geographic, visual, as well as linguistic boundaries.

The enigmatic Monkey shares with Eeyore an ambivalent position as the least capable characters in their respectful diegesis, while at the same time also the most capable. In addition to Monkey's mysterious supernatural ability to move objects by mental power, Tarkovsky also presents her as remarkably gifted at poetry, and beyond the "normal" mental capacity of children her age (2012, 163). Like Eeyore, who expresses himself in musical compositions, a nonverbal form of articulation, Monkey embodies an artistic abstraction of everyday speech. *Stalker*'s direct reference to poetry fleshes out the use of this medium of expression in the apparatus to put in words the inherently inexpressible mode of being mentally disabled. In Itami's *Quiet Life* characters do not recite poems, and the film seems antithetical to Tarkovsky's poetic approach to filmmaking. Yet the construction of episodes into a cinematic narrative that characterizes Itami's adaptation is in line with Charles Inouye's suggestion regarding *Tampopo*, Itami's most critically acclaimed film, as showcasing a cinematic form of *renga* (linked-versed), a Japanese poetic genre (2001, 135). Poetry, as *Stalker* insinuates, is thus the form of expression with which mental disability is articulated between the two versions of *Quiet Life* and the medium that links not only film and literature but also life and fiction. Although somewhat latent in the film adaptation, poetry performs a more palpable role in articulating mental disability in the novel on which it is based. However, poetry articulates mental disability as a relative condition within the apparatus, not with recitable verses, but rather by shedding light on the aporia that the apparatus exposes.

THE APORIA OF MENTAL DISABILITY AS THE ANXIETY OF INFLUENCE

Itami adds in the adaptation two sequences that do not appear in the novel, both of which ironically present mental disability as a problematic category. First is a sequence where the father, in a public speech, recalls the moment when his son finally started to talk, at the age of six, repeating names of birds he had heard on cassette recordings. The second is the film's ending.

Following a conversation on the phone with her mother (who seems to be overestimating her husband's recovery from depression), Mā-chan asks Eeyore how to title the diary she has been writing about their life without their parents. In response, Eeyore proposes the title of the novel, and of the film as well, *Shizuka na seikatsu* (*Quiet Life*). While the Japanese *shizuka*, like the English word "quiet," means calm or lack of motion—attributes that indeed characterize the novel—it also means the absence of sound. In this respect, the title can be read ironically: the disabled Eeyore is a composer who is able to hear sounds or music even in silence, in his mind, while his abled and more articulate sister struggles to find the right words.

Both added sequences present two diverging visions of mental disability. Whereas in the first sequence Eeyore, and the mental disability that he represents, are an object, in the second sequence he is the capable active agent who defines the narrative in his own terms, like one of his own compositions. As such, Eeyore—who shares a metempsychosis with Monkey from the cinematic adaptation of *Roadside Picnic*—manifests a notion of mental disability as an apparatus, an inextricable state of cognitive ability and disability that is constantly being redefined against other epistemological states. He projects an incongruous image of mental disability, one that allows a flexible articulation, not of a permanent condition, but rather of a fluctuating range of cognitive dissonance.

As noted already, Ōe's main source of influence is the mentally disabled Hikari. Ōe himself explained that the aim of his novels was to give his disabled child a voice, a task he has found, not long after *Quiet Life* was published, unsatisfactory given his son's recognition as a composer (1995, 89). His mindfulness about the medium of narrating life is on display in his later novels as well, but even before his artistic position is indicative of the conundrum of being influenced as a source of his own vulnerability. He openly acknowledged this precarious state of writing about disability in a speech delivered at an international conference on rehabilitation that was held in Tokyo in 1988:

> Essentially, in writing a novel about a handicapped child one is building a model of what it means to be handicapped, making it as complete and comprehensive as possible yet also concrete and personal. Nor is the model confined to the handicapped person alone, but something that encompasses the world around him, and by extension, the world we live in. (1996, 44–45)

The writer's position and the adaptive filmmaker's as well are therefore interlinked with multiple sources, a situation in which the "original" novel becomes an open question. Reality or truth should have limits or borders, where the public and the private are distinguished from one another, but articulating one as separated from the other is, in this case, an impossible task, an aporia.

Jacques Derrida somewhat subverts the "original" Greek term "aporia" to signify both projection and protection "of a task to accomplish, or as the protection created by a substitute, a prosthesis that we put forth in order to represent, replace, shelter, or dissimulate ourselves" (1993, 11), two usually different meanings that the term juxtaposes. Both versions of *Quiet Life* represent in this sense of the aporia the double role of protecting and projecting, but in line with the notion of mental disability as an apparatus, it is not clear whose self is being projected and who is protected. Indeed, this is a dynamic situation that is in a constant state of flux and ambiguity. Hikari Ōe is, in the most banal interpretation, the object of protection and projection, but he also serves as the means to protect his seemingly mentally capable relatives and he allows them to project a better public image of themselves, as the main source of their artistic creativity.

Aporia as a conundrum in the context of this chapter characterizes a notion of anxiety that binds Ōe and Itami with a vast network of influences. This aporic sense of anxiety within the apparatus recalls Harold Bloom's famous discussion on the anxiety of influence. In his preface to the 1997 edition of *The Anxiety of Influence*, Bloom writes that anxiety is less of a psychological matter within the author and more of a quality achieved by the work. Influence is a metaphor "that implicates a matrix of relationships-imagistic, temporal, spiritual, psychological-all of them ultimately defensive in their nature" (1997, xxiii). Seen in this light, the aporic anxiety is the consequence of one's "strong" misreading of a literary work, and by extension, also of the film adaptation in the case this chapter discusses. Hikari is the object of protection, but at the same time he is a source of influence, and therefore also of anxiety.

Ōe identifies William Blake as another influence in envisioning a state of being mentally compromised. Blake serves for him as a mediator into his own disabled son's unknowable state of being. In one interview, Ōe admits that Blake enables him to "conceive the model human environment in a cosmic context" (Ōe and Yoshida 1998, 373). As Alice Hall explains, Ōe finds in Blake an "understanding of the relationship between literature and imagination" (2016, 3), or a way to assume in his mind other states of being. Michiko N. Wilson argues that a sense of absence of knowledge in Blake's poem "The Little Boy Lost" motivates many of Ōe's works (1986, 61–62). Yet, the lost boy in this respect is not necessarily the son, but also the author himself who is lost in an aprotic apparatus of compromised epistemologies. Blake's influence is thus not just the poetic language required to depict unfathomable worlds, but also a nonfigurative mode of reading with which to compose a representational apparatus where one imagines alternative yet concrete mentally disabled experiences.

One part of *Quiet Life*, which does not appear in the film adaptation, demonstrates the anxiety of influence in the sense discussed above, as a mixture of abstraction and prosaic life stemming from Blake. In this section of the novel, Mā-chan recalls verses from the poet's *Last Judgement* in which dead children scream before being baptized; in a following dream, she sees herself and Eeyore as such children in what she interprets as a Blakean desert. After she wakes up, she explains to herself that she and her brother must have appeared as children because of her brother's "head disorder" (1996, 125–26) (*atama no shogai*) (1995, 152–53).[2] That is, as Hikari's guardian while her parents are away, she performs not only as his protector, but rather, she also assumes his compromised position as her own, hence forming a unique sense of anxiety.

A more representational (albeit indirect) example of Blakean influence that appears in both versions of *Quiet Life*, one that also underscores the inherent sense of anxiety in this experience, is a sequence where Mā-chan worries about the title of her brother's recent composition "Sutego" or "Abandoned Child." The apparent anxiety surrounding the title is whether Eeyore feels abandoned by his parents. Both the novel and film adaptation reveal that this is not actually the case, but the episode appears in a chapter of the book where Mā-chan acknowledges that her father is the one who faces mental difficulties including one "in which a mere seclusion of his person at a place of shelter offered him no solution at all" (1996, 30). The film, as already mentioned, more directly (again, even if somewhat comically) portrays the father as suffering from chronic depressive disorder. Thus, being abandoned as part of the apparatus of mental disability signifies an acute existential distress or a disabled state of mind.

Language plays a doubtful advantageous role in the apparatus. On the one hand, it is a tool used by the mentally capable subjects, the father and Mā-chan (who writes the diary). On the other hand, however, words seem to escape their control at significant points, much like meaning does in poetic abstraction. Furthermore, the written word itself has only a secondary role in the visual medium of film. As such, mental disability in the apparatus is an aporic experience. It is not only a representational matter, but rather it is also and more so a multifaceted process of deciphering verbal and visual codes of a mental zone. Doing so by watching/reading situates the subject in a compromised position from where mental disability is articulated, even if not in communicable language.

CONCLUSION: NERVOUSNESS AND REPETITION

In a 1975 study about Ōe's literature, Hasumi argues that the author's literature employs a singular form of repetition (*hanpuku*). He explains that this is not a return of the same object, but the process of individuated fabrication (*netsuzo*) in rotation with different objects, an excessive and preposterous birth of the self (1975, 71–72). However, the writer's almost obsessive focus on mental disability that began in earnest with the 1964 novel *A Personal Matter*, which depicts the birth of his mentally disabled child, showcases more than a matter of literary theme or style. It is more than an ethical consideration or personal evocation of critical engagement with an ambivalent way of thinking. It is an aesthetic principle that leads from Ōe's work and the novelist's life into Itami's film, an a-historical repetition that reimagines how life with mental disability can be conceived even by those identified as able-minded.

It is neither the literary source nor the film adaptation that gives rise to this idea, but rather the fragile interaction between them. Ato Quayson proposes the term "aesthetic nervousness" to describe interactions between not just disabled and nondisabled characters, but also and more so the relationship between the reader and the text, the way an able-minded reader interacts with the representation of disabled characters. He writes:

> Ultimately, aesthetic nervousness has to be seen as coextensive with the nervousness regarding the disabled in the real world. The embarrassment, fear, and confusion that attend the disabled in their everyday reality is translated in literature and the aesthetic field into a series of structural devices that betray themselves when the disability representation is seen predominantly from the perspective of the disabled rather than from the normative position of the nondisabled. (Quayson 2017, 222)

This is not to say that works of fiction aestheticize the world from the perspective of a disabled character, but rather that it is the disabled position itself that is being aestheticized from the perspective of an assumed able-minded reader. Quayson limits his discussion to interactions with fictional characters and representations of disability, but in the case of *Quiet Life* the two are unavoidably intertwined. Itami reads Ōe's fiction about his son with a similar sense of nervousness that manifests in his interactions with his nephew Hikari Ōe in real life.

Unanswerable questions about what is represented, who is represented, and who is representing, rotate in a circular, not linear fashion between *Quiet Life*'s two versions as an aporia. Awareness of the unbridgeable gaps between literature/film situates readers/viewers in rotating imaginable states beyond binary oppositions of mental ability/disability, textual/visual representations, and audible/inaudible expressions, as these refer in a perpetual cycle to one another within a binding apparatus. Being disabled, unknowledgeable, or unarticulated is therefore akin to being dispositioned in a wrapped mentally stable category. It is this unsettling sense of trepidation, anxiety, or nervousness that ultimately fosters an articulation of a cognitive dissonant existence in the sprawling worlds of *Quiet Life*.

NOTES

1. The Japanese language does not differentiate between singular and plural nouns. *Shizuka na sekatsu* has been translated into English as *A Quiet Life*, but it could also be "*Quiet* Lives." For the purposes of this chapter, I do not go so far as to render the title into the plural "lives," but I nonetheless omit the singular marker "A" to leave some ambivalence as for whose life or lives are being referred to in the novel and its cinematic adaptation.
2. It might seem that the words Ōe uses are somewhat offensive. Indeed, the common Japanese term for people with disability is *shogai-sha*. However, as Miho Iwakuma points out, the common label can etymologically signify not only people with hardships or difficulties but also "polluted people" (Iwakuma 2005, 132).

WORKS CITED

Agamben, Giorgio. *What is an Apparatus?: And Other Essays*. Stanford: Stanford University Press, 2009.
Baudry, Jean-Louis, and Alan Williams. "Ideological effects of the basic cinematographic apparatus." *Film Quarterly* 28, no. 2 (1974): 39–47.
Bird, Robert. *Andrei Tarkovsky: Elements of Cinema*. London: Reaktion, 2008.
Bloom, Harold. *The Anxiety of Influence: A Theory of Poetry*. New York: Oxford University Press, 1997.
Brinch, Sara. "Tracing the Original: The film *Invictus* and 'Based on a True Story' Film as Adaptation." In Jorgen Bruhn, Anne Gjelsvik, Eirik Frisvold Hanssen (eds.), *Adaptation Studies: New Challenges, New Directions*. London: Bloomsbury Publishing, 223–44, 2013.
Derrida, Jacques. *Aporias*. Translated by Thomas Dutoit. Stanford: Stanford University Press, 1993.
Hall, Alice. *Literature and Disability*. New York: Routledge, 2016.
Hasumi, Shigehiko. *Ōe Kenzaburō ron*. Tokyo: Seidosha, 1975.
Hutcheon, Linda. *A Theory of Adaptation*. New York: Routledge, 2013.
Ihara, Kei'ichirō. "Shōsetsu to eiga: Shizuka na sekatsu ha ikana nishite akushon eiga ni nattaka." *Kagoshima Daigaku Hōbungakubu Kiyō Jinbungakka Ronshū* 80: 67–78, 2014.
Inouye, Charles Shiro. "In the Show House of Modernity: Exhaustive Listing in Itami Jūzō's *Tanpopo*." In Dennis Washburn and Carole Cavanaugh (eds.), *Word and Image In Japanese Cinema*. Cambridge: Cambridge University Press, 126–46, 2001.

Itami, Jūzō. "Eigaka ni tsuite." In Ōe, Kenzaburō. *Shizuka na seikatsu*. Tokyo: Kōdansha, 291–307, 1995.
Iwakuma, Miho. "Culture, Disability, and Disability Community: Notes on Differences and Similarities Between Japan and the United States." *Atenea* 25 no. 1 (2005): 131–42.
Jameson, Fredric. "Afterword: Adaptation as a Philosophical Problem." In Colin MacCabe, Kathleen Murray, ad Rick Warner (eds.), *True to the Sprit: Film Adaptation and the Question of Fidelity*. New York: Oxford University Press, 215–34, 2011.
Johnson Vida T., and Graham Petrie. *The Films of Andrei Tarkovsky: A Visual Fugue*. Bloomington: Indiana University Press, 1994.
Martin, Sean. *Andrei Tarkovsky*. Harpenden, Herts, England: Kamera Books, 2011.
Mulvey, Bern. "Nonfiction as Deconstruction: Shishousetsu and Oe's 'Teach us to outgrow our madness.'" 欧米言語文化論集 (2012): 221–239.
Ōe, Kenzaburō. *Teach Us How to Outgrow Our Madness: Four Short Novels*. Translated by John Nathan. New York: Grove Press, 1977.
Ōe, Kenzaburō. *Jizokusuru kokorozashi: Gendai Nihon no essei*. Tokyo: Kōdansha, 1991.
Ōe, Kenzaburō. *Shizuka na seikatsu*. Tokyo: Kōdansha, 1995.
Ōe, Kenzaburō. *A Quiet Life*. Translated by Kunioki Yanagishita and William Wetherall. New York: Grove Press, 1996.
Ōe, Kenzaburō. *A Healing Family*. Translated by Stephen Snyder. New York: Kodansha International, 1996.
Ōe, Kenzaburō. *The Changeling*. Translated by Deborah Boliver Boehm. New York: Grove Press, 2010.
Ōe, Kenzaburō, and Sanroku Yoshida. "An Interview with Kenzaburō Ōe." *World Literature Today* 62, no. 3 (1988): 369–74.
Quayson, Ato. "Aesthetic Nervousness." *The Disability Studies Reader* (2013): 202–13.
Skakov, Nariman. *The Cinema of Tarkovsky: Labyrinths of Space and Time*. New York: Palgrave Macmillan, 2012.
Strugatsky, Arkady and Boris. *Roadside Picnic*. Translated by Olena Bormashenko. Chicago: Chicago Review Press, 2012.
Wilson, Michiko N. *The Marginal World of Ōe Kenzaburō*. Armonk, NY: M.E. Sharpe, 1986.
Yomota, Inuhiko. *Ajia no naka no Nihon eiga*. Tokyo: Iwanami Shoten, 2001.

Chapter 11

Adapting Autism in Telenovelas

Venevisión's **La Mujer Perfecta** *and the Trace of* **Esmeralda**

Martín Ponti

The proliferation of streaming services has evinced the popularity of serialized programming worldwide. Korean dramas, Turkish soaps, and Latin American telenovelas, among others, compete daily for viewers far beyond the limits of their linguistic and geographic borders. While the popularity of video on demand (VoD) services have disrupted the primacy of broadcast networks, or at best modified viewer habits, episodic programming continues to drive the growing library of streaming services. As reported by the website Programming Insider, notwithstanding the popularity of VoD, broadcast networks such as Televisa in Mexico continue to attract viewers through telenovelas, as they consistently rank within the top five programs on air (2017). Similarly in the United States, Spanish language broadcast networks like Univisión and Telemundo produce and distribute serialized dramas not only for the U.S. Latinx market but for global consumers of melodrama worldwide. Univision's rebroadcast of Televisa's hit telenovela *Vencer el desamor* (2020), *translated to Overcoming heartbreak (all translations from Spanish are my own unless otherwise noted)*, held the number one position in its time slot for both networks. The centrality of telenovelas as the main television genre in Latin America and in the U.S. Spanish-language market is not a recent trend, but rather one that began as radio serials lost popularity due to the emergence of television in the Americas throughout the late 1950s.

The beginning stages of television production vary by country. Whereas Cuba pioneered telenovela production in 1952, in its launch of the melodramatic serial *El Derecho de Nacer* by the CMQ network, Mexico produced its first telenovela in 1958, with the release of *Senda Prohibida* by *Telesistema Mexicano*. Telenovela scholar Nora Mazziotti categorizes this early period as the "initial stage" of telenovela production ranging from the 1950s up until the implementation of videotape in the 1960s (2006, 30). It is within this initial period where broadcasters began experimenting with the genre by remaking successful radio serials and adapting literary romance novels for the small screen. Thus adaptation has always been a prominent practice in the telenovela industry. In the following two decades, as each network developed its own aesthetic, Venezuelan and Mexican media industries commercialized their works throughout the Spanish speaking world, enabled by technological advances. The transnational success of Venezuelan melodramatic productions like *Esmeralda* (1970), produced by Enrique Crousillat for Venevisión, and its subsequent adaptation *Topacio* (1984) produced by the now defunct Radio Caracas Television (RCTV) network, were texts penned by Cuban exile writer Delia Fiallo. The success of this story turned the actress Lupita Ferrer who played the titular character of Esmeralda, into a transnational and global personality as it enabled her to have a career throughout Latin America and Europe. The success of the show also resulted in four televised adaptations (1984, 1997, 2004, 2017). Since the initial stage of telenovela production, actors, scripts, technicians, and telenovelas circulated widely as serialized drama competed for viewers globally.

Considering this uninterrupted trend of sustained production and distribution, as a researcher of melodramatic serials I find it pertinent to reassess the 2010 Venezuelan television season. The season opened without a locally produced telenovela and the launch of one did not occur until almost the end of the year. While this trend might not sound like an anomaly, especially when one considers how viewing habits have changed due to VoD, in the case of Venezuela, there are other factors that require consideration. The absence of a nationally produced serial signals yet another sign of how shifts in Venezuela's political and economic processes have direct repercussions on their media industries. As a consequence, the political, social, and cultural movement known as the Bolivarian Revolution, led by then-president Hugo Chavez, espoused an anti-imperialist rhetoric and favored a state-led economy buttressed by a series of social policies meant to redistribute the wealth of concentrated oligopolies, such as those in telecommunications (Ramírez Alvarado 2007, 292). As an example, on May 27, 2007, RCTV ceased to exist as the government terminated the network's license to operate as a terrestrial broadcast network. The highest court of law, the Supreme Tribunal of Justice, upheld the National Commission of Communication's decision to order RCTV to transfer its equipment to the newly formed state media television company: Televisora Venezolana Social (TVes). Given the political and economic panorama of the country, other remaining networks, such as Venevisión, redirected their business models to focus on its international market out of its U.S. Miami affiliates. Again this shift ignored its internal market, to the detriment of its own national programming, but secured its presence outside its national borders.

While this chapter contextualizes the reasons for a decrease in nationally produced telenovelas in Venezuela, the primary focus considers the industry's standard practice of adaptation as a key strategy to return to serialized fiction, as evidenced through Leonardo Padrón's creation of the hit telenovela, *La Mujer Perfecta (LMP)*. In short, the plot line of *LMP* centers on Micaela Gómez (played by Mónica Spear), a poor young woman with Asperger's syndrome. She falls in love with Santiago Reverón (played by Ricardo Álamo), a successful plastic surgeon known as Dr. Botox. Santiago is married to Gala Moncada (played by Ana Karina Manco), who is portrayed as an aging and over-the-top telenovela diva struggling to regain her once prominent position on television. At the onset, the plot line replicates the traditional telenovela formula of a love triangle where the narrative rests on the character's need to resolve their economic differences, coupled with a man's dilemma to choose between two women who compete for his affection. However, Padrón builds and expands on these themes as a way to deconstruct and decenter patriarchal ideologies present in traditional melodramatic texts. As I argue, the success of the show rests on Padrón's ability to adapt the telenovela, from a genre originally created to entertain, to a site for social change and inclusion. Padrón creates a realist drama with scientific rigor in order to educate viewers on autism. While *LMP* is a love story in its most basic formula, the main theme and plot line is dedicated to Micaela's journey as a person who is diagnosed as having Asperger's syndrome. As a clarifying point, according to the website Autism Speaks, since the publication of the *DSM-5* in 2013 by the American Psychiatric Association, Asperger's syndrome is no longer diagnosed as a standalone disorder. Now Asperger's is part of a larger umbrella in the Autism Spectrum Disorder (ASD) (Autism Speaks, n.d). While I acknowledge this change, I continue to refer to Asperger's throughout this chapter, as the telenovela *LMP* was created and released prior to the revised diagnosis.

In addition to this initial analysis that considers adaptation and the reimagining of the telenovela genre in order to inject realism to a historically traditional program, I also propose a second prong to this layered analysis. Padrón's adaptation cannot occur without revisiting the stylistic and thematic formula established by the paradigmatic success of telenovela writer Delia Fiallo. She formed part of the initial stage of telenovela production and continued working in the industry throughout the 2000s. In 1970, Fiallo scripted the successful Venezuelan telenovela *Esmeralda*. Fiallo's story arc focuses on a young peasant's journey to discover love and her true identity as a blind person. While *LMP* and *Esmeralda* are told in completely different ways, the latter's legacy is so ingrained in the viewers' telenovela imaginary, that it is impossible to create a telenovela in Venezuela about disabilities and ignore the paradigmatic legacy of Fiallo's work. Therefore, Padrón's dual adaptation of both the genre and narrative of *Esmeralda* allow for the renewal of the telenovela formula as it presents a socially forward treatment of neurodiversity on serialized television.

Underpinning this dual analysis of adaptation I underscore adaptation as industry practice that capitalizes on the success of previous media content in order to guarantee renewed viewers. There is also an important element that the research on adaptation generally fails to consider, which all the chapters in this edited collection highlight: adaptation provides writers and creators the opportunity to revisit and "breathe new life to tired narratives" (Hardin and Kiernan 2022, 3). At the same time, adaptation operates as a corrective tool to update narratives that we now understand as detrimental to underrepresented and marginalized groups. In other words, as the editors of this collection support, adaptations remedy "past inaccuracies . . . making them accessible and relevant for contemporary viewers" (Hardin and Kiernan 2022, 3). Thus this research stands at the crossroads of adaptation and disability studies, as it explains how Latin American melodramatic narratives embed issues of neurodiversity into their content.

THE TELENOVELA AS AN ADAPTED GENRE

Working and researching adaptations proposes a series of problems, particularly associated with perceptions of degrees of fidelity and quality. As Linda Hutcheon explains in *A Theory of Adaptation*, even though cultural recycling and the adaptation of artistic forms is a common and accepted practice in our postmodern era, there still exists a tendency to distrust the value of such work (2006, 3). Others, such as Naremore (2000), address critics' use of negative terms such as "culturally inferior" and "belated" when assessing adapted works (6). Even the term "desecration" figures into critics' assessment (Stam 2000, 54); as Stam explains, part of the negative connotations afforded to popular cultural adaptations of literary works into films stems from the strict hierarchy that has existed in Western societies between the superiority of the written word, defined as "logophilia" versus the lesser, the visual, "iconophobia" (58). There is also the issue of fidelity, which has generated a whole series of adaptation studies with the main focus to discern the level of precision of transposing one text into another form (Hutcheon 2006, 7). Aligned with Hutcheon, this chapter discards the above past trends in adaptation studies in favor of a nuanced and an encompassing definition of adaptation, as highlighted by Hutcheon in the following three points:

An acknowledged transposition of recognizable other work or works . . . A creative and an interpretive act of appropriation/salvaging . . . An extended intertextual engagement with the adapted work. (2006, 8)

I value these three descriptive elements expressed above, as they inform my understanding and interpretation of *LMP* as an adapted text. As highlighted by Hutcheon, an adaptation does not imply a one-to-one relationship between the original and the remake, but rather includes multiple intertexts that affect the interpretation and adaptation of the text. Second, there is an interpretative element that is involved in the appropriation and reshaping of a text, an interpretative model that I deduce is not limited just to the creator, but those who are actively consuming the text, in this case the viewer. And lastly, that adaptations can be understood via a relay of texts, a sort of palimpsest of original and competing texts, that make up the totality of the adapted work. These three elements are key in interpreting the way Padron adapts the telenovela genre. In short, the telenovela as a genre is already part of an adapted text, since it must conform to a strict set of genre requirements that are replicated in each iteration. Furthermore, since the inception of the telenovela, the industry has deferred to adaptations as an industry practice, as the telenovela emerged from adapted radio serials, classic novels and films. The foundational history of the telenovela is very clear in articulating the role played by adaptation.

In 1952 television arrived in Venezuela, and a year later, the now defunct Televisa bought out by Venevision, produced its first telenovela, *La Criada de la Granja* (1953). This first attempt at a telenovela aired live in fifteen-minute episodes and was based on the adapted work of Guy de Maupassant's novel *Histoire D'une Fille De Ferme*. Venevisión's main competitor, RCTV had its first major hit a decade later with the adaption of *El Derecho de Nacer* (1965), originally created by the Cuban Felix B. Caignet, as a radio serial in 1948. The success of Caignet's work situated the serial as an international success throughout Latin America, becoming the standard and model for future telenovelas. Multiple radio versions were produced throughout the Americas and when Cuba began experimenting with television, the format was adapted to the small screen, becoming the first Cuban telenovela (Ramírez Alvarado 2007, 188). As evidenced here, adaptations became the most salient strategy to create serialized television programming. This industry trend continues up to the present as both broadcast networks and VoD continue to attract and secure viewers through serialized narratives.

As part of the continued commitment to adaptation, Venezuela remade mostly Cuban and Mexican hits as part of its industrial strategy. After the Cuban revolution in 1959 and the elimination of private networks on the island, media players including actors, screenwriters, and producers were exiled and contributed to the emerging television industries in the Americas. This is the case of Delia Fiallo who was hired by Venevisión and RCTV to adapt her library of hits for the local market. Fiallo was responsible for instilling her distinctive style to the genre. Its style became inseparable from that of its lead writer, known for her highly sentimental heroines whose ultimate goal of marriage and family came to fruition after overcoming obstacles mostly linked to social mobility within a strict class system. A clear example is *Esmeralda* produced in 1970–1971, loosely based on Fiallo's 1952 radio version, later remade into a second telenovela in 1985 titled *Topacio*. Both versions of the telenovela were crucial in Venezuela's entrance into the transnational media market since its success led to its distribution throughout Latin America, Spain, Eastern Europe, and Asia. This early success solidified Venevisión and RCTV in their ability to commercialize and distribute telenovelas globally. When seeing *LMP*, it is impossible to not recognize themes and aesthetic qualities originally found in the paradigmatic 1970 telenovela *Esmeralda*.

UPDATING ESMERALDA: MEDICAL NARRATIVES AND MELODRAMA

In Fiallo's 1970 original telenovela *Esmeralda*, the main story arc centers on the titular character who is a blind peasant woman. Following the traditional telenovela formula, Esmeralda's blindness serves to construct her character as weak, innocent, and in need of protection, which she will find in her future husband Juan Pablo Peñalver. There is also a love triangle, since Juan Pablo dates socialite Graciela, the daughter of family friends and someone whom both families want to see united, due to their common upper-class background. Running parallel to this story arc, the show also presents the theme and plot of mistaken identities as Esmeralda is really the daughter of the Peñalvers. Esmeralda and Juan Pablo were switched at birth due to her father's wish for a male firstborn. Consequently, while Juan Pablo leads a life of privilege, Esmeralda grows up impoverished in the countryside. Lastly, during a momentary break in their relationship, Esmeralda dates an ophthalmologist who will operate and cure her blindness. Once she recovers her vision and identity, Esmeralda and Juan Pablo marry, providing narrative closure.

The similarities in thematic and basic plot elements between *Esmeralda* and *LMP*—established in the female leads with disabilities, love triangle, mistaken identities, and class differences—resonate and clearly position the melodramatic elements, specific to telenovela codes. Also the role of mistaken identities plays an integral role in both productions but with varying ideological frameworks. Fiallo's story, fashioned out of traditional melodrama, situates the switching of babies, one blind and one poor, as a crisis, as a generator of dramatic tension. Esmeralda is the true heir of the Peñalver's but grows up poor as her intransigent *machista* father can only accept a healthy male firstborn. It is this traditional context that allows the parents to discard their child due to her gender and disability without framing that decision as a criminal act. Instead, the story presents their actions as a mistake that Esmeralda will understand and forgive. Inversely, the male baby received all the benefits and rights afforded to a Peñalver's by their high social status. The romance that ultimately emerges between Esmeralda and Juan Pablo forces the family to confront its past and once all is forgiven, order is restored and the couple marry. Ideologically, the story suggests the possibilities of class reconciliation through the eventual safeguard of patriarchal heteronormativity. While it is recognized that Juan Pablo is not the Peñalver's biological son, his marriage to the rightful heir does not endanger the family's patrimony as it remains in the hands of the same family. Thus, the common melodramatic trope of reversal of fortunes does not apply, at least for the female protagonist. Instead, Esmeralda experiences a restoration in terms of her familial and societal status. The only element that one could categorize as a reversal refers to her disability. Fiallo's character was born blind but through the help of a doctor and love interest, Esmeralda is able to see, facilitating the possibility to return to her biological parents and reclaim her love of Juan Pablo.

While it is clear Fiallo did not intend to discuss the causes of blindness or attempt to change people's perception of those living with disabilities, as does Padrón with Asperger's, both writers employ medical conditions in telenovelas to accentuate the genre's requirement for melodramatic tension. As Carolina Costa-Alzuru argues in relation to Fiallo's work:

> Did famous Cuban writer Delia Fiallo spend months researching the different causes and consequences—behavioral and social—of blindness before writing her landmark telenovela Esmeralda? It does not seem so. Esmeralda's blindness was not intended to generate knowledge or elicit reflection but was a dramatic way to accentuate the traditional telenovela female protagonist code. (2013, 2)

Here, Costa-Alzuru emphasizes, any socially relevant and contemporary approach to health issues on telenovelas exist for dramatic effect, as entertainment occupies the genre's prerogative. In a study on Venezuelan telenovelas and uses of myths, Alirio Aguilera argues that medical discourses in melodrama function as an element to "dramatize" underpinning a sensationalist tone. Aguilera claims the *tone* is heightened by a tendency to incorporate into the story arc unrealistic outcomes brought upon by a "miraculous rehabilitation" (1992, 11). For Aguilera melodramatic serials do not offer scientific-medical rigor as the goal is not to inform, but to generate in viewers an emotional reaction by the character's pain and or recovery. Thus, miracles are not included as a means to impart a religious or supernatural element to the story, but rather operate and serve to parallel the characters' moral barometer. That is, characters constructed as evil acquire a disease or a disability as a punishment, and the hero's goodness is rewarded with the miracle of recovery. The inscription of a moral code in relation to medical issues is in part tied to the ideological worldview of melodrama. Melodramatic texts construct Manichaean characters that represent very clearly delineated conceptions of "good" and "evil." Telenovela scholar Nora Mazziotti characterizes this extreme Manichean construction of illnesses and recovery for its punitive effect (2006, 82). As mentioned previously, characters are either awarded with a cure or with a disease based on their moral standing allowing melodrama to open up a space where the character's moral fortitude surfaces to overcome evil, to endure pain, or accept their limitations (Mazziotti 2006, 84). Furthermore, Mazziotti contends that melodramatic texts naturalize medical issues by how often telenovelas incorporate medical props, characters portraying medical professionals, and sets that recreate spaces such as hospital rooms and doctor offices (2006, 81).

The overrepresentation of medical topics as suggested by Mazziotti as well as the recurring themes of miracle cures as a measure of a character's moral compass (Aguilar and Acosta Alzuru) results in a questioning of the social and communicative value of telenovelas. The question that arises confronts researchers of melodrama and serialized television as it questions whether the telenovela as a genre provides viewers with tools to understand and make informed choices regarding medical issues. Ultimately, the question also underpins whether serialized programming can operate as socially responsible content that corrects past inaccuracies while enlightening viewers. In responding to these research questions, I propose the *spectrum* approach. Melodrama as a genre already has the tendency to favor binary themes, structures, and ideologies. However viewers and overall consumers of serialized content do not have to limit their interpretation and understanding of such texts in binary ways, but can contend, reject, and or question the inner workings of melodrama in multiple and disruptive ways. This approach suggests that viewers have agency to interpret and connect with content in ways that differ from the ideological framework that a genre/cultural product may invoke or form part of its essence. In part, viewer agency to interpret from their experience is due to the recognition that viewers are not a homogenous block; viewer interpretation and connection to a media text is on a spectrum. For example, some viewers may find pleasure in regressive telenovelas that portray a rigid patriarchal worldview, not because they subscribe to such views, but rather viewer pleasure is derived from counternarratives that viewers impose on the texts they consume.

Just as viewer consumption of melodramatic serials exists on a continuum, the same applies to the industrial imperative of the genre. In other words, the telenovela industry is not a monolithic block that operates on a fixed and ever-evolving linear path. As multiple scholars have argued, just as there are multiple Latin American nations, there are different models of telenovelas that each country and corresponding network actively produce. Even though telenovelas over time have incorporated more accurate representations of health issues, there are moments where the health issue discussed receives a regressive and anachronistic treatment, not because it is unaware of the changes, but because the particular type of telenovela may employ medical issues as a catalyst for dramatic tension over accuracy. A clarifying example includes the development of the *Entertainment-Education* telenovela model developed by Miguel and Irene Sabido in Mexico throughout the 1970s. In their model, telenovelas were written first to educate and then to entertain, and thus topical issues are represented following accurate information for that time. The couples' telenovelas produced by *Televisa*, *Ven conmigo* (1975) (*Come with me*), and *Nosotras las mujeres* (1984) (*We, Women*) dealt with issues of adult literacy and family reproductive planning, respectively (Kawamura and Kohler 2013, 93). However, this does not imply that *Televisa*, since it produced these highly informative educational and entertaining programs in the 1970s, continues to do so consistently in the present. Instead, we see how even in the same network, regressive and progressive stand side by side competing against each other. This industry practice generates consequences for viewers who must make decisions about not only the type of programming they will consume but also how they choose to consume and make sense of these messages. In this chapter I argue rather than having to select between creating a regressive/progressive narrative, Padrón shifts between these two forms in the same telenovela. This grants Padrón the ability to capture a wide segment of viewers since those looking for a more traditional telenovela will find it here, as well as those who want a more progressive and updated storyline. Thus, Padrón through both his adaptation of elements of the classic telenovela *Esmeralda* and his infusion of elements of the *entertainment-education* model of telenovela production can vacillate between the two. Considering the economic and social context of the Venezuelan industry mentioned previously, a shrinking industry with less nationally produced content for viewers, this allows Padrón, with one production, to offer multiple viewing experiences.

Once the connection between Fiallo and Padrón's work is established, it is also important to consider the role of representing disability on melodramatic serials, such as telenovelas. The use of medical issues and contemporary health topics have historically been included in telenovelas, in part, this is due to the fact that, at its core, melodrama has always deferred to medical issues as a way of communicating a message. Accordingly, this chapter necessitates a closer look at melodrama, as it informs the structure of the telenovela. In the classic text *The Melodramatic Imagination*, Peter Brooks provides an in-depth study of the origins of melodrama. Brooks defines melodrama not within the fixed parameters of a genre but rather develops the notion of melodrama as *expressionistic aesthetic: a mode of excess* that has influenced the imagination of modern literature and culture (1995, vii–viii). In short, melodrama as a mode of expression attempts to make sense of a society's battle between good and evil in a secularized world, where innocence and goodness always triumphs over evil. While Brook's develops his work on melodrama to explain this mode in a series of writers in the nineteenth and twentieth century, his conception provides clarity in understanding the application of this mode onto other genres influenced by melodrama. The telenovela, thus, can be understood as a form of melodrama, as its aesthetic and thematic composition borrows heavily from this form. As defined by Brooks:

> Melodrama is indeed, typically, not only a moralistic drama but the drama of morality: it strives to find, to articulate, to demonstrate, to "prove" the existence of a moral universe which, though put into question, masked by villainy and perversions of judgment, does exist and can be made to assert its presence. (1995, 20)

In this quote, one could simply substitute "melodrama" for "telenovela," and the definition still applies for the second term. Brooks also elaborates on how this mode overrepresents characters with physical and mental disabilities. "There are blind men, paralytics, invalids of various sorts whose very physical presence evokes the extremism and hyperbole of ethical conflict and manichaeistic struggle" (1995, 56). In his chapter titled *The Text of Muteness*, Brooks probes further, arguing that melodrama always presents an inherent paradox. At the same time, in classic melodrama there is often a preference for including a mute character, who cannot precisely speak and communicate their intentions; forcing the character to communicate through bodily gestures. This requires the actor playing the character to deploy "all of his dramatic power to convey meaning" (1995, 61). Brooks connects gestural communication in melodrama as the evolution and influence of pantomime found in the early melodramatic theater, where the gestural was considered nonarbitrary and a *universal* form of communication (1995, 68). With time the mute character has adapted to depict other forms of disability, allowing the character, figuratively and rhetorically, to carry out the role of the *mute* to communicate and express their moral worldview without words, but through their disability.

Delia Fiallo's 1970 *Esmeralda* figuratively continues the trope of the mute character, but now through Esmeralda's blindness. As a classic telenovela heroine, Esmeralda must communicate her innocence and purity, yet words are not enough to convey this idea, and thus the character must resort to bodily gestures as a form of communication. As a telenovela convention, actors portraying blind characters generally overplay gestural and facial expressions that are supposed to convey their disability to audiences. Rhetorically, Esmeralda's blindness puts her in a situation where she *cannot see* the cruelty of the characters around her, allowing her to not be influenced by their intentions. Her blindness also operates to invoke a sense of sympathy and connection to the character on the part of viewers who can *see* how the titular character contrasts with the evil character's true motives. This rhetorical use of blindness as a recourse of theatrics and as a way to build dramatic tension is also adapted by Leonardo Padrón in *LMP*. Although Padrón adapts blindness to Asperger's, both conditions refer figuratively and rhetorically to the text of muteness, as suggested in Brook's writings. While blindness and Asperger's are clearly very different conditions, within the scope of melodrama they operate at the same level. Both Micaela and Esmeralda due to their disabilities employ a different language from which to communicate with others; the characters surrounding both female heroines have difficulty understanding their actions and quickly resort to categorizing them as strange and crazy.

NARRATIVIZING AUTISM ON *LMP*

As an adaptation of the 1970 *Esmeralda*, Padrón's *LMP* oscillates between embracing traditional elements of Fiallo's work, while at the same time furthering the entertainment-education value of the telenovela. In this section, I exemplify through three key scenes the ways in which the adapted texts incorporate Asperger's syndrome in its advancement of social issues. At the same time, these examples elucidate my understanding of the inner workings of adaptation as a common practice of the industry. The first scene analyzed focuses on the main character of Micaela in relation to the narrative strategies employed to present her to viewers for the first time. Second, I explore the ways characters relate to her and use derogatory epithets such as "strange" and "crazy," when they fail to understand her Asperger's. Lastly, the third scene expands on the concept of domesticity, a common theme found in classic telenovela formulas where the young ingénue is ultimately molded to conform to the needs of a patriarchal and heteronormative worldview. It is through these three key scenes that viewers are presented with a telenovela on a spectrum that oscillates between regressive and progressive.

The first episode reveals the ways Padrón presents a character with autism to viewers. Micaela is introduced via voice-over allowing her to express her frustration when people perceive her as strange. She states: "Yesterday someone told me that I was a strange girl. My family has told me this my whole life, but as of now no doctor has told me what's wrong with me" (Padrón 2010). Padrón's use of first-person voice-over operates as a television and film convention that creates necessary intimacy and space to reveal to viewers the main character from the perspective and voice of the protagonist. At the same time, the voiceover allows Micaela to speak candidly about her main concern: people failing to understand her. The scene proceeds with a montage of Micaela taking pictures throughout Caracas as she further recounts how there are messages and linguistic registers that escape her understanding, such as the expression "to have butterflies in your stomach" to mean someone is in or falling in love. Micaela states that she is trying to understand that expression because she would like to be in love. Her inability to understand figurative language is a clear sign that viewers receive about her Asperger's, although this is something that the character and viewers are unaware of at the start of the serial. It is through the repetition of similar scenes, such as when she misinterprets figurative language followed by a doctor's visit, that explains to her that it is all part of her Asperger's, and that allows for audience understanding. In the initial episode, Padrón, within the first three minutes, exemplifies through the character's perceived strangeness—her Asperger's syndrome—as the melodramatic hook from which to create a connection between the protagonist and the viewer. Both viewer and character are implicated in their search to understand her story, and while this approach is much more nuanced in comparison to the presentation of Esmeralda as blind, both telenovelas similarly employ the characters' condition as a convention of dramatic tension, since viewers are unaware of Micaela's autism. By the end of the seventh minute, the character explains that unlike her sisters who have fallen in love multiple times, she has never experienced those feelings. Thus, the story clearly delineates that the main issue, as in all telenovelas, dictates a narrative predicated on a sentimental female protagonist whose main goal is to decipher who they are as they search for love. This common theme of finding love connects to the traditional telenovela code found in *Esmeralda*.

In the second key scene I interpret here the viewer remains uninformed regarding Micaela's Asperger's. My assessment contends that the narrative attempts to generate viewer interest in the story by raising the question and not providing the reason for Micaela's behavior. Instead, at this stage, the story continues to push the narrative about Micaela's erratic, strange, and crazy behavior, based on the negative words used by characters to describe her; I argue this leads to viewers wanting to distance themselves from those characters and assess the situation differently. There is a sense of empathy that is generated in viewers when other characters describe her in negative ways. Viewers who consume telenovelas are familiar with the genre, which generally stipulate that the main character (as in this case Micaela) is the heroine whom we must root for and connect with her worldview. Also in the scenes where she is described negatively, the viewer has been able to see the full development of the episode; at the end viewers are more likely to empathize and feel bad for what has happened to Micaela, rather than criticize and ridicule her as do some characters. For example in episode one, we learn that Micaela is not able to keep a job since she is too honest with customers. In this specific scene, Micaela is working as a waitress and meets Santiago as he is dining. She answers his questions about the restaurant's offerings very honestly which leads her boss to fire her. She runs out of the restaurant upset and it starts to rain which frightens her, this sensory-based fear is further impacted by the noise from the street f and traffic. Micaela is disoriented due to her hypersensitivity to the lights and sounds of the city. Due to this raised anxiety she is unable to see that Santiago is attempting to help her. As Micaela is unable to verbalize her feelings, she hits Santiago and runs from the conflict. Santiago remains perplexed and as he explains the situation, a friend ends the conversation with the following line: "*esa muchacha está loca*" (that girl is crazy). As the episodes progress the terms used begin to shift from "strange" to "crazy," even though by the first half of the telenovela most characters know that Micaela has been diagnosed with Asperger's.

The shift in terminology from strange to crazy continues to build throughout the serial. For instance, in episode 127 when Micaela is talking to Santiago's ex-wife Gala she shares that she enjoys talking to Ronaldinho, her pet guinea pig. Gala responds with the insulting term *piazo e' loca*. The literal translation to this expression is "a big piece of a crazy woman" and Micaela replies as follows:

> Asperger's is a syndrome one is born with. It's a neurological condition, it's not a state of psychosis. But I see that you use that term "crazy" to make me feel inferior. . . . I thought that you having breast cancer would have changed the way you perceive and value others. . . . I hope you never feel excluded and that you never have to feel the shame of being made fun of, as you have made fun of me. (Padrón 2010)

The exchange taking place between Micaela and Gala responds to the genre's code to create dramatic tension between the protagonist-antagonist. This exchange forces viewers to take sides with the protagonist, as is the convention in telenovelas, as the narrative constructs Micaela as *good* and Gala as the antagonist. Gala's constant ridicule also helps in establishing the idea that her insensitivity to neurodiversity is something that viewers should not support. Instead, they should feel empathy for Micaela who, in tandem with viewers, learns about Asperger's. In a traditional telenovela, one without medical particularity, the Micaela-Gala conflict would have played out as a confrontation where the antagonist offends the lead by referring to her lower socioeconomic status. Instead here, while Gala is portrayed as rich, the class conflict is replaced by Micaela's disability. Nonetheless, the insult is troubling since it refers to things that the character cannot change. If one reads Micaela's message decontextualized from the serial, her message potentially suggests that her psychosis is a sign of delirium added to the fact that Micaela equates autism to cancer. However, when considering the context of her words, the character attempts to convey the importance of having empathy. Micaela reminds Gala that while their conditions are different, both have been rejected by others. Gala has been excluded from working due to her cancer, and Micaela has been fired from most jobs due to their inability to understand her. Instead, she urges Gala to reconsider the damaging repercussions of her words.

Lastly, the third key scene in *LMP* shows in part the ways in which Padrón adapts elements of the classic 1970 telenovela *Esmeralda*. In setting up this scene, it is important to understand how Padrón is resignifying the classic telenovela model that ideologically builds a narrative where domesticity is a key theme. Domesticity is understood here as a patriarchal ideology that requires women to remain within the space of the home—the private sphere—while men occupy a more central and public space. Within this framework, marriage and childbirth are the only viable options for women. In telenovelas, this has historically been represented through the trope of the poor uneducated peasant woman who is enlightened/civilized by a rich and educated man. Once she is "domesticated" through his help, she can marry and join the upper class. In *Esmeralda*, the characterization of the titular character as innocent and pure is constructed via connections to her status as a rural peasant in counterpoint to the urbanity and knowledge of Juan Pablo, a doctor from Caracas. In their initial meeting, Esmeralda bites Juan Pablo since she heard a gunshot, as he is hunting, and she can smell the residue of the bullets on him. Before biting him, she warns him that he should leave and not kill any more animals, or she will turn into a snake and bite him. He is amused and also taken aback as he considers her a "strange" girl when she bites him. This scene is reminiscent of the scene described earlier where Micaela hits Santiago during their first meeting. In both telenovelas female characters react out of fear and anxiety, leaving the male protagonist in shock but intrigued. In *LMP*, the notion of the need to domesticate Micaela is further developed once they have been married.

By episode 72, Micaela and Santiago are married and living together; however, it is explained that due to her Asperger's syndrome she is unable to quickly adapt to new conditions—she is unable to sleep next to her husband. To remedy the situation, Santiago builds a large bed that occupies the whole living room; this way they can sleep in the same bed. Santiago explains to Micaela that the idea came from reading Antoine de Saint-Exupéry work, *The Little Prince*. In that text, the young boy wants to play with a fox, but in order to do so, he must first domesticate the fox. As he utters these words, Micaela adds, "To domesticate is to establish a relationship between a person with an animal, like the horseman and the mare." To which Santiago adds, "It can also mean to get accustomed to one another." While his definition softens the animal connotation, he ends the scene with the following words, "I did all this to domesticate you," and the episode concludes with them having sex. While in the scene, there is an attempt to resignify domestication not as an act of male domination, the message is unable to completely shatter the sexist ideology, as it is her husband who guides her into married life. Santiago's use of the term further fuels the argument that Padrón's work operates on a spectrum that oscillates between presenting realistic issues regarding neurodiversity and between the need to satisfy viewers who consume traditional telenovelas. In the same scene, we learn the difficulties a person with Asperger's can have in establishing relationships, as well returning to outdated gender constructs that see the need to domesticate women. It is precisely Padrón's ability to establish this paradox of represented ideas that makes *LMP* a successful telenovela as multiple viewers can consume the work based on their particular views.

CONCLUSIONS: MELODRAMA AND ITS ADAPTATION

For more than fifty years, telenovelas have occupied a central role on Latin American television. Even with the proliferation of streaming services that offer diverse programming, melodramatic serials continue to engage viewers through the retelling of emotionally charged narratives. Scholars have attributed the genre's success in mobilizing primal human emotions that transcend linguistic, geographic, and sociocultural boundaries far beyond Latin America. While their assessment of the genre is accurate, I argue for the necessity to explore industry practices, such as the role of adaptation to standardize, reproduce, and circulate telenovela production. That is, adaptations, reboots, and remakes occupy a central role not only in supporting telenovela production but also in securing its place within a highly globalized industry. Most importantly, telenovela adaptations allow creators to resignify a genre that has been considered regressive due to its traditional representations of race, class, gender, as well as disability. Part of the adaptation process requires authors to revisit the main melodramatic codes as a starting point to connect with viewers familiar with the genre, and then use the opportunity to entertain responsibly.

As demonstrated here, Padrón's *LMP* accomplishes the feat of creating a text that exists on a spectrum. In other words, Padrón's telenovela is a hybrid form of melodrama that not only borrows and adapts classic telenovelas but also pushes melodrama to new and socially relevant areas. My interpretation is facilitated by my understanding of the adaptation process as one that does not necessitate fidelity when adapting one text into another form. This means that adaptations can include thematic and character elements that transfer from one text to the other without having to have a complete and identical transference of the plot. This is the case with *Esmeralda* and *LMP* where the adaptive process focuses on the similarities between the heroines in both texts; both characters have disabilities that lead them to communicate differently from other characters. At the same time, viewers have influence over the adaptive process since it is really their understanding and familiarity with telenovelas that allows them to understand the conventions of the genre. It is this engagement with multiple texts that signify an adaptation, as in this case, the viewer's telenovela imagination emerges from their previous viewing/consumption habits.

WORKS CITED

Acosta-Alzuru, Carolina. *Telenovela adentro*. Vol. 115. Editorial Alfa, 2016.

Acosta-Alzuru, Carolina. "Dear Micaela: Studying a telenovela protagonist with asperger's syndrome." *Cultural Studies Critical Methodologies* 13, no. 2 (2013): 125–37.

Acosta-Alzuru, Carolina. "Beauty queens, machistas and street children: The production and reception of socio-cultural issues in telenovelas." *International Journal of Cultural Studies* 13, no. 2 (2010): 185–203.

Acosta-Alzuru, Carolina. *Venezuela es una Telenovela: melodrama, realidad y crisis*. Caracas: Editorial Alfa, 2007.

Autism Speaks. n.d. "What Is Asperger's Syndrome." Accessed August 10, 2021. https://www.autismspeaks.org/types-autism-what-asperger-syndrome.

Brooks, Peter. *The Melodramatic Imagination: Balzac, Henry James, Melodrama, and the Mode of Excess*. New Haven: Yale University Press, 1995.

Carroll, Rachel, ed. *Adaptation in Contemporary Culture: Textual Infidelities*. A&C Black, 2014.

Hardin, Whitney, and Julia Kiernan. "Introduction: Adaptations of Mental and Cognitive Disability in Popular Media." *Adaptations of Mental and Cognitive Disability in Popular Media*, edited by Whitney Hardin and Julia Kiernan. Lexington Books (2022): 1–13.

Hutcheon, Linda. *A Theory of Adaptation*. New York: Taylor and Francis, 2006.

Kawamura, Yoko, and Connie Kohler. "Applying Sabido's entertainment-education serial drama strategy to serve local radio audiences in the United States and Japan." *Critical Arts* 27, no. 1 (2013): 91–111.

Matelski, Marilyn J. "Telenovela: As our worlds turn: The birth and rebirth of Cuban serial drama." *The Journal of Popular Film and Television* 38, no. 4 (2010): 186–92.

Mazziotti, Nora. *Telenovela industria y prácticas sociales*. Bogotá (Colombia): Grupo editorial norma, 2006.

Mazziotti, Nora. *El espectáculo de la pasión: las telenovelas latinoamericanas*. Buenos Aires: Ed. Colihue, 1995.

Naremore, James, ed. *Film Adaptation*. New Brunswick, NJ: Rutgers University Press, 2000.

Padrón, Leonardo, writer. *La mujer perfecta*. Directed by César Bolívar and José Luis Zuleta, featuring Mónica Spear and Ricardo Álamo. Aired 2010–2011, Venevisión.

Programming Insider. "Monday Final Ratings." 2020. Accessed May 1, 2021. https://programminginsider.com/monday-final-ratins-vencer-el-desamor.

Ramírez Alvarado, María del Mar. "Escenarios de comunicación en una Venezuela polarizada: del Grupo Cisneros a la Ley Resorte." *Zer (Bilbao, Spain)*, 12, no. 22 (2007).

Stam, Robert. "The dialogics of adaptation." *Film Adaptation*. New Brunswick, NJ: Rutgers University Press, 54–76, 2000.

Chapter 12

Female Representations of Autism and Disability in Telenovelas

La Mujer Perfecta

Andrea Urrutia Gómez

When I was in primary school, I used to watch TV during the afternoons by myself after classes. One of the few distractions accessible to most Latin American audiences is the telenovela; its melodramatic plots and exaggerated performances are pure escapism. Through the screen, the public follows explorations of the human condition, albeit in a very stereotypical manner. Like many other Latin Americans, I grew up following the fights between the millionaire villain and the poor, but honest, protagonist. However, as much as I enjoyed them, it was difficult to see myself reflected in the unrealistic characters and stories. Growing up, my teachers repeatedly commented about my way of speaking, akin to a robot, and my lack of ability and interest in socializing with the other children in my classroom. Despite this, they were happy because I usually finished my homework early. I was obedient, attentive, and quiet. It would take me two more decades to get a diagnosis of Asperger syndrome, and more years to understand what it meant—an understanding that my teachers did not recognize, nor did any of the adults around me. Decades later, I realize that one of the reasons behind this circumstance is the absence or misrepresentation of autistic people in mass media such as telenovelas.

In this chapter, my goal is to address how a distinctive media production that is as widely consumed and culturally ingrained by Latin American audiences as the telenovela reproduces harmful representations of autistic and disabled people. I do this first by analyzing the telenovela genre in a comprehensive way and then exploring a (partial) counterexample, the Venezuelan telenovela *La Mujer Perfecta*, which aired in 2011 and whose protagonist is a woman diagnosed with Asperger syndrome. I chose this program because of its rarity (while the show was popular in its home country of Venezuela, the production gained international notoriety due to the death of the main actress, Mónica Spear, in 2014) and its intended goal of rendering the realities of neurodiverse people on television; ten years after it first aired, it remains an exception among representations of neurodiversity and disability in its genre.

I begin with a discussion of the theoretical framework employed for the analysis about telenovelas, and then offer an exploration of telenovelas' mostly ableist and misogynistic depictions as related to the individual model of disability, depictions which establish disability as a punishment for villains or an obstacle to be surmounted by its heroes or heroines. The chapter then outlines autism, neurodiversity, and the medical model of disability, scrutinizing the genre of the telenovela; and the selected case study of *La Mujer Perfecta* explores heterogeneous depictions of an "extraordinary" disabled and autistic woman. To close, I focus on the potential contributions of *La Mujer Perfecta* in combatting discussed stereotypes and stigmas. Throughout the chapter, I also tackle the heavily gendered connotations in telenovelas, especially the reproduction of hegemonic femininity in the region, and how stereotypes based on gender and disability feed from each other to produce complex misrepresentations within this genre.

TELENOVELAS AND THE IDEOLOGICAL CONSTRUCTION OF DISABILITY

To begin, I introduce competing definitions of telenovela, which guide this analysis through attention to key concepts such as representation, stereotype, and stigma. Cassano describes the telenovela as

> a cultural production that talks about the different national industries, a set of stories that mobilize and affect people's lives, a consumption that requires rituality, a reading and an instance of dialogue with its audiences . . . by representing life, it also shapes and constitutes it. (2014, 2)

Building upon Hall, Lugo, Melón, and Castillo (2010) argue that the narratives executed in telenovelas enact a discursive imposition whose purpose is naturalization. Moreover, Bermúdez Jaimes (2007) describes the telenovela as a cultural matrix that simultaneously feeds on and affects the recognition of popular sectors and gender polarities. Indeed, it is impossible to discuss telenovelas without gender, which is part of a conceptual structure that translates into historically patriarchal domination. It is justified on naturalized foundations, such as sex, to make sense of "culturally defined value systems" (Ortner 1974, 71). Padilla de la Torre (2005) explains telenovelas as being comprised of gendered everyday elements, which serve as references for highly ritualized statements of femininity. In other words, this mass media genre shapes a fixed audience that is attentive to its sequential deliveries, who then recreate certain elements from the telenovela in their daily lives while also anticipating others to dictate what they consider correct with respect to gender and society itself.

Although in recent decades, telenovela plots are more finely written, its moral component is mostly transparent. Triumphant outcomes are frequent for characters who embody what is designated as desirable or aspirational, such as romantic love, individual effort, and family sacrifice (especially if the character is a woman). Its origin is located in the emigration of Cuban broadcasters of radio soap operas in the middle of the twentieth century to its development in Latin America as a mass spectacle. Historically, telenovelas can be recognized as adaptations of nineteenth-century feuilletons, sentimental novels of the eighteenth century, and popular fairy tales (Arroyo Redondo 2006). Like these earlier genres, one of the telenovela's primary characteristics is the balance between immutable elements, such as one or several heterosexual romantic stories, and innovation that make a character unique. Telenovelas also require realistic depictions, even if these depictions question the context in which they are written (Arroyo Redondo 2006) or if they go against ethical codes. For instance, the plot of the Brazilian telenovela *Bellísima* (2005) which strives to depict the corruption scandals that affected the government of the Workers' Party, the villain Bia Falcão ends up escaping her crimes without major repercussions. Moreover, the telenovela's verisimilitude is ensured through engagement with the spectators; emotions are exalted to involve them, and in this way, the telenovela "constitutes both a unit of meaning and a unit of production" (Bermúdez Jaimes 2007, 71). As a result, telenovelas portray formulaic worldviews, which are easily consumed by the viewing public; however, in its pretension of depicting everyday lives in Latin American realities, disabled lives either do not appear or are misrepresented.

In Latin America and the Caribbean, people with disabilities represent around 13 percent of the population (Duryea, Salazar Salamanca, and Pinzon Caicedo 2019), but this percentage does not correspond with the number of depictions of disability on television. In Argentina, this amount reaches 9 percent per day: "a low figure . . . that shows a clear and constant invisibility of the issue" (AFSCA 2014, 17); more than half of the characters with disability portrayed in Colombian telenovelas broadcasted between 1998 and 2005 were supporting roles (Bermúdez Jaimes 2007). These figures show that telenovelas maintain the patterns found in other television and popular media productions, specifically a weak recognition of disabled lives. Indeed, both the cultural industries and the audiences that consume these productions are guilty of perpetuating pejorative imaginaries of disability (Wilde 2014), maintaining the position that disability is unusual, even invisible. According to Bhabha (2007, 1994), a stereotype, like those often associated with disabled characters, is the basic element of colonial discourse theory, whose first property is ambivalence. That is to say, what determines the stereotype is not something natural or given, but rather the fixity that it seeks to impose in order to ideologically construct the "other." If the construction of meaning is accompanied by potential transformations, silence denotes as much as the explicit enunciation of disability itself. The media and entertainment industries help to ensure that stereotypes about disability and other differences are repeated and spread, generating "truths" while keeping those who seek to constrain them in their place. When disability is portrayed in telenovelas, characters' otherness is constantly reinforced, positioning disability as a main attribute. For example, in the 2004 Mexican telenovela *Rubí*, its titular anti-heroine belittles the main protagonist Maribel, because she has a paralyzed leg and walks with a limp. Several characters throughout the story treat Maribel compassionately, reinforcing "disability as a quality before which we must have pain and mercy" (Solís 2019, 76). Yet, this character remains primarily understood only by her disabled body, which is employed as a narrative tool to underline Maribel's uniqueness.

Stereotypes of disability act within the framework of ableism, which, quoting Toboso, is "an attitude or discourse that devalues disability, compared to the positive assessment of bodily integrity, equated to a supposed essential human condition of normality" (2017, 73). In turn, representations of disability, such as those offered in telenovelas, are a

> social and historical production that is modern and colonial, inscribed in the modes of production and reproduction of a society . . . framed in a system of an invented classification of subjects, that reproduces a hegemonic order based on relations of asymmetry and inequality. (Yarza et al. 2019, 22)

Stereotypes, ableism, and disability operate within the coloniality of power and the fiction of modernity, where gender is also situated. In these ways, telenovelas depict idealized versions of lived and unequal experiences, based on cultural and historical relationships where gender and disability meet. Consequently, telenovelas falsely propagate the very real presumption that both gender and disability are valid sources of otherness.

ABLEISM, MENTAL DIFFERENCE, AND THE INDIVIDUAL MODEL OF DISABILITY

With the aid of selected examples, I turn to the individual model of disability and its connections to coloniality, gender, and mental difference to argue how most representations of disability in telenovelas are restrictive and harmful. In Latin America, ableism is reflected in media representations, mainly according to the medical model of disability. The most widespread understanding of disability follows the individual model: the result of a physical and/or mental condition, because of which the individual cannot carry out the activities that would allow them a decent life. This model determines disability by relative factors and often culminates in the contention that to be disabled is a death sentence. In Latin America, this model is deeply influenced by earlier Catholic understandings of disability as the consequence of immorality and sin wherein disabled people are only realized as individuals who must "recover" (Bariffi and Palacios 2009). In relation to this model, the term "stigma" is applied when a physical characteristic of an individual or a group evokes a negative response from people who do not carry it, which responds to the distortion of existences and ends up incarnating a deviation from the established norms (Sánchez and Mercado 2011).

For instance, in *Juegos Prohibidos*, a telenovela from Colombia, the supporting character Gentil becomes paralyzed after an accident. His character is set as an example of the repercussions of "moral excess" due to his previous lifestyle of partying and promiscuity. After the accident, he calls himself "a burden," stating he "simply does not have a life." However, once Gentil has repented for his immoral behavior, his character sheds his disability and is able to walk to the altar on his wedding day. Here, disability is a temporary circumstance which Gentil must overcome in order to regain his identity and his life—implying that a disabled life is not worth living (Bermúdez Jaimes 2007). Disability stigmatizes him: he is seen as unable to enjoy life, due to previous immorality. This example illustrates how disability is depicted as an impediment to surpass through astounding moral efforts made by the disabled individual, which are never demanded to his social environment or to any public institution. This is also seen in *Rubí* when near the end of the story, the able-bodied antagonist has an accident and her leg is amputated. Realizing what happened, she screams: "I can't be crippled [. . .]; I'd rather be dead than crippled!" In this case, disability is presented as a punishment, wherein the disabled person is especially aware of its stigma because she once used it to victimize another disabled character. In this way, physical disability is understood as an element that sets the character apart and compounds her villainous qualities (Solís 2019).

While the above examples refer to physical disability, mental difference has also been understood as a shortcoming in telenovela narratives. Characters who live with mental difference are depicted as a threat to social order, either due to it or because they have failed to be remedied through treatment (Solís 2019). Unlike physical disability, which is attributed to both male and female characters, in telenovelas, mental disability is usually assigned to female roles that symbolize the moral compass of the plot. As discussed, telenovelas establish a status quo founded on hegemonic interpretations of gender and disability, qualifying their representations according to ethical standards of disability as a product of immorality or an obstacle good people can transcend. Women are regularly portrayed as a potential danger to order (Cassano 2014), reiterating the conventional message that femininity is never completely rational and must be tamed and controlled by civilized and logical men. In the telenovela, mental difference and disability signal the immorality of the female role, and the former directly affects women's behaviors without a corporeal signifier. For this reason, mass media and telenovelas have, at first glance, usually portrayed mentally disabled female characters as aggressive, unpredictable, and dependent.

To date, there have been many roles in telenovelas where women have been explicitly written as having some kind of diagnosis related to mental difference. For instance, the villain Roberta in the 2017 Mexican telenovela *Me declaro culpable* has bipolar disorder and is characterized as a danger to her family. Mental difference is a recurrent trope that is instilled in numerous portrayals without being disclosed, where certain actions and demeanors are presented to the audience as its signifiers. I still remember when Tamara shaved her head in the also Mexican production *El Privilegio de Amar* from 1998; the scene represented the outcome of her actions against the protagonists and her suffering for not being romantically reciprocated. Afterward, Tamara is called "crazy" and "irrational" by other characters. According to Cynthia Klitbo who performed said role, "I was impressed to see the transformation to madwoman" (Klitbo 2020). Mental difference in female villains, especially, tends to manifest in harmful ways, as they menace their relatives with threats of suicide to obtain what they want like Roberta, kidnap their rivals' children like Tamara, and commit murder as both characters do. These representations are based on stereotypes that link disability and mental difference to mistrust. Following the individual model of disability, even if they are not overtly identified as disabled women, these characters become a metaphor for evil that is punished in the end. Often these female characters, just like Roberta and Tamara, die because they represent the opposite of what a woman should be, and how an (abled) individual should implicitly abide.

In these ways, stigma and stereotype work together in telenovelas' plots. The former indicates visually and corporeally what should be pitied or avoided according to the moral qualities of the disabled role. The latter provides the discursive background that transmits to the public how to understand disability through the storyline, discarding the othered possibilities of mental difference. Such erasure provokes marginalization of disabled people, and especially of disabled women: its reiteration by the media comes from the colonial context from which it feeds itself, namely contemporary asymmetric structures of power (Fernández-Cid Enríquez 2010).

LA MUJER PERFECTA: A CASE STUDY

The remainder of this chapter offers a critical analysis of the Venezuelan telenovela *La Mujer Perfecta*, which aired in 2011. It cast Mónica Spear as Micaela and Ricardo Álamo as Santiago in the main roles and enjoyed its highest ratings during its broadcast in its home country. The telenovela follows the stories of six women who are seeking perfection, which might mean physical beauty, fame, money, romantic love, or a successful career. The protagonist is a woman who is initially portrayed as eccentric and gullible and is later diagnosed with Asperger syndrome and eventually acknowledged as the perfect woman. The remaining subsections discuss autism and the medical model of disability, gendered portrayals of exceptionality, and potentials and limits to alternative representations. A primary purpose of this section is to explore the possibilities and limitations in telenovela portrayals of gender and disability, with attention to the specific tropes affecting (mis)representation of autism as exemplified in *La Mujer Perfecta*.

The Medical Model of Disability and Autism

The medical model of disability, its connections to autism, Asperger syndrome, and neurodiversity are all reflected in *La Mujer Perfecta*. As was discussed earlier in this chapter, in the telenovela, ableism shapes itself under the individual and medical models of disability. The medical model supports a standardized and "western" parameter of how the human (body) should be. This model aligns with the accepted theoretical framework of eugenics, which was present, in Latin America in the nineteenth and twentieth centuries and which shaped public policies in the region along with positivism and social Darwinism (Suárez and Guazo 2005). These worldviews determined a scale of bodies and individuals, ranking who should be part of the newly formed countries' population and workforce (Jarrín 2010). Consequently, the idea of disability as "inferior" and reprehensible as transmitted to the next generations remains. For instance, during my time as a volunteer for an autism awareness organization, many people new to the diagnosis of their relatives believed these people would forever stay in a childlike and helpless state. Their only reference was what they had seen in movies or television, and they were so convinced being autistic was loathsome that a lot of them had kept it a secret; they saw their relatives as forever dependent on them, even describing them as a "cross to bear."

This is also generalized across various media; the disclosure of physical disability and/or obtaining a diagnosis is handled as a climactic moment in fictional stories, biographies, and even journalistic reports. In *La Mujer Perfecta*, for instance, there is a clear delineation between before and after (the revelation of) the protagonist's diagnosis: the impact of receiving an "official" name to categorize Micaela's traits and behaviors from a legitimized source is glorified. It begins her on a path of medical identification and self-exploration, with her family reacting in various ways to the recognition of what was previously presumed to be bizarreness and, even, laziness.

The exact diagnosis the protagonist receives is Asperger syndrome. However, this is a term no longer advocated by psychiatry because the diagnostic criteria were inexact and unreliable (American Psychiatric Association & American Psychiatric Association 2018). Despite this, it is still employed in popular media and in Latin American education and health systems, including the Peruvian one where I obtained my diagnosis. Currently, however, what used to be differentiated as Asperger syndrome has been subsumed into the autism spectrum, which comprises a range of neurological differences. Following Trimmer, McDonald, and Rushby (2017), Asperger syndrome is linked to deficits in social communication and social interaction in multiple contexts as well as a repetitive, restricted range of interests and activities, which are often performed repeatedly.

Asperger syndrome is named after Hans Asperger, who based his research about "autistic psychopathy" on children he treated during the Nazi regime in Austria. His research included clinical treatment of certain patients as well as the hospitalization of others at facilities where "euthanasia" was practiced (Czech 2018). As a result, Asperger syndrome has become a loosely used label to indicate persons who supposedly have "less" autism and, consequently those diagnosed with Asperger's are often deemed as closer to "normalcy." Its legacies remain: I have a close relative with whom I grew up, and who was diagnosed as autistic when he was four years old. He was considered to live in a "worse" state than me because his autistic expressions such as echolalia and motor tics were more easily recognizable. This led to his infantilization and involuntary isolation; while at the same time, the perception that my state was "better" than his consequently led to my own denial of psychological care and accommodation. Social expectations dictate that autism is expected to be lived as blatantly deviating from social norms and "normal" corporealities; however, as implied by the choice of "spectrum," autism has a multifaceted range which is widely unidentified. For instance, *La Mujer Perfecta*'s first episode shows Micaela working as a waitress in a temporary position. It is later revealed she cannot retain a job for a sustained period and has several social complications when living without her family or her knowing for sure why. Before her diagnosis, she is portrayed as firmly different from the rest, but not "extremely," and is expected to contribute financially to her family.

Unlike Asperger syndrome, neurodiversity refers to the various neurological conditions that appear as a result of variations in the human genome (Rodríguez-Giralt 2017). It is an expression critical of the false equivalence between mental diversity and inability. However, the autism spectrum is usually depicted by media productions as a monolithic situation, with a very notorious quirk or a unique talent to signify its difference, along with social clumsiness. The concept of neurodiversity is nonexistent on highly consumed performances, removing what they consider might alienate audiences and continuing harmful stereotypes. Subsequently, it "appears to glamorize eccentricity and devalue the ordinarily abled" (Belcher and Maich 2014, 109), reproducing portrayals without the discomfort of meltdowns and the effect of traumatic encounters due to marginalization.

Gendered Portrayals of Exceptionality

Inspiration porn and other damaging representations of autism inform many of the sexist tropes found in the telenovela. This term was coined by Stella Young (2014) to describe testimonial productions about disabled and neurodiverse people whose purpose is to make the neurotypical and abled public feel better about them, by awakening minimal interest to what they would never pay attention to in their daily life. *La Mujer Perfecta* falls into this discursive trap: Micaela is formulated as a character with "a fragile quality to it" (Acosta-Alzuru 2013). For example, at a party, when thieves break in, they instruct her to collect the other guests' belongings and she obeys, even asking out loud for those possessions being hidden by party goers. As a result, she is considered an accomplice and is taken to the police station. The fact that Micaela does not grasp why she should have not complied with the instructions of the robbers partially illustrates how people with the same diagnosis tend to interpret information literally. This event is justified later by the extremely naivete Micaela possesses as an autistic person, as someone who is so "pure" and "kind-hearted" that she is innocence incarnated. Her actions become inspirational by highlighting the supposedly neurotypical and abled audience's abilities for social communication and interaction and demonstrating a lived existence "despite" her neurodiversity.

To render these concrete aspects in a telenovela is not detrimental, but in *La Mujer Perfecta* they are histrionic recourses that portray a character so incomparable she is, indeed, perfect. Here lies the paradox of this analysis: at the same time that the telenovela reproduces misrepresentations that fixate on the (stereotypical) abnormality of autistic and disabled people, the genre also covers aspects of their daily experiences that are scarcely portrayed in other television programs. Through examples like her encounter with the thieves, *La Mujer Perfecta* argues that a person who is not vain and does not long for material ambitions is the perfect woman; this person is Micaela because of the morality and candor supposedly granted by her Asperger's, which makes her inspirational. Additionally, her ascribed "perfection" is not merely an outcome of her actions. Instead, the selection of Asperger syndrome as a trait for the heroine presents a tacit argument that her benevolence is innate.

Examples from *La Mujer Perfecta* also build on the embodiment of "exemplary" femininity. Anchored by Marianism, the assumption of female spiritual superiority (Fuller 1995); female leads of telenovelas are frequently virgins whose life aspirations culminate in maternity and domesticity. For Cassano (2014), the telenovela and its representation of women are processes of this gender construction; each storyline delivers a valid and schematic rendition. By conforming to these traits, Micaela personifies a set of moral values that establish her as a heroine and a victim on the side of "good." This nonthreatening portrayal of womanhood converges with a particular kind of ableism; if neurodiverse people are epitomized as transparent and noble, a neurodiverse woman is located on the extreme of exceptionality. As a result, a side to this misrepresentation is a supposed innocence, which corresponds to an infantilization of autism, and the reinforcement of disability as a source of exclusionist motivation. Even in front of harmless eccentricity, as in *La Mujer Perfecta*, disabled characters are still signaled as "other" and are dehumanized: Micaela and her disability are idealized to a degree that she is less of a person and more of a female archetype.

The consequence of inspiration porn is to render the disabled not subjects but objects—inspirational objects, but objects after all. This approach falsely reinforces the stigma of people within the autism spectrum. Concurrently, misogyny perpetuates femininity as illogical; as incapable of complete autonomy—othering women. Heroines, in this context, are never completely independent because women are thought of as intrinsically tied to their families, caring for them and ensuring this perpetuation. As a consequence, disabled and autistic women are considered doubly defenseless. The concrete effects of such distortions are the lack of support for the autistic and disabled population's social inclusion (Lugo, Melón and Castillo 2017), where women bear the worst part of this neglect.

The medical model and the individual model of disability are thus embodied in characters who are characterized as victims of their disability, which is further assumed as a loss. This is the great accomplishment of *La Mujer Perfecta*: it does not equate disability with limitation. Unlike other telenovelas, it does not show characters that resign themselves to their "shortcomings," or whose disability is intrinsically linked to depravity. Nevertheless, it does depict a protagonist who accomplishes extraordinary achievements "in spite of" their disability. As a result, we are still far from representing disabled people living and working in a variety of ordinary situations, showing multifaceted sides of their humanity (Cunha and Pinto 2017).

Potentials and Limits to Alternative Representations

One of the most powerful elements of telenovelas is the testimonial portrait of the daily life of its viewers. Its direct consequence is to validate and encourage their participation in witnessing "other" daily lives. Tufte (2007) explains that the constant marginalization of the audience is channeled into a cultural citizenship through telenovelas. These media productions mainly target Latin American masses, including many underprivileged populations who do not have access to costly cultural industries (Bermúdez Jaimes 2007). Women are the target audience and the family is the basic interpretive community of the narratives, on account of the telenovela being "a television genre that is culturally accepted as typical of women, who from childhood find blueprints in their characters to observe and imitate about femininity" (Padilla de la Torre 2005, 161–62). In these ways, the telenovela acts as a medium intentionally crafted to aid the repetition of inequalities inherent to modern and colonial societies, namely sexism. The impact of this genre is based in rituality, proximity to everyday life, and discursive imposition. Then again, the audience is never completely passive in front of what is communicated to them, texts are always understood and appropriated by viewers in various manners, such as resistance to or identification with (negative) caricatures (Lugo, Melón, and Castillo 2010).

At the same time, *La Mujer Perfecta* demonstrates how relevant gender is to a telenovelas reception. Micaela's frankness about what she is experiencing during the development of a love relationship was criticized by the audience and later mocked in a comedy show, for dialogue such as "I didn't know that being next to a body like this you could feel so good" and specifically for a scene where she declares she wants to have sex again (Acosta-Alzuru 2013). Her overt declaration is contrary to the way sexuality is usually portrayed in this genre and, as such, functions as a threat to the misogyny usually represented in telenovelas. In a misogynist society, the only purpose of female sexuality is motherhood; however, in contrast, Micaela defies this stereotype by enjoying sexual pleasure. *La Mujer Perfecta*'s viewers and press commentators highlighted the limits that socially tolerated gender identities are not supposed to cross. However, even though there are glances of defiance to standard representations of gender and disability, the telenovela does not completely escape the stereotyped pathways of femininity and ableism. The female lead gets a traditional happy ending. Following the canonical resolution of the genre, Micaela gets married and has a daughter, who shares the same diagnosis as her mother (Acosta-Alzuru 2013). One promising glimpse of hope resides in the creators choosing to make her daughter neurodiverse; autism is not relegated to the past, but its presence is proclaimed in the present, showing its potential in the future as a desired event and not as a scourge to be suppressed or cured (Kafer 2013).

In this telenovela, traditional representations of femininity are defied, but not abandoned. Similarly, it challenges stereotypes about disability and autism, without completely leaving them behind. One of the approaches found in *La Mujer Perfecta*'s storyline is distancing from the individual model of disability explored in the second section. Instead of portraying difference as a hardship to be overcome by the disabled person, Micaela's narrative arc is closer to the social model of disability, which Bariffi and Palacios (2009) define as a construction and a mode of social oppression, which is the result of a society that does not consider or have people in mind with disabilities. In these ways, they question the idea of a supposed standard norm of being human. The social model of disability further argues that society in general prevents the full development of the person with a disability: exclusion comes from the environment. In *La Mujer Perfecta*, the protagonist's continuous attempts to maintain a job are limited because she does not follow social appropriateness, which also restricted her access to education. Similarly, disabled people are situated in heterogeneous locations of power in Latin America by incorporating exclusions resulting from both (but not exclusively) ableism and gender disparities. In this telenovela, the plot makes it clear that Micaela's class origins and low family income made an accurate diagnosis unattainable and her journey exposes crude situations where other disadvantages interact, as often happens to people within the spectrum. The potency of the social model relies on highlighting that the paradigm of humanity opposed to disability is determined by more than this concept, which is demonstrated in *La Mujer Perfecta*. In fact, Micaela's character faces multiple sources of oppression, which in turn are shown to come from exterior conditions as the social model argues.

The writing in *La Mujer Perfecta* follows the social model, profiling not only the difficulties the protagonist goes through as an autistic woman but those provoked by social exclusions independent of her neurodiversity and/ or her disability. Nonetheless, its capacity to tackle entrenched stigmas is restricted by the fact that its discursive proposition of neurodiversity, disability, and gender is not incarnated by an autistic, disabled woman. One of the main criticisms toward popular media is that the number of people involved in the industries it brings together who are disabled is very few. Those who show themselves as the faces and bodies of people with disabilities utilize these representations for profit and professional prestige, and this includes the actress who played Micaela in *La Mujer Perfecta*. Mónica Spear was an able-bodied and neurotypical woman, by her own admission. This telenovela cannot be considered completely inclusive when disability and neurodiversity are only selected topics, not incarnated realities intervening directly in the resulting cultural performances.

CONCLUSION

To conclude, this chapter intended to answer what happens when an identity that has been repeatedly stripped of its humanity is shown in a more nuanced way, in a cultural media production as predominant in Latin America as the telenovela. *La Mujer Perfecta* accomplishes the move away from detrimental portrayals that obey the individual model of disability and define disability as hindrance. It also presents a neurodiverse woman as desirable and as someone who enjoys her sexuality, opposing constant misrepresentations of the autism spectrum and femininity more broadly.

La Mujer Perfecta possesses the great value of differentiating the many identities explored throughout the present analysis: disability, neurodiversity, and Asperger syndrome. It avoids stereotypical personifications of other tropes such as mental difference, leaning into the social determinants that limit disabled lives. Therefore, in many ways, this telenovela represents the heterogeneity found among autistic people and often omitted from media depictions. Tufte (2007) calls the "hybrid sphere of meaning" the border area between the public and the private, where the telenovela acts as a socializing agent for new or little-known ways of life. As a result, telenovelas like La Mujer Perfecta have the potential of gaining the spectators' acceptance of nonhegemonic gendered identities and might subvert the stereotypes about disability found in other television programs. Acosta-Alzuru recounts how, in the telenovela, "every key moment . . . was carefully researched, written, and performed" (2013, 7). She also comments on the reshooting of the first scenes after both lead actors asked its author for a meeting, to grasp the nuances of the relationship between them brought about by the inclusion of an autistic protagonist. This strength was recognized after La Mujer Perfecta's broadcast: its creator, Leonardo Padrón, later won the Rafael Ángel García Award for Writer of the Year and received a public tribute from the Centre for Evaluation and Integrated Diagnostics of Developmental Disorders (CEDIAD) (Acosta-Alzuru 2013). Mónica Spear became a spokesperson for Asodeco, a nonprofit institution for the inclusion of people with disabilities; she was also the godmother of the Asperger Foundation of Venezuela (Fundasperven). However, *La Mujer Perfecta* was an anomaly, a "one-day flower" that does not appear to have left any sort of precedent in this television genre. While researching for this chapter, it was almost impossible to find another autistic character in telenovelas. Recent examples only depict autistic children like in *Quiero amarte* (2013), *Eva la trailera* (2016), and *Vencer el desamor* (2020), which maintains the infantilization of autism and limited representations of its lived realities.

Ultimately, while La Mujer Perfecta was a step forward, it was and is not enough. It still leans on medical meanings of disability and ableist tropes like inspiration porn, which locate its protagonist outside normalcy. These tropes interact with hegemonic mandates about being a woman, mandates which the character embodies, articulating multifaceted stigmas. Consequently, her story development fits within expectations of personal growth through her sentimental involvement with a heterosexual partner and embracing maternity.

Telenovelas and other televised productions still reflect popular views about those outside the hegemonic, patriarchal, and medicalized norm, which excludes incarnated and first-person critiques and demands. Because the telenovela as a genre is formulated to induce exacerbated feelings in order to maintain spectators' attention, it could very well reflect multifaceted everyday lives of disabled individuals, and particularly of disabled women, as *La Mujer Perfecta* attempted. However, one media production alone will not transform Latin American audiences' perspectives about structurally oppressed identities. More manifold and "fused" portrayals are needed in telenovelas and other popular media genres that reflect the true day-to-day occurrences of all Latin American citizens, and notably of those of us who have been constantly omitted from these narratives. From the point of view of someone excluded from said narratives, the exhortation for media and entertainment creators to play an active role in the nondiscriminatory treatment of physical and mental disabilities and differences is necessary, in order to expect real repercussions on the quality of life of disabled populations.

BIBLIOGRAPHY

Acosta-Alzuru, Carolina. "Dear Micaela: Studying a telenovela protagonist with Asperger's syndrome." *Cultural Studies? Critical Methodologies* 13, no. 2 (2013): 125–37.

American Psychiatric Association and American Psychiatric Association. *Manual diagnóstico y estadístico de los trastornos mentales: DSM-5*. Buenos Aires: Editorial Médica Panamericana, 2018.

Arroyo Redondo, Susanna "La estructura de la telenovela como relato tradicional." *Culturas Populares. Revista Electrónica 2* (mayo-agosto 2006), 20pp.

Bariffi, Francisco and Agustina Palacios. *El modelo social de discapacidad: orígenes, caracterización y plasmación en la Convención Internacional sobre los Derechos de las Personas con Discapacidad*. Madrid: Cinea, 2009.

Belcher, Christina and Kimberly Maich. "Autism spectrum disorder in popular media: Storied reflections of societal views." *Brock Education* 23, no. 2, Spring (2014): 97–115.

Bermúdez, Jaimes and Gloria Isabel. *Representaciones de la discapacidad en las telenovelas colombianas que transmiten los canales privados de cubrimiento nacional*. Masters diss., Universidad Nacional de Colombia, 2007.

Bhabha, Homi. *El lugar de la cultura*. Buenos Aires: Manantial, 2007 [1994].

Cassano, Giuliana. "Mirando la Telenovela desde el Género. Natacha: De la Domesticidad a la Agencia." *Ação Midiática – Estudos em Comunicação, Sociedade e Cultura*, no. 8 (2014): 1–14.

Collier, Jane and Michelle Rosaldo. "Politics and gender in simple societies." In *Sexual Meanings*, edited by Sherry Ortner and Harriet Whitehead, 275–329. Cambridge: Cambridge University Press, 1981.

Cunha, Maria João and Paula Campos Pinto. "Representações mediáticas da deficiência. Um estudo longitudinal na imprensa." *Sociologia, problemas e práticas*, no. 85 (2017): 131–47.

Czech, Herwig. "Hans Asperger, National Socialism, and "race hygiene" in Nazi-era Vienna." *Molecular Autism* 9, no. 29 (2018): 1–43.

Den Houting, Jacquiline. "Neurodiversity: An insider's perspective." *Autism* 23, no. 2 (2018): 271–73.

Duryea, Suzanne, Juan Pablo Salazar Salamanca and Mariana Pinzon Caicedo. *Somos todos: Inclusión de las personas con discapacidad en América Latina y el Caribe*. Washington: Inter-American Development Bank, 2019.

Federal Authority for Audiovisual Communication Services (AFSCA). *Monitoreo de las Discapacidades en la TV. Tratamiento de la temática y representación de las personas con discapacidad*. Buenos Aires: AFSCA, 2014.

Fernández-Cid Enríquez, Matilde. "Medios de comunicación, conformación de imagen y construcción de sentido en relación a la discapacidad." *Política y Sociedad* 47, no. 1 (2010): 105–13.

Fuller, Norma. "Acerca de la polaridad maranismo machismo." In *Lo Femenino y lo Masculino: Estudios Sociales sobre las Identidades de Género en América Latina*, edited by Gabriela Arango, Magdalena León and Mara Viveros. Bogotá: Third World Editions, Ediciones UniAndes, and Gender, Women and Development Studies Programs of the Universidad Nacional de Bogotá, 1995.

Jarrín, Alvaro. *Cosmetic Citizenship: Beauty, Affect and Inequality in Southeastern Brazil*. PhD diss., Duke University, 2010.

Kafer, Alison. *Feminist, Queer, Crip*. Indianapolis: Indiana University Press, 2013.

Klitbo, Cynthia. "Cynthia Klitbo se sorprende al verse en El privilegio de amar." Interview by Tlnovelas. *Tlnovelas*, March 24, 2020. Video, 6:21, 2020.

Lugo, Nohemí, María Elena Melón and María Concepción Castillo. "La representación del autismo en las narrativas de fan fiction.net: los espacios de afinidad como oportunidad para la negociación de sentido." *Palabra Clave* 20, no. 4 (2017): 948–78.

Ortner, Sherry. "Is female to male as nature is to culture." In *Woman, Culture and Society*, coordinated by Michelle Rosaldo and Louise Lamphere, 67–88. Stanford: Stanford University Press, 1974.

Padilla de la Torre, María Rebeca. "Ser mujer se aprende, enseña, disfruta y sufre. Telenovela, cultura e identidad de género." *Culturales* I, no. 1 January–June (2005): 143–76.

Rodríguez-Giralt, Israel. 2013. "El concepto de neurodiversidad." *Expdem*, October 17, 2013.

Sánchez, Sebastián and María Teresa Mercado. "Narrativa audiovisual y discapacidad. Realización televisiva comparada de los Juegos Olímpicos y Paralímpicos de Pekín 2008." *Zer* 16, no. 31 (2011): 89–107.

Solís, Patricia. "La visión de la discapacidad en la primera etapa de Disney: Blancanieves y los 7 enanitos, Alicia en el País de las Maravillas y Peter Pan." *Revista de Medicina y Cine* 15, no. 2(2019): 73–79.

Suárez, Laura and López Guazo. *Eugenesia y racismo en México*. Mexico City: Universidad Nacional Autónoma de México, 2005.

Toboso, Mario. "Capacitismo (ableism)." In *Barbarismos queer y otras esdrújulas*, edited by María Rosón Lucas Platero and Esther Ortega, 73–81. Barcelona: Bellaterra, 2017.

Trimmer, Emily, Skye McDonald, and Jacqueline Ann Rushby. "Not knowing what I feel: Emotional empathy in autism spectrum disorders." *Autism* 21, no. 4 (2017): 450–57.

Tufte, Thomas. "Soap operas y construcción de sentido: mediaciones y etnografía de la audiencia." *Nueva época*, no. 8 June-December (2007): 89–112.

Wilde, Alison. "Spectacle, Performance, and the Re-Presentation of Disability and Impairment." *Review of Disability Studies: An International Journal* 6, no. 3 (2014): 34–43.

Yarza de los Ríos, Alexander, Alfonsina Angelino, Carolina Ferrante, María Eugenia Almeida and, María Noel Míguez Passada. "Ideología de la normalidad: un concepto clave para comprender la discapacidad desde América Latina." In *Estudios críticos en discapacidad: una polifonía desde América Latina*, coordinated by Alexander Yarza de los Ríos, Laura Mercedes Sosa and Berenice Pérez Ramírez, 21–44. Buenos Aires: Consejo Latinoamericano de Ciencias Sociales – CLACSO, 2019.

Young, Stella. "I'm not your inspiration, thank you very much." Filmed April 2014 at *TEDxSydney*, Sydney. Video and transcript, 9:04, 2014.

Index

ableism, 36–37, 40, 51, 135, 208–11, 213
adaptation: defined, 3–4, 55; fidelity, 159; graphic novel series to film, 159; novel-to-film, 10, 173–85; studies, 175; transmedia, 3–4
AJ and the Queen, series, 28, 31–32
Alias, comic book series, 10, 141–43, 145–54
American Born Chinese, comic book, 61, 64
apparatus, 176–84
Asperger's, 56–61, 197–201, 205, 211–14, 217. *See also* autism
Atypical, series, 9, 57, 64, 71–72, 75–85
autism, 9, 35–40, 46–51, 59, 61, 67, 76, 82–83; comics depictions, 55–68; imagination, autistic, 84; pathologizing of autism, 63; research on, 65; telenovelas, in, 205–6, 211–16; violent autistic stereotype, 61–63

Bakhtin, Mikhail, 30
Batgirl, comic book series (reboot by Gail Simone), 145
Bloom, Harold, 182–83

colonial subjects, 35, 37, 49, 50
Curious Incident of the Dog in the Night-Time (2004, Haddon), 55, 57, 58

de Man, Paul, 25–26
Derrida, Jacques, 182
Diagnostic and Statistical Manual of Mental Disorders, 17; homosexuality in, 17
Diagnostic and Statistical Manual of Mental Disorders IV (DSM IV), 6, 56, 93
Diagnostic and Statistical Manual of Mental Disorders V (DSM V), 23–24, 57; Asperger's in, 57; BDSM in, 23; gender non-conformity vs. gender dysphoria in, 18
disability studies, 4–8, 35–36, 80–81, 90–91, 93, 143–45, 148; "deep ethics" approach, 7–8, 95, 98–99; mental disability, inattention to, 5; social model, 4–5, 73, 79
disidentification, 24–25, 27
displacement, 82–85
drag, 9, 20–21, 23–26, 28–30, 32

Elsinore, game (2019), 123–37
Esmeralda, telenovela (1970), 188, 192–93, 195–98, 200, 202
"Eugenic Atlantic" period, 37, 40, 43–44
eugenics, 43–44

Forrest Gump (1994), 74–75

Foucault, Michel: apparatus, conception of, 176–77

gaze: ableist, 36–37; ageist, 36; imperialist, 37; medicalizing, 48, 49; neurotypical, 59
gender expression, 18
gender identity, 18
Guru (2018, RuPaul), 25
Gypsies. *See* Romani

Hamlet (Shakespeare), 123, 124
Heroes in Crisis, limited series comic book, 145
Hutcheon, Linda, 4, 159, 161, 179, 190–91

Iron Man 3 (2013), 145

Jameson, Frederic, 4, 118, 176
Jessica Jones, series, 10, 92, 141–43, 145–54

Legion, series, 9, 89–91, 95–100
L'Enfant sauvage (*The Wild Child*) (1970), 35–52
Letting It All Hang Out (1995, RuPaul), 19–21
LGBTQ+communities, 17, 24, 31

mad studies, 6, 136
melodrama, 103–8, 111–12, 114, 116–17, 187–90, 192–97, 201–2
Memoire and Report on Victor of Aveyron (1806, Itard), 35, 36
mental difference, 22; representation of, 2–3, 9–10
mental disability, 173–85
mental health conditions/mental illness, 10; anxiety, 6, 30, 94, 103; bipolar, 93, 103; depression, 6, 30, 93, 94, 103; dissociative identity disorder, 1, 93, 95; "madness," 129–34; PTSD, 10, 21, 92–93, 142–54; schizophrenia, 89, 91, 97; trauma, 143, 158–71
moral disability, 10, 103–16
La Mujer Perfecta, telenovela, 11, 191–93, 197–202, 205–6, 211–18
myth, 103–5, 108, 116–18, 193–94

narrative and narratives, 6–8, 11, 94; biomedical, 7, 90, 93–97, 100, 192–97, 209, 211–13; comics narratives, 55–68, 89–100, 141–54, 158–71; coming of age, 71–85; fidelity, 9; film, 103–5, 108, 118; rehabilitative coming-of-age, 72–75; rhetorical lens, through a, 93–95; superhero, 91–95, 100, 141–54; trauma, 142–54, 158–71
neurodiversity, 2, 5–6, 9, 18–19, 35, 58, 91, 190, 206, 211–13; neurodivergent, neurodivergence, 5–6, 26; neurotypical, 5–6

One Flew Over the Cuckoo's Nest, (1962, Kesey), 1
Ophelia (2006, Klein), 125–27, 129–30, 134–37
Ophelia (2018), 125–27, 134–37
Ophelia, character, 10, 123–37

people of color, 36, 40–42, 44, 48–51, 65
performance theory, 23; re-accentuation, 23–24, 30–32
Postal, comic series, 55–64
postcolonial theory, 35–36, 41
Prendergast, Catherine, 5–7, 91, 93, 144
prosthesis, narrative, 26–27, 103–4
prosthetic performance, 32
prosthetic self, 26–27
The Punisher, series, 142

A Quiet Life (1990, Oe), 10, 173–85
A Quiet Life (1995), 10, 173–85

racism, 40, 42–43
Rain Man (1988), 56–57, 75
Ratched, series, 1–2
rehabilitation, 72–75
rhetorics of disability, 7, 94–95, 99
Romani (Gypsies), 42–43, 50
RuPaul, 9, 19–32
RuPaul's Drag Race, series, 23, 24, 31

Said, Edward, 41
Scott Pilgrim, graphic novel series, 10, 157–71
Scott Pilgrim vs. the World, film (2010), 10, 159–71
Sherlock, BBC series, 55, 58
Silver Linings Playbook (2012), 103–12, 114–17
The Song Collector, comic, 65–68

spatiality and spatial arrangements, 9, 75–79, 81, 83
Stalker (1979), 174, 178–80
standardization, ideology of, 79–82
stimming, 35, 37–41, 49, 66. *See also* autism

telenovelas, 187–202, 205–18
trauma studies, 144, 162
trope of psychiatric hospital as prison and site of abuse, 89

Ulrichs, Karl Heinrich, 18

Where'd You Go, Bernadette (2019), 103–4, 106–9, 112–17
white savior, 37, 48–51

About the Contributors

Whitney Hardin received her PhD from Wayne State University in 2014. Her scholarly interests are often centered on exploring rhetoric's role in shaping our ideas about civic life, such as the use of institutional rhetoric to enforce notions of good citizenship; the rhetorical practices of social movements and acts of protest; and the interplay of violence and rhetoric, specifically through state-sanctioned acts of coercion or threat directed at citizens. More recently, a life-long love of video games has led her to game studies and game design theory.

Julia E. Kiernan is an assistant professor of communications at Lawrence Technological University. Her research and teaching are intimately linked and regularly examine the shifting impacts of pedagogical and curricular design in the digital humanities, translingual and transnational writing, environmental sciences, and medical humanities. Julia's favored research methodology is active research, which focuses on the impacts of listening, reflection, and feedback throughout learning processes. Her work has appeared in a number of peer-reviewed edited collections as well as the journals: *Composition Forum*, *Interdisciplinary Humanities*, *Communication and Language at Work*, *Journal of Global Literacies, Technologies, and Emerging Pedagogies*, and *Composition Studies*.

Lindsay Adams Kennedy is a visiting lecturer of English and creative writing at Lee University and a PhD candidate at Saint Louis University. Her research explores the performance, textual history, and adaptation of Shakespeare's works, as well as depictions of invisible disability in Early Modern literature. Most recently her article "Catcalls and Live Chat: Or, How Livestreamed Performances Illuminate the Early Modern Audience" was published in the *Sixteenth Century Journal*. She has also been published in the anthology *How to Teach a Play: 75 Exercises for the College Classroom* and in the Comparative Drama Conference's journal *Text and Presentation*. She has an MFA in playwriting from the Catholic University of America and is a proud member of the Dramatists' Guild.

Rea Amit is assistant professor in the Department of Modern Languages, Literatures, and Linguistics at the University of Oklahoma. He has published mainly on Asian media, aesthetics, and theory in journals such as *Philosophy East and West, Positions: Asia Critique, Participations: International Journal of Audience Research, On_Culture—The Open Journal for the Study of Culture*, as well as several book chapters in edited volumes.

Carol Donelan is professor of Cinema and Media Studies at Carleton College in Northfield, Minnesota, USA. Her interests include narrative film modes and genres and archival research in American film history. Among her publications are essays in *The Routledge Companion to Philosophy and Film, The Oxford Handbook of Sound and Image in Digital Media, A Critical Companion to James Cameron, A Critical Companion to Stanley Kubrick, Quarterly Review of Film and Video, Film History: An International Journal, The Moving Image*, and *Film Criticism*.

John W. Gulledge is a doctoral candidate at Emory University in Atlanta, where he studies early modern theater and culture, disability representation and experience, performance and/of identity, affect theory, and the history of emotions, especially feelings associated with laughter and wonder. His dissertation project is tentatively titled "Prosthetic Laughter: Feeling Disabled Performance in Early Modern England," which traces the performance and presentation of disability both on and off the stage between 1570 and 1777. John's work combines such allied fields as performance theory, health humanities, disability studies, and cognitive neuroscience to field and recover the ways premodern peoples may have (mis)understood alterity differently than we do today and, thus, have been able to access one another in more sociological, affective movements of communal, shared experience.

Martín Ponti received his PhD from the University of Illinois, Chicago. He is currently an assistant professor of Hispanic Studies at Washington College, Maryland. His scholarly interest explores melodramatic serials and Latin American telenovelas in their intersections of race, class, gender, and nation. His research has appeared in peer-reviewed journals and in edited collections such as *Screen Bodies* and in the *Journal of Gender and Sexuality Studies*

(*REGS*). In his upcoming research, Ponti explores the role of melodrama in presidential memoirs in Argentinean politics.

Anamika Purohit is assistant professor in the Department of English, Jai Hind College, Autonomous, Mumbai, India. She teaches English Literature and Communication Skills to undergraduate students from varied faculties of Arts, Commerce, and Science. She has a PhD in English from the University of Mumbai, and specializes in the fields of English Literature and Culture Studies. Her doctoral thesis examines the relationship between the geographical entity of the city-space and the literary entity of the "city text" using spatial criticism as a tool. Her noteworthy publications include "(De)constructing (Dis)placement: A Comparative Analysis of Augmented Reality in Spike Jonze's *Her* and Gil Ho Ahn's *Memories of the Alhambra*" published in *Media Integrity*, July 2019; and "The Place of the Abject: Locating a Dalit Spatiality in Selected Poems of Namdeo Dhasal" in *Asian Journal of English Studies*, April 2015.

Robert Rozema is a professor of English at Grand Valley State University in Allendale, MI. He publishes books and articles about secondary English education and is especially interested in issues of neurodiversity. His current research involves examining the literacy lives of autistic adolescents. Dr. Rozema is the editor-in-chief of the academic journal *Ought: The Journal of Autistic Culture*.

Joy C. Schaefer is senior lecturer of Critical Media Studies at Lawrence Technological University. Her teaching and research interests include cinema studies; French studies; transnationalism and postcolonial studies; representations of race, religion, gender, and sexuality; disability studies; and feminist affect theories. Her work has appeared in *The Quarterly Review of Film and Video, Studies in European Cinema, Ought: The Journal of Autistic Culture*, and *JCMS: Journal of Cinema and Media Studies*.

Guy Spriggs earned his doctorate in English from the University of Kentucky in 2018, specializing in film studies. His research examines the career of Paul Newman as a means for positioning on-screen aesthetic continuity at the center of our understanding of stardom and star studies. His recent work on horror cinema and trauma has been featured in *The Encyclopedia of Sexism in American Film* (Rowman & Littlefield, 2019) and *Blumhouse Productions: The New House of Horror* (University of Wales Press, forthcoming).

Andrea Urrutia Gómez is a Peruvian anthropologist and received her PhD from the Universidad Autónoma Metropolitana—Iztapalapa. She is also a feminist and an autistic woman, with activist experience in neurodiversity issues, as well as in sexual and reproductive health, and cyberfeminism. Body, beauty, and gender are her main research topics, having notably studied makeup and the cosmetic industry in Peru and Mexico. She is a member of the Working Group on Critical Studies in Disability of the Latin American Council of Social Sciences (CLACSO).

www.ingramcontent.com/pod-product-compliance
Lightning Source LLC
Chambersburg PA
CBHW020117010526
44115CB00008B/866